2799

THE CHELSEA GARDENER

Philip Miller 1691–1771

Frontispiece to Gardeners Dictionary *8th ed. 1768*

THE CHELSEA GARDENER

Philip Miller 1691–1771

HAZEL LE ROUGETEL

with a contribution by William T. Stearn on the
botanical importance of Miller

NATURAL HISTORY MUSEUM PUBLICATIONS
LONDON

Dedicated to all my friends
in the Garden History Society with gratitude
for their encouragement

The Publishers wish to thank The Stanley Smith
Horticultural Trust for help with this publication

Book designed by Gillian Greenwood
© Hazel Le Rougetel 1990
Published by the British Museum (Natural History)
Cromwell Road, London SW7 5BD

British Library Cataloguing in Publication Data

Le Rougetel, Hazel
    The Chelsea Gardener: Philip Miller 1691–1771.
    1. London. Kensington and Chelsea (London Borough)
    Botanical gardens. Chelsea physic garden biographies
    I. Title
    580'.74'424

ISBN 0–565–01101–4

Typeset in Garamond by J&L Composition Ltd, Filey, North Yorkshire
Printed in Great Britain by Butler & Tanner Ltd, Frome, Somerset

Contents

Preface

The most celebrated English naturalist of the eighteenth century introduced me to that century's most celebrated gardener. The present book on the latter has resulted from that fortuitous encounter.

When reading Gilbert White's *Garden Kalendar* (1751–1771) some twenty years ago, I came across an entry for 16 April 1752:

> Sowed a rose of purple double Stocks from London & Half a Row of Brompton Stocks from Ringmer. Sowed in the New Garden on the Border by the Brick Walk, Loves Lies a Bleeding, Painted Lady Peas, Larkspurs, Yellow Lupines and Double Poppies. Mem. Sow'd Radishes with the Stocks as Miller directs.

A note for 11 November 1754 stated: 'Made, earth'd and thatch'd a mushroom bed seven feet long according to Miller.' Many entries cover ambitious attempts with melons; some expressing exhilaration, others exasperation and White wrote to Miller for advice in 1759. He received a courteous reply with some seeds 'immediately from Armenia'. The results, however, did not 'look quite right' and on June 23 he recorded:

> Called in upon Mr. Miller at Chelsea and found he had 18 light of Armenian Melons in excellent order. There were about two brace & half of fruit to a light, full grown and very rough and black. He pushes his lights, it seems, quite down in dry weather and says the defect of male bloom is owing to yr. seeds being of some age.

Who was this oracle, obviously an authority on flowers, fruit and vegetables, some of them exotic? I must explain that I reached the realm of garden history somewhat late in life and was curious to learn more about Mr Miller of Chelsea. Gilbert White's account book showed he had bought a Miller's *Dictionary* in 1749 for 18s and from this he would have taken the directive for stocks:

> ... for if they are too much exposed to the Sun in the Heat of the Day, they are very subject to be eaten by a sort of Fly, as they often are when young, upon a hot, dry soil; to remedy which, you should always sow a few Radishes amongst them, which will secure them from this Mischief; for the Flies will always prey upon the Radishes, wherby your July-flowers will be preserved.

In May 1753 another copy was purchased: 'Miller's Gardeners Dictionary, new edition halfbound in exchange from Br. Benjamin – £01.14.6.' This must have been the sixth, published the year before and, as stated in the Preface, it rendered 'previous editions of inferior value' and included many rare plants and improvements in directions for culture, 'especially fruit trees, melons, ananas and the kitchen garden.' As the most detailed entries in the *Garden Kalendar* range over the years 1754–59, it would seem that this large volume was Gilbert White's constant companion and relatively high expenditure on equipment for raising melons and cucumbers (another Selborne speciality) indicated he was following authoritative advice.

I became engrossed in the *Dictionary*'s wealth of information, much of it relevant today, and asked libraries for a book on Philip Miller. There appeared to be none and this seemed an extraordinary omission although now, two decades on, I appreciate that any personal information about the Chelsea Gardener is hard to come by. I well remember talking to William Stearn about the need for such a book at a Garden History Society annual conference some time ago. He kindly said that if I undertook the research, then he would cast his expert eye over my text from a botanical viewpoint and might even make his own contribution. This was a wonderful gesture and, with typical generosity, he has lent me his own copy of the eighth (1768) edition of the *Dictionary* over many years, saying he had easier access to libraries than I had. Obviously his erudite contribution will prove invaluable to academic botanists.

Without Gilbert White's introduction to and William Stearn's collaboration with Philip Miller, the writing of this book would never have been undertaken. The eighteenth century naturalist and the twentieth century authority on taxonomic, nomenclatural and historic aspects of botany have my gratitude on its completion.

Hazel Le Rougetel
BRAMSHOTT, HAMPSHIRE, MAY 1989

Philippo Miller, Soc. Reg. Lond.
Sodali.
Horti. Bot. Chelseiani Hortulano.

Milleria quinqueflora *L.*

8

1 Miller's Place in Garden History

Philip Miller (1691–1771) was the most distinguished and influential British gardener of the eighteenth century, esteemed not only in the British Isles but throughout Europe and the British Colonies in America for his practical skill in horticulture and his wide botanical knowledge of cultivated plants. This expertise he made widely available from 1731 to 1768 in edition after edition of his *Gardeners Dictionary* and its abridged version.

From 1722–1770, a period of great progress in botany and horticulture, Philip Miller was working at the Apothecaries' Physic Garden at Chelsea. Under his care and through his enthusiastic introduction of new plants it became the most richly stocked botanic garden in Europe. Other gardeners trained there and, having gained experience under Miller, developed new botanic gardens at Kew and Cambridge. At Chelsea, concentrating on both the theory and practice of gardening, Philip Miller fulfilled the expectation of one of his early admirers, Patrick Blair, who wrote in 1721, 'I look upon him to go onward with a curiosity and genious superior to most of his occupation'.

Any account of his work cannot be confined to that small village some two miles up river from the City, and any study of Miller must include his wide circle of friends and correspondents, in this country and overseas, at a time when the Chelsea Physic Garden became a pivot of horticultural debate and plant dissemination. Miller's associates ranged from John Ray (1627–1705) to Joseph Banks (1743–1820) and, while the former would have inspired him towards industrious research and correspondence, he encouraged the latter to pursue botanical discovery. From Sir Hans Sloane, to whom he owed his appointment, he inherited a sincere dedication to the Physic Garden. With Dr Boerhaave in Leyden, he learned the value of a wide collection of plants. Through Linnaeus, the illustrious Swedish naturalist who came to Chelsea in 1736, he was persuaded to accept a new system of nomenclature and, by the example of John Bartram's journeys through virgin colonies, he appreciated the patience and courage needed in the course of botanical expeditions.

In this country curious (in the eighteenth century sense of inquisitive) gardeners showed great interest in the 'outlandish' plants then becoming available for the first time, many of them grown in the Chelsea Garden. The Dukes of Argyll, Bedford and Richmond, the Earl of Northumberland,

and young Lord Petre all grew new trees and exotic plants at Whitton, Woburn, Goodwood, Stanwick and Thorndon, estates with which Miller was associated professionally.

Amongst his friends, Richard Warner had a splendid collection of rare plants at Woodford, John Fothergill amassed an extensive display of 'Americans' at Upton and Peter Collinson, who played such an important part in their collection, grew beautiful trees at Mill Hill. Leading nurserymen began to advertise novelties; at Mile End, James Gordon had significant success with rare seeds and Robert Furber concentrated on exciting trees and plants at Kensington. A competitive spirit for growing strange plants was aroused amongst quite modest gardeners and Philip Miller's written advice was much in demand.

Thus it will be appreciated that Miller's circle was all-embracing; his correspondents both in this country and overseas included great landowners, professors of science, doctors, collectors, gardeners and nurserymen. Letters were their only form of communication albeit a hazardous one. Transport was always slow and often uncertain; mail was constantly stolen on land or lost at sea and was frequently opened en route by a government fearful of treasonable correspondence. Most of the letters were copied and later duplicates would be dispatched against such contingencies. There was no guarantee of delivery, but high postal rates were collected from the recipients who willingly paid the price, grateful for a service which survived adversity. Philip Miller was one of the most consciencious of letter writers and, in a careful hand, explained, encouraged, questioned and corrected. From his exchanges, gardeners the world over have benefited and, indeed, the Apothecaries, who were not entirely appreciative of their Gardener's achievements, did congratulate him on diligence in this respect.

Philip Miller's span of eighty years stretched from the time of William III and Marlborough's victories in France to the first decade of George III and the revolt of the British American colonies: a period of radical change in garden design. As a youth, Miller had seen the grand concept of seventeenth century French architectured gardens, encouraged in this country by Charles II at the Restoration and in some measure replaced by the Dutch taste for confined formality. A revolution against these contrived gardens was led by Charles Bridgeman, followed by William Kent and 'Capability' Brown, all exponents of landscaped expansion and with them Miller was in agreement.

He advocated incorporation of the distant prospect as background to the garden scene and emphasized the importance of wilderness, with walks through informally planted trees and shrubs, stating 'where the beautiful parts of nature are justly imitated in gardens, they will always be approved by judicious persons, let the taste of gardening alter as it will'. In his concern for the countryside, pressing for barren heaths to be usefully clad with pines, or marshes with willow and poplar to supplement timber shortage, he

As the gardens of Verſailles, Marli, and others, were extolled for their magnificence, ſo the plans of them were almoſt univerſally copied ; the deſigners, or imitators rather, only varying the parts according to the ſituation or figure of the ground ; and this was practiſed for ſeveral years, at a time, when great ſums of money were expended in gardens, which might have rendered this country the moſt beautiful of any in Europe, had a natural taſte then prevailed in the deſigning of gardens ; which is the more to be lamented, as the plantations then made, have been many of them rooted out, to make way for the alterations and improvements which have been ſince introduced. Many perſons, I am ſenſible, will have it, that, in the deſigns of gardens, the taſte ſhould alter from time to time, as much as the faſhion of apparel ; but theſe cannot be perſons of judgment ; for wherever there are natural beauties in a country, they will always pleaſe perſons of real knowledge ; and frequently it is obſerved, that perſons of but little ſkill in the art of gardening, are ſtruck with theſe beauties without knowing the cauſe ; therefore where the beautiful parts of nature are juſtly imitated in gardens, they will always be approved by judicious perſons, let the taſte of gardening alter as it will.

Philip Miller on gardening [GD]

It may interest the reader to know that the *Gardeners Dictionary* (1768) was set in the same typeface – Garamond – as this book

demonstrated a keen sense of economy and comprehension of the wider scene of husbandry. Indeed, as well as its obvious use to botanists and horticulturists, Miller's *Gardeners Dictionary* provides many interesting aspects of eighteenth century cultivation both at home and abroad for historians generally.

Acclaim of this great gardener can be quoted from one who knew him personally. Having met Miller not long before he left the Physic Garden, John Rogers (1752–1842) added some reminiscences as an appendix to his book, *The Vegetable Cultivator* (1839). He regarded him as a benefactor to mankind: 'Medicine, botany, agriculture and manufactures are all indebted to him' and rated the *Dictionary* 'as the first bright beam of gardening issuing from the dark cloud of ignorance in which it had previously been enveloped; but having once broken through, it had continued to shine with increasing splendour for the last century. It may be almost said to have laid the foundation of the horticultural taste and knowledge in Europe.'

The final edition of the *Dictionary* in Miller's lifetime, 1768, remains botanically important even now, because it records the introduction of so many plants and provides them with names still used; while horticulturally it describes eighteenth-century gardening practices, some of which are still relevant today. Readers of the *Dictionary* soon come to realize that Philip Miller, co-ordinator of half a century's discoveries and conclusions, became a counsellor for every cultivator of the day and stands as a prominent figure in the world's history of gardening.

2 The Apothecaries and their Garden

Throughout the ages medicine and botany have been intertwined. Indeed, botany as a science grew out of the study of plants for medicinal purpose. At universities, where professors of medicine taught botany, physic gardens became a necessity for the practical study of plants. Although the Vatican has records of a physic garden in 1277, it was not until the sioteenth century that centres of learning, first in Italy and then elsewhere, began to establish their gardens of medicinal plants. In this country they followed still later; at Oxford in 1621, Edinburgh in 1670 and Chelsea in 1673.

In his *Memoirs of the Botanic Garden at Chelsea*, Henry Field writes:

> Many of the members of the Apothecaries' Society in the seventeenth and eighteenth centuries were distinguished for their scientific attainments ... That all of them were good citizens and honourable men will be readily conceded from a consideration of the very constitution of the Society and from a perusal of the Bye-Laws, by which the Society is governed and there is reason to believe that they were also practitioners of the healing art. But it is not so generally known and acknowledged that some of them in their day held high positions in the scientific world, nor has sufficient commendation been bestowed upon the whole body for their unselfish zeal in the promotion and encouragement of the study of Natural History, and especially Botany, as an essential element of medical education.

The Apothecaries of London were originally members of the City Company of Grocers. It would appear that they can have had little in common with their trading companions, except in the sale of medicines. The Gardeners had already obtained their Charter in 1606; the Apothecaries felt they also warranted separate identification. James I, champion of the sciences, upheld their claim and part of the instrument of independence, granted in 1617 is worth quoting:

> Whereas very many Empiricks and unskilful and ignorant Men ... do abide in our City of London ... which are not well instructed in the Art of Mystery of Apothecaries, but ... do make and compound many unwholesome, hurtful, deceiptful, corrupt and dangerous medicines and the same do sell ... and daily transmit ... to the great peril and daily hazard of the lives of our subjects ... We therefore weighing with ourselves how to prevent the endeavours of such wicked persons ... thought necessary to disunite and dissociate the Apothecaries of our City of London from the Freedom of the Mystery of

Grocers ... into one body Corporate and Politic ... to whom in all future time the management of those inconveniences might be given charge and committee ... after the manner of other Companies.

The Grocers did not take kindly to the breakaway and, with the support of the Lord Mayor, the Commons were approached to revoke the decision. However, the King stood by his Apothecaries and their independence, although the City did not openly acknowledge them until seven years later, when they were allowed to take part in the river procession on Lord Mayor's Day, using a hired barge for the occasion, since as yet they lacked funds for such ceremonial trimmings. By 1632 they had installed themselves in their own Hall, Cobham House in Blackfriars, where they embarked upon regularizing their trade and setting examinations for their Apprentices.

For studying botany in the field they did not have far to go. Hampstead Heath, the fields of Battersea and Islington, and banks of the river through the villages of Chelsea, Wandsworth, Hammersmith and Putney provided rich hunting grounds for plant collectors and daily expeditions could be made from the City. The more enquiring ventured further afield and a young Yorkshireman, Thomas Johnson, apprenticed to a Mr William Bell in 1620, paid particular attention to botanical discovery. He qualified in 1628 and before the year was out had made 'simpling voyages' to Kent and Hampstead Heath with nine companions, all in some way associated with the Company. The published accounts of these journeys and the plants found, 250 in Kent and 72 more in Hampstead, were the first records of the herborising expeditions which were to become a regular part of the Apprentices' training in botany. Later he wrote of expeditions to the Isle of Wight, the West Country and Wales.

Although plants were being collected throughout this country and many were beginning to arrive from overseas, as yet the Apothecaries had no place where they might cultivate and study them scientifically. They were anxious also to find a mooring place for their four-oared ceremonial barge, with a cabin in the stern. In the seventeenth century the broad water of the Thames was used far more than the narrow and often bad roads for practical transport and festive occasions. Up river some two and a half miles from Blackfriars was a convenient creek and there the fertile land had long produced fruit and vegetables for the City. The Apothecaries looked no further; they approached Charles Cheyne, a Chelsea landowner of some substance, who agreed, in 1673, to let the Society a three and a half acre plot at a rent of £5 per annum.

The site for the new garden had a river frontage to the south, was bounded on the east by Swan Lane, which led to the tavern of that name and on the north by Cox's Close. In 1676 an arrangement was made with the widow of William Gape, a past Master of the Company, for plants to be transferred from her Westminster garden to Chelsea and work began on the building of a brick wall around the property. The first gardener on record was named Piggot, apparently a dishonest one, as he was dismissed for overcharging. He was followed by Richard Pratt in 1677, whose salary of £30 a year warranted an experienced gardener. However, all was not well; plants were stolen, work left undone and general advantage was taken of distant authority at Blackfriars. After due consideration the Company levied high subscriptions on members to help with garden maintenance and decided to plant 'Nectorines of all sorts, Peaches, Apricocks, Cherryes and Plumes', as well as herbs specifically for medicinal teaching.

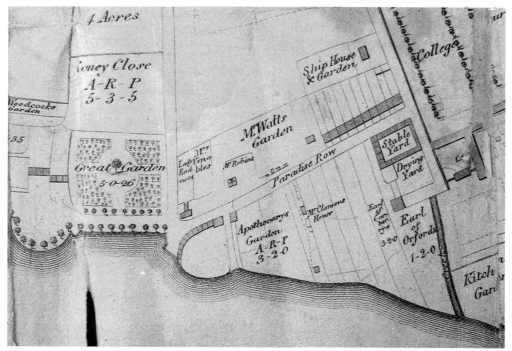

Part of a map of Chelsea surveyed in 1664 by James Hamilton

They made a water gate in the south wall and built a boathouse large enough to accommodate three barges, thereby gaining rent paid by two other users. John Watts, one of the Apothecaries who had contributed to the cost of erecting the wall, was in 1680 appointed to manage garden affairs at a salary of £50 per annum, with additional labouring help. A Garden Committee was formed and agreed to the building of a greenhouse at a cost of £138. Two years later the first noteworthy visitor arrived from overseas, Dr Paul Hermann, Professor of Botany at Leyden. They agreed upon an exchange of plants and later Watts journeyed to Holland, with a grant from

Plaque on the Swan Walk wall of Chelsea Physic Garden

the Company of £10 towards travelling expenses, to collect plants for Chelsea. This was the first record of contact with a physic garden on the continent and so, within a few years, the Apothecaries' garden had established itself in botanical circles.

In Watts's time four cedar trees were planted at Chelsea: two near the river frontage of the garden and two further back. A young medical man, Hans Sloane, wrote to John Ray of his wonder 'to see the *Cedrus Montis Libani*, the inhabitant of a very different climate' thriving in the Garden. In 1732 these trees produced cones, the first in this country. The two innermost trees were cut down in 1771 as they were considered to be impoverishing the soil and shading the flowers in the Garden, but the others stood guard by the watergate for another hundred years and no doubt caused interested comment from river travellers. The last was felled in 1912.

By 1685, although more established and better organized, the Garden was proving a heavy expense for the Company, which made a proposition to Mr Watts. For an annual sum of £100 he was to take on the care, culture and management of the Garden for a term of seven years from Michaelmas, to keep in repair the stove, greenhouse and other buildings and utensils contained in them, to make a catalogue of the plants and, an additional commercial perquisite, to be allowed to sell surplus fruit and plants for his own benefit. It was also decided that the Master, Wardens and Assistants should pay for a key giving them access to the Garden. The date of the plaque on the Swan Lane wall is 1686, by which time it was considered that the Garden had become 'effectively arranged'.

John Evelyn recorded in his Diary, August 6, 1685:

> ... to see Mr. Wats, keeper of the Apothecaries Garden of simples at Chelsey; where there is a collection of innumerable rarities of that sort: Particularly, besids many rare annuals the Tree bearing the Jesuits bark, which had don such cures in quartans: & what was very ingenious the subterranean heate, conveyed by a stove under the Conserveatory, which was all Vaulted with brick; so as he leaves the doores & windowes open in the hard(e)st frosts, secluding onely the snow, &c.

The tree mentioned (*Cinchona*) grew on the slopes of the Andes and was the source of quinine. Its bark was brought back to Europe by the Countess of Chinchon, wife of the Spanish Ambassador in Peru. Jesuit missionaries had also taken it to Rome, from where an Apothecary named Robert Talbot had obtained medicine to cure Charles II of ague. Scarcity limited its purchase to the wealthy and quinine did not become available generally for the treatment of malaria for another two hundred years, when the Dutch successfully transplanted trees to the East Indies.

John Watts proved not the most able of administrators and when his term expired, charge of the Garden passed to Samuel Doody, an Apothecary with a London practice, who collected all manner of natural history specimens and was a prolific writer on the sciences. With four others: Petiver, Dare, Bromwich and Jones, he was granted a 21-year lease of the Garden, though no official record of this arrangement exists. On Doody's death in 1706, the Court of Apothecaries agreed to lease the garden to a joint stock of ninety subscribers, amongst whom Isaac Rand was prominent. James Petiver, Apothecary to St Bartholomews and the Charterhouse, became Demonstrator of Plants.

Under the new regime, herborising expeditions received some impetus. They had been increased to six a year; five for the Apprentices, conducted by the Demonstrator and one, the General Herborising, for Members only. The Apprentices, marshalled early, were allowed no encumbrances in the way of umbrellas or overcoats. Each slung a tin collecting box over his shoulder and an attendant of the Company carried a receptacle for larger discoveries. They would stop at an inn for a midday meal, discuss their finds and be instructed particularly on their medical properties. One annual excursion was made to the Woodford area of Essex, where undoubtedly they would have visited 'Harts', the home of hospitable Mr Richard Warner, an avid herboriser himself, as well as a collector of exotics from overseas. The General Herborising was also conducted by the Demonstrator who led his more expert colleagues further afield, sometimes to the coast where they

A VIEW of a Piece of WATER at Woodford Row. in Essex. With the Adjacent Country.
To Richard Warner Esq.r of Woodford this Plate is inscribed by his most obliged humble Serv.t Will.m Bellers.
Published 17 Jan.y 1774 by Rob.t Sayer Map & Printseller, in Fleet Street, and John Boydell, Engraver, in Cheapside.

Woodford Row, Essex in the eighteenth century

would remain for a couple of days or more. Plants collected were exhibited at a dinner in July to Members and their guests, and a general discussion followed a talk by the Demonstrator. Stewards were appointed to bear the cost of the entertainment and on one occasion Petiver wrote to Dr Sloane about fixing the next Herborising, 'and Putney Heath being a place not this year visited, I have determined ye Bowling Green there for ye lecture of Botany, where we shall dine on Tuesday next.' These working dinners provided an excellent opportunity for convivial exchanges on botanical discovery.

One of Petiver's friends was James Sherard (1666–1738), brother of the diplomat, William, who did much for botany at Oxford. He had studied at Chelsea in his apprenticeship days and his highly successful practice in Mark Lane enabled him to retire early to Eltham in Kent and to devote the rest of his days to his garden of rare plants, many of which were sent home by his brother from the Near East. In 1704 Petiver and Sherard carried out a botanising expedition in a stylish manner, travelling together in a two-horse chaise with a servant. Their progress through Kent resulted in both a gastronomic and botanic appreciation. They comment on the Mayoress of Winchelsea's excellent punch, 'each bowl better than the former one', and at Dr Fuller's in Sevenoaks they enjoyed 'venison pasty, plus the strongest drink in the country'. After a day's botanising near Tunbridge Wells, they relished 'a bottle of pretty good Madeira and a couple of large rabbits, well dressed'. Nevertheless, they did not forget the main object of their expedition and kept a careful record af all the plants found, though they commented that had the journey been made a month or two sooner, they would have found a greater number of rarities.

An Apothecary who obviously appreciated the garden at Chelsea was Dr Samuel Dale (1659–1739) who left instructions for his botanical books and dried specimens to be preserved there. In 1692 he published a *Pharmacologia*, an early work on drugs and medicines, which showed his wide botanical knowledge and where he gratefully acknowledged help from Sloane, Ray, Sherard, Doody and Petiver. Samuel Dale practised at Bocking in Essex, where his garden of curiosities prompted a visit from Petiver and Sherard when on a tour of East Anglia. John Martyn (1699–1768) was another distinguished physician–botanist who lived in Chelsea where he practised medicine. He was frequently at the Physic Garden, seeking information for his *Historia Plantarum Rariorum* (1728–37). He held the Chair of Botany at Cambridge for thirty years, although he ceased lecturing in 1735 and that University's Botanic Garden was not established until 1762 (see Chapter 17).

By 1713 the Chelsea Physic Garden again needed help and the Trustees for the Management imposed various levies on Members and Apprentices to raise funds. As the original lease had expired, a new Committee was appointed to consider how best to make the garden viable. Although Lord Cheyne had earlier offered the Apothecaries the freehold of the land for £400, this was far beyond their means. They had even been forced to give up the prestigious Company barge, unable to afford the cost of its repair and the wages of the bargemaster. Petiver died in 1718 and left his collections to his great friend, the recently knighted Hans Sloane, who was now the owner of the Manor of Chelsea which included the Garden. Here was a sympathetic listener to whom the Apothecaries could turn – one with an extensive knowledge of medicine and botany, who was to play an important part in the history of the Garden.

3 The Garden's Benefactor

Hans Sloane was born in Killyleagh, County Down in 1660, the third son of parents of Scottish descent. At the age of sixteen he became seriously ill, probably with tuberculosis, and was compelled to rest in Ireland for three years. This adversity he turned to good advantage, for here was time to devote to his beloved natural history. Once recovered, he decided to study medicine in London and took lodgings with Nicholas Staphorst, a chemist who most conveniently lived next door to the Apothecaries' Hall in Blackfriars, where he attended lectures on medicine and pursued the study of botany with John Watts at the Chelsea Garden. Thus Hans Sloane began the thorough grounding on which he was to build his successful career. During this time he became acquainted with John Ray, the great English naturalist, and Robert Boyle, the philosopher, both of whom gave help and encouragement to the young man.

He continued his studies in France at the Royal Garden of Plants in Paris under Joseph Pitton de Tournefort, a French botanist who had already made expeditions to Spain, Greece and Asia Minor, and later produced a new classification of plants, accompanied by descriptions of the genera. After Sloane had quickly gained his degree as Doctor of Medicine from the University of Orange (southern France) in 1683, he continued his medical studies at Montpellier under another botanist, Pierre Magnol. Together they travelled in search of plants, sometimes joined by William Courten, who became Sloane's lifelong friend. At the end of 1684 he returned to England, fully qualified, and was taken on by Dr Thomas Sydenham as an assistant in a busy London practice.

About this time a detailed correspondence, lasting for twenty years, started between Sloane and Ray. The aged naturalist was thus kept in touch with London affairs when compelled to stay in Essex on account of ill health and slender means. In 1705 he wrote that he doubted whether he would see the winter through and early in the next year he died, leaving a last, unfinished letter to his young friend. One of the first he had received from Sloane reported on a new hothouse at Chelsea and listed the exotics already growing there. He told of botanising in Sheppey and, excitedly, of a chance to visit the West Indies as physician to the Duke of Albemarle, recently appointed Governor of Jamaica. Sydenham's unenthusiastic reaction was outweighed by John Ray's wise encouragement and expectation of achieve-

*Hans Sloane memorial
in the Chelsea Physic
Garden*

ment. Sloane himself reckoned that such an opportunity to travel and at the same time pursue the practice of physic was too good an opportunity to miss. He had recently been elected a Fellow of the Royal Society and of the College of Physicians; the future was open for furtherance.

In Jamaica, as well as tending the Governor's household, he looked after many islanders who had great faith in him. He also collected natural history curiosities and plants before the appointment ended with the Duke's death. The first publication resulting from this tour abroad was *Catalogus Plantarum quae in Jamaica* (1696), reviewed favourably by John Ray for the *Philosophical Transactions* of the Royal Society, his faith in the young collector fully justified. This was but a resumé of the botanical part of a much more detailed work to follow in due course. The first folio volume of Sloane's *Natural History of Jamaica* was published in 1707, the delay of the second, until eighteen years later being due, he explained, to the demands of his busy practice in Bloomsbury (he also attended the Royal Family) and to putting his vast collections into some sort of order. These included his own from Jamaica, others from his friend, Courten, and still more from Holland, where, in 1711, he had sent Petiver to buy the collections amassed by Dr

Hermann, the Leyden Professor of Botany. Petiver also bequeathed his own collection to Sloane and it had taken him many years to bring all this material into an orderly array.

In 1695 Sloane had married the wealthy widow of a Jamaican planter. Of their four children, a boy and a girl died as infants and two daughters, Sarah and Elizabeth, became the wives of George Stanley and Lord Cadogan respectively, both husbands proving dutiful correspondents with their father-in-law on matters of health and horticulture. Due recognition was soon to come to the industrious doctor: in 1716 George I created him a baronet, an honour as yet conferred on only one other physician. Three years later he became President of the College of Physicians and in 1727 Physician-General to the Army. He followed Sir Isaac Newton as President of the Royal Society and held this office until 1741, making generous financial contributions, one in particular of importance to botany.

He had purchased the Manor of Chelsea, including the Apothecaries' Garden, from William Cheyne in 1712. This was not, as some believe, originally owned by Sir Thomas More, but a later manor belonging to Henry VIII, where the young Princess Elizabeth lived for a while. The new owner had long been acquainted with the village on account of his association with the Physic Garden. He would undoubtedly have watched with anxiety the growing troubles over finance and staff during the next ten years and, by 1722, the abandonment of the Garden was a possibility. At this juncture, although he was not yet living at Chelsea, Sloane intervened as saviour and benefactor of the Garden.

For a yearly payment of £5 he conveyed that piece of his estate to the Apothecaries Company, with one particular proviso: that every year fifty dried specimens grown there in the same year be supplied to the Royal Society of London. Under this arrangement the Society received more than 3000 plants; all to be carefully listed in the *Philosophical Transactions*. Frequent references to inspection and study by Fellows of these acquisitions from Chelsea are to be found in the Journal Books of the Royal Society and the specimens are now housed in the British Museum (Natural History).

As future Apothecaries might well have been tempted to sell the site for building, Sloane insisted on another clause:

> If the Society shall at any time convert the Garden into buildings for
> habitations or to any other uses, save such as are necessary for a Physic
> Garden, for the culture, planting and preserving of trees, plants and flowers,
> and such like purposes, then it shall be lawful for Sir Hans Sloane, his heirs
> and assigns to enter upon the premises and to hold the same for the use and
> benefit and in trust for the said President, Council and Fellows of the Royal
> Society, subject to the same rent and to the delivery of specimens of plants.

This wise precaution preserved the Garden for posterity.

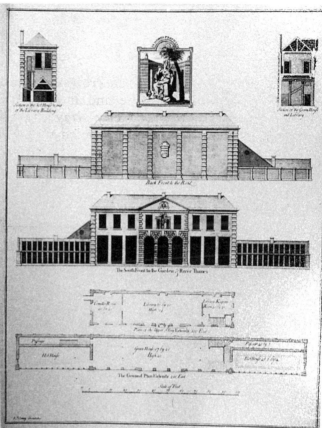

'Plan of ye intended improvements to be made in your Physic Garden at Chelsea'
c.1732, Edward Oakley, architect

Sir Hans also helped with maintenance; he gave the Society £100 to repair the steps to the river and was certainly instrumental in gaining another £100 from the College of Physicians. He laid the foundation stone of the new greenhouse and later gave 150 guineas for its repair. In 1733, the Apothecaries erected a marble statue by Rysbrack to their most generous benefactor and placed it in one of the rooms of the orange house, but in 1748 it was moved to the centre of the garden, where a replica stands today.

Sloane also became concerned in another local matter: the controversy over the King's Road. Originally a mere footpath through fields, Charles II had decided it was a better route to Hampton Court than one to the North, through the village of Knightsbridge. At this time the King's French gardeners were making extensive improvements to the Palace gardens and frequent inspection was necessary. The land was therefore made into a coach road, allowing farm labourers and market gardeners access to the fields, but during the reign of George I, this long-established route was closed by the Surveyor General and only a few privileged people were allowed to use it. Sloane petitioned the Lords Commissioner of H.M. Treasury, who decided in favour of the request and once again tenants of the lands adjoining King's Road in Chelsea were allowed free passage with their carts and horses, and their ditches, invaluable for drainage and cattle stops, were reopened. Thus, the Lord of the Manor was acclaimed by both workers on the land and consumers of their produce.

Once the tenure of the Garden had been guaranteed, measures had to be taken to ensure its successful progress. In November 1721, Sir Hans received a letter (Sloane MSS 4046 f 168. See opp.) from Patrick Blair, a scientist whose *Botanick Essays* (1720) had received much attention. He wrote of a Mr Philip Miller:

> I own I am not personally acquainted with him. The reading of my Botanick Essays and the Experiments he has successfully made in pursuance of what I have advanced there has created in him an earnestness to correspond with me. I have of late had two letters from him, in which he has shown such an easy and familiar way of expressing his thoughts, such a delight for improvement and so much exactness and dilligence in the making of observations that I look upon him to go onward with a curiosity and genious superior to most of his occupation.
>
> The enclosed experiments will, I doubt not, excuse this my freedom in endeavouring to give him this opportunity of becoming acquainted with you. His knowledge in the improving of ground, it seems has now redounded to his disadvantage. His Landlord, designing profit himself by it, by raising his rent or otherwise proposing to turn him out. He therefore earnestly begs of me that since you deservedly have the nomination of an Gardner to the Chelsea Garden, which I understand is now vacant, that I would address you in his behalf that at least you would accept of him as an Candidate if there are other competitors and, if found sufficiently qualifyd you would propose him accordingly as you shall find he deserves. He tells me he is already acquainted with Mr. Miller and Mr. Rand. I'm ready to believe yowl admit of their recommendations all I presume to say of him is that he writes me he shall be really dilligent and the enclosed specimens he has grown which I hope yowl puruse make it look as if he would prove so.

Evidently Sir Hans supported this glowing testimonial as the appointment was made the following year. It has been said that Philip Miller worked at the Garden before 1722 and that this referred to his promotion. It had also been said that his father had been employed there. However, from Blair's letter it is clear that there was another Mr Miller working at Chelsea as Isaac Rand's assistant (acknowledged in the Preface of his *Essays*), hence the resulting confusion.

During his retirement in Chelsea, when well over eighty, Sir Hans directed the arrangement of his enormous natural history collections from a wheelchair. Many famous people came to view the grandiose exhibition: the Prince of Wales judged it to be 'an ornament to the nation', as indeed it was to become. Pehr Kalm, a Swedish naturalist and pupil of Linnaeus, was amazed by the diversity of stones, insects, East and West Indian butterflies,

Honoured Sir   Boston 10ber 30 172¾/44   No 166

I did my self the favour some time ago to present you with several Species of the Absynthia maritima indigenous upon this Coast If the dryd specimens has not given such an Idea of the distinctions as appeared to me while they were growing perhaps the planting them in so many different pots along with their native soil may clear up what difficultys still remain about them of which if youl be pleasd to inform me I shall endeavour to give you better satisfaction

The Bearer hereof Mr. Phillip Miller Gardiner is the cause of my troubling you with this second Letter. I own I am not personally acquainted with him The reading of my Botanick Essays and the experiments he has since successfully made in pursuance of what I have advanced there has created in him an earnestness to correspond with me. I have of late recd two Letters from him in which he has shown such an easy and familiar way of expressing his thought such a delight for improvements and so much exactness and diligence in the making of observations that I look upon him to be endowd with a curiosity and Genious superiour to most of his occupation

The enclosed experiments will I doubt not excuse this my freedom in endeavouring to give him this opportunity of becoming acquainted with you His knowledge in the improving of Ground it seems has now redounded to the disadvantage His Landlord designing profit himself by it by raising his rent or otherwise proposing to turn him out He therefore earnestly begs of me that since you deservedly have the nomination of an gardiner to the Chelsea Garden which I understand is now vacant that I would address you in his behalf that at least you would accept of him as an Candidate if there are other Competitors and if found sufficiently qualifyd you would preferr him according as you shall find he deserves He tells me he is already acquainted with Mr Miller and Mr. Rand I am ready to believe you Admit of their recommendations all I presume to say of him is that he writes me he shall be very diligent and the enclosed specimens he has given me which I hope youl peruse make it reasonable if he would prove so I am with all due respect Your most obliged humble servt

                                                    Ja. Blair

Chelsea Old Church

corals, humming birds, all manner of snakes, animals and birds, and a surprising assortment of peculiar footwear. In addition to the collection was his magnificent library of 4800 volumes, 'all bound in superb bindings'. Philip Miller had taken Kalm to visit the old man in 1748 and although they were 'obliged to shout loud', they discussed the Jamaican venture of sixty years earlier, John Ray's correspondence and Kalm's impending visit to America. Sir Hans maintained his insatiable curiosity until the end: weekly visits from George Edwards, a natural history artist and Librarian of the College of Physicians, kept him aware of events in the two spheres to which he had devoted his life.

He died in 1753, in his ninety-third year, having made arrangements for his great collections, valued at £80,000, to be left to the nation, on the condition that £20,000 be paid to his daughters. After long debate in Parliament, the condition was accepted and the collections were moved to Montague House to become the nucleus of the British Museum. Chelsea Old Church has a monument in memory of Sir Hans Sloane; but additional permanent memorials are the streets, square, crescent and terrace in the Chelsea area, named after its magnanimous citizen.

In one way or another a great many people owed much to this benevolent physician and he gave to Philip Miller an opportunity which would ultimately benefit botany and horticulture throughout the world. Two years after his appointment at the Chelsea Garden, Miller played a major part in producing *The Gardener's and Florists's Dictionary*. This was dedicated to Sir Hans Sloane and provided

> ... an opportunity publickly to acknowledge the many obligations I lie under your person. As it was your generous gift of the Physic Garden to the Worshipful Company of Apothecaries that encouraged the supporting of that Garden for the improvement of Botany and so consequently was the Occasion of my being employed in a service so agreeable to my natural inclinations, so the favourable opinion you have had of my abilities, when you was pleased to recommend me to that worshipful Company, with the several instances I have since had of your generous inclinations to encourage the Art and me, will ever lay me under the greatest obligations to endeavour to answer that character you was please to give of me and herein humbly hoping to approve myself what I most desire to be thought of ...

Indeed, over the next forty-five years, Philip Miller repaid his patron through a diligence rarely equalled.

Hans Sloane memorial, Chelsea Old Church

4 Philip Miller in Chelsea

Land around the Thames to the west of the City had long attracted tillers of the soil. First came the farmers and then more specialist cultivators: market gardeners, nurserymen and florists. All appreciated the rich soil and the proximity of a large river for easy transport of their produce. At one time London suppliers had been importing Holland's renowned out-of-season fruit and vegetables for special occasions; but with William III came those skilled in the art of 'forcing' and at the beginning of the eighteenth century Richard Bradley claimed that the kitchen gardens which

> exceed all the others in Europe for wholesome Produce and a variety of Herbs are those at the Neat-Houses near Tuttle-fields,* Westminster, which abound in Salads, early Cucumbers, Colliflowers, Melons, Winter Asparagus and almost every Herb fitting the Table; and I think there is no where so good a school for a Kitchen Gardener as this Place: tho' Battersea affords the largest natural Asparagus and the earliest Cabbages. Again, the Gardens about Hammersmith are as famous for Strawberries, Raspberries, Currants, Gooseberries, and such like; and if early fruit is our Desire, Mr. Millet's at North End, near the same Place, affords us Cherries, Apricocks and Curiosities of those kinds, some months before the Natural Season.

The productivity of the area impressed Pehr Kalm on his visit later in the century. He described Chelsea as a little village a couple of miles from London where the Thames ran between nurseries and market gardens, 'of which there are a frightful number'. He observed that here there was no need to grow trees from seed; one could buy them in various sizes, 'cultivated and clipped' at a moderate price on account of many competitive tradesmen. The same was true of market produce; some growers concentrating on just one crop so that 'whole tracts, like large arable fields, were sown with only cabbages or asparagus', and he also appreciated the local economy in forcing asparagus through the necks of broken bottles.

In his *History of Chelsea* (1869) George Bryan remarked how the King's Road was once almost exclusively occupied by farmers and gardeners and one of its greatest attractions for many years afterwards was the preponderance of nursery and floricultural grounds to be found there. There was, for example, an interesting garden near the site of Sloane Square owned

---

* Commemorated in Tothill Street, by St James's Park Station.

by John Fraser (1750–1811), who had crossed the Atlantic to collect plants in the wilds of North America and, on the site of Colville Terrace, James Colvill's nursery displayed hitherto unknown flowers to excite general admiration. By 1811 this nursery had over 30,000 square feet of glass.

No better environment could therefore have been found for Philip Miller when he came to Chelsea in 1722. His father, a Scotsman, had been gardener to a gentleman at Bromley before founding his own market gardening business at Deptford and, in the diary of Pehr Kalm, details about Miller's early life are found. Kalm had gained his information from 'trustworthy men': Richard Warner (c.1713–1775) and Peter Collinson (1694–1775), both good friends of Miller and the somewhat verbose account ran:

> Mr. Miller's father was a nurseryman, who followed occupation all his life. He began to instruct his son, this Philip Miller, in the art from his earliest years, as he had an uncommon liking for that occupation. As the man throve, so he spared no expense in also causing his son to have a sufficient education in various languages, and other sciences, which profit and adorn a man. Miller quickly assimilated all that his father had himself taught him, within theory and practice of ornamental and kitchen gardening. At the same time he went through all books which had appeared in England on these sciences. An industrious intercourse with other enterprising nurserymen in this town and

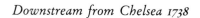

Downstream from Chelsea 1738

in the country round made him still more proficient. But he did not stop with this. A change of soil, climate, etc. often caused a plant which can, according to ordinary rules, be transplanted at one place, not to admit of this being accomplished with the same advantage at another place, but particular treatment is often required at each place.

His thoughts were therefore turned upon travelling. He was well off and had therefore no difficulty in accomplishing this. To travel out to foreign countries without having first made himself acquainted with what remarkable things there are to be found at home, he held neither for wisdom or usefulness. He therefore travelled through the greater part of England, observing everything, but was equally careful to inspect all ornamental and kitchen gardens, and to make himself at home and acquainted with all horticulturalists, for he was of the opinion that he could learn something useful which he did not know before at least from some of them. He conversed with them on all matters connected with their business and had his trouble often many times repeated with the useful wrinkles he gained. As agriculture had so near a connection with horticulture therefore he kept at the same time an observant eye on everything which occurred in rural economy, particularly the cultivation of ploughed lands.

After he had travelled through England he started on his foreign travels and thus explored Flanders and Holland, because he knew that there were also great horticulturalists there and with the science and management of ornamental and kitchen gardens which there reached a high pitch of excellence. Whether he, besides the aforesaid lands, also explored other districts, I have not understood.

After this comprehensive study of every aspect of horticulture, Miller came to the conclusion that his preference was for ornamental gardening and he established his own nursery in St George's Fields, Southwark, later the site of King's Bench Prison. There, as Blair had so persuasively pointed out to Sloane, he diligently tilled his soil to cultivate the beautiful flowers and shrubs of which, in later writings, his own appreciation was always apparent. Only one direct reference to this period has been discovered. This may be found in most editions of the *Dictionary* and *Kalendar*, and refers to Monthly [Autumn Damask] Roses. Miller had been forced to transplant some of these just as they were coming into flower, but by cutting off all the buds, placing them in a wet trench and watering continuously until they became established, he was able, in August and September to pick flowers 'as fair as those produced in June'.

Today the Victoria and Albert Museum stands on part of the renowned Brompton Nursery run by the talented garden designers George London and Henry Wise. Here the King's exotic evergreens were housed during the winter and plans were made for extensive alterations at Hampton Court and for the great gardens at Blenheim and Longleat. When both London and

Wise were absent, Stephen Switzer was sometimes in charge of the nursery. He was the author of some works on gardening, but he lacked the experience to produce a much needed comprehensive practical guide book. Having heard of Miller's industry, he made the suggestion to him and thus the idea of a small *Dictionary* was conceived.

Published in 1724, it contained a message to the reader:

We whose names are underwritten do approve and recommend this book as highly useful and necessary for all lovers of gardening. Thomas Fairchild at Hoxton, Robert Furber at Kensington, Robert Smith at Vauxhall, Samuel Driver at Lambeth, Moses James at Standgate, Obadiah Lowe at Battersea, Christopher Gray at Fulham, Benjamin Whitmill at Hoxton, Francis Hunt at Putney and Wm. Gray Jr. at Fulham.

These ten were leading nurserymen in the London area around 1720 and Miller, writing to Blair the following year, acknowledged their help. Thomas Martyn (who early in the next century brought out a revised edition of Miller's later large *Dictionary*) said of the signatories 'I have reason to suppose that the above were united in a society for the improvement of gardening, that Mr. Miller acted as their secretary and that the work was in some degree the produce of their joint efforts'. This was also borne out by the inclusion of catalogues at the end of the book, looking very much like contributions from various nurseries and it is evident that those recommending the work did so with an eye to business.

The Society of Gardeners met every month, usually at Newhall's Coffee House in Chelsea. Thomas Fairchild (1667–1729) was already known for his *City Gardener*, with its advice on flowers, evergreens and shrubs suitable for London gardens and another member, Robert Furber, who experimented with many new trees and plants in his Kensington nursery numbered a horse chestnut with a scarlet flower amongst his novelties. He apprenticed his son, William, to Philip Miller at Chelsea in 1722 at a premium of £4 (Soc. of Genealogists, TS 'Apprentices 1710–1762', ref. 9/186). To each meeting members brought rare plants for general discussion and in due course they decided to publish their findings in a series of illustrated catalogues. The first, covering trees and shrubs (Miller may have been instrumental in choice of subject) appeared in 1730 (see Chapter 12, p. 99). However, this ambitious project was taken no further because Fairchild had died in 1727, Miller was becoming preoccupied with his own writing and, after some dissension, the Society was disbanded.

Philip Miller married a Miss Kennet, probably not before he was well established at Chelsea. She came from outside the parish as there is no entry of this marriage in the Register Books nor is there mention of the marriage of her sister, Susanna, to Georg Ehret, the botanical artist, in 1738. However, parish records show that three of the Miller children were baptised at

Chelsea Old Church: Mary in 1732, Philip in 1734 and Charles in 1739. Although there were instances of many infant deaths, for example four children of Dr Thos. Percifull died in nine days in November 1733 and Dr John Martyn's twins, John and Eulalia, died within a year of their baptism in 1737, there appear to have been no such tragedies in the Miller family and we may suppose these were their only three children.

A contemporary of young Charles Miller was Dr Martyn's son, Thomas, baptised in 1738. They attended the same school in Chelsea, became firm friends and many years later were to work together at Cambridge in the interests of botany. An entry among the baptisms at the Old Church in April 1741, names the son of George Dennis Ehret (an approximation of the artist's second name, Dionysius, seems as near as the Parish Clerk could get) as George-Philip, almost certainly after his uncle by marriage.

Under the new Rules and Orders for the Management of the Physic Garden, drawn up in 1722, 'convenient accommodation for the Director and Gardener' was to be provided and by 1727 the new orangery, or greenhouse, was complete. This was not a greenhouse as we know it; in the eighteenth

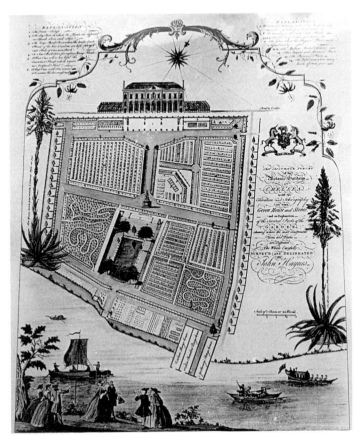

Plan of Chelsea Physic Garden by John Haynes (1751): note the gap in the wall (top right) to Miller's house

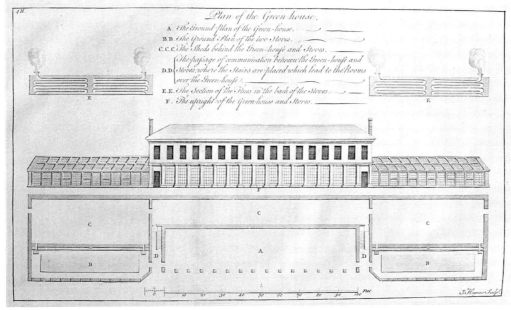

Plan of the greenhouse [GD]

century these buildings were of brick with large windows. It was planned in 1725 and an engraving by Sutton Nicholls shows it at the north side of the garden, 300 feet long with forty-one windows on the ground floor. The upper storey of 180 feet provided accommodation for the library, committee room and living quarters for the gardener.

There the Millers may have lived for a short while. However, in August 1734, a month after their first son was baptised, Philip Miller appears in the Parish Rate Books as occupier of a house in Swan Walk, for which he paid a half yearly rate of 14/–, reduced to 10/6d. two years later. When compared with rates levied on other houses in the road, this would indicate only a modest establishment. The map of Chelsea Physic Garden, engraved by John Haynes in 1751, clearly shows a gap for a small gate in the north-east corner of the garden wall to provide easy access to the gardener's home, the main gate being on the river frontage. In 1751 the Garden Committee recommended Miller be given an allowance of £4 a year to compensate him for the £4 increase in the rent of his house. However, the Court of Apothecaries took the view that Miller had been paying the increased rent for some years and declined to sanction the proposed allowance.

Ten years later a note in the Minutes of the Garden Committee states that Miller had asked for a residence to be built in the Garden, but this was refused. Later in 1761 the Committee ordered Miller to 'hire a house lately called the New Tavern for his residence, provided the rent does not exceed £20 per annum'. Whether he did this is questionable, as in the following months he made a kitchen in the east end of the greenhouse. This may have been for meals during the day while living elsewhere, or perhaps it was to make existing accommodation there more adequate for his use. It is evident that he did live there in his later years as the Minutes of 1771 agree to provide his successor with lodgings in Chelsea, 'until such time as Mr. Miller has quit his apartments in the greenhouse'.

Doggett Coat and Badge race finish

While the young Millers lived in Swan Walk, eighteenth-century Chelsea provided many diversions for their amusement. The anniversary of the accession of George I, 1 August, was marked by an exciting event on the river. In 1715, Thomas Doggett, an Irishman who had made a successful career in London as an actor, theatre manager and author, instituted a race between six young watermen, donating the prize of an ornate jacket, cash in pocket and silver badge to the winner. The course was rowed from the Old Swan near London Bridge to the White Swan at Chelsea and thus dwellers in the Walk were conveniently placed to view the finish.

The river also provided a tremendous variety of fish and certainly the Millers would have taken advantage of this from the Garden frontage. Faulkner's local *History* mentions trout, pike, carp, roach, dace, perch, chub, barbel, smelt, flounder, shad, lamprey and eel all being caught in the river off Chelsea and also records nine salmon weighing 171½ lbs. being landed there in May 1664.

David Loudon's Bunn House c.1730

Prelates and princes and lieges and kings
Hail for the Bellman who tinkles and sings,
Bouch of the highest and lowliest ones,
There's a charm in the sound which nobody shuns,
Of 'smoking hot, piping hot, rare Chelsey bunns'.

Thus ran the old rhyme, extolling the produce of the Bunnhouse, situated between Union and Westbourne Streets. Even Dean Swift wrote with enthusiasm of this speciality of Richard Hand, who had the honour to serve the Royal Family. On Good Friday there was great merrymaking, when as many as 200,000 buns were sold to those who came to the Easter Fair and its various side shows. At other times the Bunnhouse became more respectable, opening the gardens behind its premises where, discreetly in grottos, fashionable customers of the eighteenth century dallied and nibbled.

Don Saltero's Coffee House

The Coffee House of Don Saltero was another attraction. The owner was, in fact, a Mr Salter, one-time servant to Sir Hans Sloane, who had collected many curios rejected by his master on their travels. These he assembled in his Chelsea Knackatory in 1695, an establishment which proved popular for the next hundred years. Sir Richard Steel wrote in the *Tatler* 'When I came into the Coffee House, I had not time to salute the company before my eye was diverted to 10,000 gimcracks round the room and on the ceiling'.

The Chelsea China Factory, established at the corner of Justice Walk in 1745, under the efficient management of a Mr Sprimont provided yet further scenes of energetic business. Many of the floral designs for this china, whether taken from prints or fresh exotic blooms, were obtained from the nearby Physic Garden and Philip Miller must have been in touch with the factory. The porcelain produced at Chelsea was said to compare with Dresden's fine china and there was always keen competition amongst dealers who waited at the doors to purchase pieces as soon as they emerged from the ovens.

Miller must surely have taken the family on local botanising expeditions to Chelsea Heath, the large stretch of common land to the north of the Fulham Road, where they could search for plants important to the Physic Garden. Probably they took friends as well: George-Philip Ehret and Thomas Martyn, both of whom inherited an interest in botany from their respective artistic and academic fathers. At other times they would collect along the river bank and the younger Martyn was to write many years later of *Crocus vernus*, 'I remember, when a boy, to have seen it in considerable quantity in Battersea meadow, near the mill'.

Certainly the Miller boys would have helped in the Garden. Young Philip was employed there for a time before going abroad, taking over during his father's trips into the country where some landowners sought his practical advice, particularly with regard to establishing plantations of hitherto un-known trees from abroad. Miller would also wish to discuss and inspect rarities being cultivated by his contemporaries. He was impressed by a fine *Annona triloba*, American custard apple or pawpaw, flourishing in Christopher Gray's nursery at Fulham. To exchange experience on raising rare seeds, he would visit James Gordon's thriving shop in the City's Fenchurch Street, many of the seeds sold there harvested from Gordon's own nursery between Mile End and Bromley. Miller commended him for success with *Kalmia latifola*, and Peter Collinson knew of no other man who could raise the 'dusty seeds of the Kalmias, Rhododendrons of Azaleas' as he did.

In the Garden, Miller had to give time to those who might call seeking particular plants or information on their culture. In 1752 Horace Walpole instructed his brother, Ned, to collect tea seed; Gilbert White came a few years later to discuss difficulties over growing melons at Selborne; and Charles Hatton selected two pots of passion flower, 'lusty and strong' in April 1760. Every day the diary had to be filled; an important day-to-day record of garden affairs was imperative for his writing and current work for his publishers called for continued attention, because throughout his long life editions of the *Dictionary* and the *Abridgement* needed revision and extension. Additionally and importantly, for from this so much resulted, there was extensive correspondence to be dealt with.

Philip Miller in Chelsea

In his Preface to the *Gardeners Dictionary*, Miller invited communications on 'new experiments in relation to this art' and, at a time when scientific work was developing rapidly, this request alone would have attracted a large response. Additionally there would be questions relating to horticulture and agriculture in Britain covering a diversity of subjects, from seed selection to estate enterprise. There was also the constant exchange of letters, seeds and plants with his overseas correspondents. All were answered at length in a meticulous hand and, from a closer study of these letters, much can be learned of this gardener who was to be acknowledged as the greatest of his time.

5 Correspondents in England and Scotland

From the exchange of letters with eight very diverse correspondents over nearly fifty years, some insight can be gained of Philip Miller, although personal references are only occasionally made. There is evidence of the writer's early energy and enthusiasm being replaced by latter-day physical inactivity and associated irritability, but throughout his letters, Miller's exceptionally wide knowledge, generously shared, on every aspect of horticulture – its science, practice and literature – is impressive. Each small request is invariably met, each question carefully considered, points either debated with an academic botanist or explained to an amateur gardener with patient thoroughness.

Patrick Blair, in his letter of recommendation to Sir Hans Sloane (1721) referred to an exchange of correspondence with Philip Miller. A month later he wrote again, expressing gratification that observations in his *Botanical Essays*, published the year before, 'had been confirmed by experiments made by some curious gardeners, among whom is Mr. Philip Miller'. He quoted fully from Miller's letters on pollination of tulips by bees and on cross-fertilisation of white and red cabbage, and these observations were passed on to the Royal Society (*Phil. Trans.* 31 216–221, 1721).

During 1724–25 Miller frequently wrote to Blair with information on the Physic Garden and his own literary work. On one occasion a dozen young myrtles had been dispatched, at a shilling apiece, although Miller much regretted he was unable to pack them himself on account of injuring his leg while 'a-herborising by water'. He commiserated with Blair over his failure with certain seeds and promised to send him rare plants. A prophetic note was penned, 'We have in flower several exotics in vast perfections and I doubt not that we shall be able to manage the most tender plants in ye world with these stoves.' Among his achievements at Chelsea were some pine-apples considered fine enough to be presented to the King by Sir Hans Sloane. At this time, Miller told Blair that he had been working with Nathanael St André, 'the famous anatomist', examining structures of plants and he believed that together they would make some curious discoveries. A postscript exemplifies Miller's independence, an attitude which ultimately caused friction with his employers: 'Pray take no notice to any body what I sent you, for some of our Company is for making a law that I should part with nothing without the consent of the company.'

An early correspondent of both Miller and Blair was Dr James Douglas (1615–1742), whose paper on the cultivation of saffron, as presented to the Royal Society, was included by Miller in the *Dictionary*. He was always willing to acknowledge and incorporate authoritative information and appreciated how Douglas had carefully surveyed the growth of this commodity in the Saffron Walden area between 1723 and 1728. Douglas was glad to acknowledge Miller's help and told the Royal Society that he had received some coconuts 'germinated in this country by the industrious Mr. Miller, by whose care and skill they were brought to this perfection; and besides he very freely communicated to me for the good of the publick his own methods in management in raising them which I here desire may be read in his words.' Thus each promoted the other's knowledge.

Dr Richardson (1663–1741) of North Bierley near Bradford was an eminent botanist who had studied in Leyden for three years, lodging with Paul Hermann, Professor of Botany. He was a good friend of Hans Sloane, on whose behalf Miller wrote with thanks for plants and later passed on a prescription for gout: patience and flannel. Richardson reciprocated with a promise of 'a pott of Woodcocks by Sam Haggers, a Kendal carrier', although most commissions between Chelsea and Yorkshire were undertaken by one working from Bradford.

In September 1726 Miller reported to Richardson that he was making a comprehensive catalogue of seeds saved from the previous year and would be forwarding it with *Martyn's Synoptical Table of Medicinal Plants* and a list of exotics at Chelsea. In the following year, having recently seen madder, *Rubia tinctorum*, grown and processed for dye in Holland, he asked if this commodity was grown in the north of England. He told Richardson that a Dutch gentleman had given him *Frageria chiloensis*, a native strawberry from the Spanish West Indies, but although Miller had not yet seen the fruit he quoted A. F. Frézier who 'in his Voyages says it grows as big as a pullet's egg ... a great rarity'. The first decade of Martyn's *Historia Plantarum* was forwarded with a list of twenty-eight plants sent to North Bierley and twenty-four wanted for Chelsea. In 1730 Miller makes a specific request for 'cuttings or a small part of your sort of Cistus's, which is a tribe of plants that we have very few of'.

Four years later Miller sent seeds collected by the late William Houstoun (c. 1695–1733) in Carthagena (i.e. Cartagena, Colombia) and anticipated many more

since his whole time is to be employed in collecting and in such countries where no Botanist has yet been. When any seeds arrive from him I will take the first opportunity of sending you a share and in return shall trouble you for some Northern and Welsh plants which I hope we shall make proper conveniency to receive into our Garden in a short time; for several of those which you were so good as to furnish me with a few years since are lost for want of proper soil and situation, the natural earth of our Garden being too light and dry and the bottom too warm.

There seems to be no further record of this amicable exchange between Miller and Richardson after 1734.

From a letter dated February 1735 ending 'your obliged and affectionate servant', it is apparent that the poet, Alexander Pope, knew Miller well. He had written on behalf of a friend 'whose great curiosity in fruit has been terribly disappointed by the nurserymen'. Pope requested 'cuttings of the Chaumontell, a French Pear and of the Vingoleuse and Epine d'Hyber'. He asked for them to be clearly marked, packed in damp moss and sent to Lord Cornbury's by Oxford Chapel, 'where I am to be around generally any morning before ten if you ever have time to call'. At this time Pope was busily engaged in constructing two new ovens, stoves and a hothouse for pineapples at Twickenham, so it is more than likely that there was further correspondence or discussion with Miller on exotics.

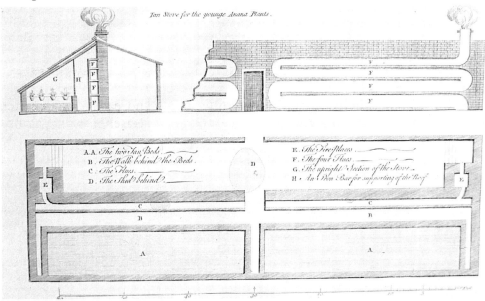

Tan stove for young pineapples [GD]

Pope also confirmed that Miller was widely read in high circles because when staying in Bath in 1743, he wrote to the Earl of Marchmont about a meeting there with Lord Chesterfield who had told him that 'your Lordship is got a-head of all the Gardening Lords and that you have distanc'd Lord Burlington and Lord Cobham in the true scientific parts, but he is studying before you and has here lying before him those Thesaruru's from which he affirms you draw all knowledge, Miller's *Dictionaries*.'

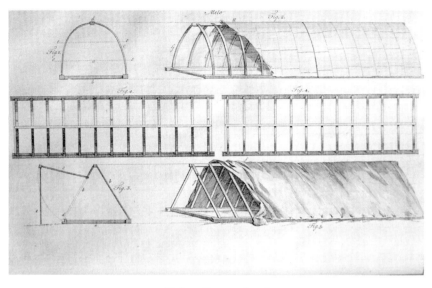

Melon frames [GD]

Another literary gentleman to follow Miller's advice was Gilbert White, author of *The Natural History of Selborne*. He possessed two editions of the *Gardeners Dictionary* and in his own *Garden Kalendar* (1751–1771) recorded 'sow'd radishes with the stocks as Miller directs' (this was to divert the attention of a destructive fly). He carefully 'made and earth'd and thatch'd mushroom bed according to Miller' and followed precisely his directions on growing cucumbers with gratifying results. He was not as successful with melons because even 'Miller's very fine old seed produced abominable fruit' and after trials covering five years he wrote to Chelsea for guidance. With his reply (*Natural History of Selborne*, Ed. Bell 2: 341, 1877) Miller sent cantaleupe seeds from Armenia, in his opinion the best, and advised using dung rather than tanners bark for the hotbed, with a good depth of loam for rooting. This was a condition not easily achieved at the Physic Garden because, Miller added, 'we have very little loam within a favourable distance'. He wondered if Gilbert White had seen the last edition of the *Dictionary* (the seventh, 1756–59) where he had incorporated all the latest improvements in the culture of the cantaleupe melon. However, in spite of expert advice the new melon seedlings at Selborne did not flourish and so on 23 June 1750, as his *Kalendar* recalls, Gilbert White called on Miller at Chelsea and took due note of the correct procedure. Not long afterwards his hotbeds produced 'fine, large, beautiful fruit, just like Miller's' and so six years of patience were rewarded.

In the seventeen-forties Philip Miller acted as adviser to the Fourth Duke of Bedford at his Woburn estate. There are five letters written by Miller within fifteen months in 1748–9 to Robert Butcher, Chief Agent at Bedford

House in Bloomsbury Square. Apparently indisposition had, in March 1748 prevented him from working on a plan for winter shelter of orange trees. By July he hoped to be able to meet Butcher at Cheam, a property where the fourth Duke had spent his early married life; but only if the weather proved favourable, 'for I have had the Rheumatism so bad of late, as to make me fearful of riding in the wet'. In the following May, Miller again reported illness, being just recovered from a fever and subsequent attack of rheumatism, so wished to postpone a visit to Woburn. However, this must have been countered by an urgent request from Butcher as two days later Miller sent his servant with a note, agreeing to meet at Bedford House by four o'clock in order to get as far as St Albans that evening.

These letters to Butcher present a somewhat different picture of Miller. Correspondents previously mentioned were independent gentlemen to whom Miller paid due deference and where little deviation detracted from the subject discussed; whereas with Butcher, another employee, his tone was far less formal and he found time to dwell on his health, the weather and even mentioned his own servant.

In complete contrast were letters between Chelsea and Scotland covering the period from 1737 to 1758 and presenting a spirited academic exchange. Miller had told Richardson that he hoped to correspond with Dr Alston, King's Professor of Botany in Edinburgh ... 'a man of learning and has good skill in distinguishing plants and a great share of modesty'. Both Charles Alston and Alexander Monro of Edinburgh had studied at Leyden and maintained close association with that university. Richard Pulteney* believed that these two doctors, together with Rutherford, Sinclair and Plummer were responsible for Edinburgh's reputation as one of the finest medical schools in Europe, and Miller preferred Alston's *Medical Essays* to 'all the Modern Books of Physick'.

In a long letter to Alston in 1737 Miller discussed classification of plants according to Tournefort, 'no person was ever more exact in all the Synonimes'. On the other hand, Linnaeus, who had visited Chelsea a few months earlier, came in for severe criticism: '... he has demolished not only Species but Genus without the least reason for so doing but that of having his method establish'd and made universal, which I venture to affirm will be of very short duration'. Although Linnaeus had spent four days at Chelsea in July, when the plants in the Garden were perfect, he had concentrated on dried plants – this to Miller was unforgiveable. Miller concluded this letter to Alston with a note on his own intentions – to add figures to supplement the *Dictionary* – 'my scheme is to give the characters of each Genus after the manner of Tournefort, which are all drawn from the growing plants and

* Author of *Historical and Biographical Sketches of the Progress of Botany in England from its Origin to the Introduction of the Linnaean System* (1790)

I hope soon to send you the abridgment of the Gardeners Dictionary, which is almost reprinted, and the three Vol. thrown into one alphabet. I am also busy in revising and altering the two Vol. in folio, and reducing them into one alphabet, and to add figures of the uncommon, or more useful plants. My scheme is to give the characters of each Genus, after the manner of Tournefort, which are all drawn from the growing plants, then to add one, two, or more plants of the most beautiful, useful or rare species of each Genus. I can add no more at present, but that I am

Sir your most sincere
Humble Servant.
Philip Miller

Extract from Miller's letter to Alston, *1737*

then to add, one, two, or more plants of the most beautiful, useful or rare species of each Genus.'

His letter to Alston of February 1755 runs to three folio pages (he hopes the 'long scribble' will not prove tiring) and is the most authoritative considered so far. He judged the current *Transactions* of the Royal Society to be unworthy of publication, the fault lying with the Secretary. Alston opposed the concept of sex in plants and Miller criticised his paper on the 'Generation of Plants', having himself closely studied hemp, mercury, briony, cucumber and mulberry in this connection. He also quoted Père Laval's *Voyage de l'Afrique Occidentale* on the fertilisation of palms. The third page of this letter is devoted to a discussion on the naming of the Indian Pink [*Dianthus chinensis*] mentioned in Alston's *Essays* and here Miller quoted from many sources including the *History of Carolina*, the *Flora Virginica* and a Doctor Brown writing in *The Gentleman's Magazine*, December 1751.

The other species from which Plumier took the characters of his Genus Arapabaca, grows in Jamaica, and the Leward Islands, where it is used as an Anthelmintic and has been found of great service. this is figured and an account printed of its vertues given by Docto Brown, in the Gentlemans Magazine for December 1755. but the Doctor has given it the Title of Anthelmia from its vertues, supposing the plant a non descript, the seed he sent to England, which grew with me, and I soon found it was the Arapabaca quadrifolie of Plumier. this is an annual plant, but perfects its seed well in the stove, its common name in the country is Worm Grass. I fear this long scribble will tire you, so shall only add

I am Sir your most obedient
Humble Servant
Philip Miller

Chelsea Feb. 4th 1755

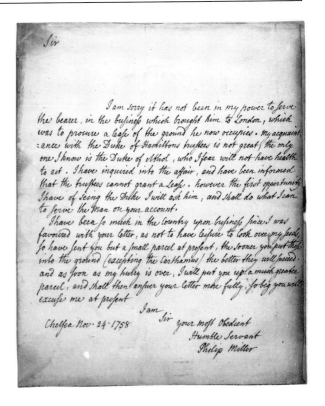

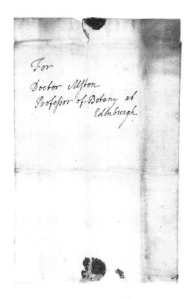

*Letter from Miller to
Alston, 24 Nov. 1758*

Alston replied to this in 1756, his minute writing condensing to a single sheet thoughts which Miller's careful copper-plate would stretch to three, and concluded that Edinburgh lagged behind Chelsea in some reading – he had not seen the *Voyages* until quite recently. He agreed in part with its author, disputed the theories of many others and expanded at length on his own theory concerning the fertilisation of the date palm. May 1758 brought a brief letter from Miller: he had been preoccupied with business in the country and could only send a small parcel of seeds.

James Justice (1695–1763), Principal Clerk to the Court Session in Scotland, was an enthusiastic botanist and gardener, particularly interested in the Dutch skill with bulbs. A long letter from him to Miller in 1730 was brought to the attention of the Royal Society and in this he related his experience with inarching (grafting) for exotic trees, the climate of Midlothian not being as rigorous as one might imagine. He goes on to describe his *Ananas* (pineapple) in fine fruit, coffee berries colouring, guajavas about the blossom, 'in short all my Exotics are in a mighty prosperous thriving condition in the Stoves as well as the Greenhouse'.

Here was a gentleman with a partiality towards those particular fruits whose cultivation was one of Miller's specialities and Justice refers to their happy association in the Preface of his *British Gardener's New Director chiefly adapted to the Climate of the Northern Counties* (4th ed. Dublin, 1765).

> Mr. Miller, of whom I must always retain the highest sense, both for the Knowledge I have received from his Labours, and more particularly that Friendship and Communicativeness with which he always treated me, was blessed with a more favourable Situation in the Progress of his Experiments, by enjoying the kind Influence of the Sun (the Parent of Vegetation) in so high a Degree as to have the Vine in full ripeness on the natural Wall, without the assistance of Art; and could we all experience the same Felicity, I need not have communicated my Observations or my Countrymen wanted an other Tutor ...

Thus Justice gave Miller his due, at the same time ensuring a place on northern bookshelves for his *Director* alongside Miller's *Dictionary*.

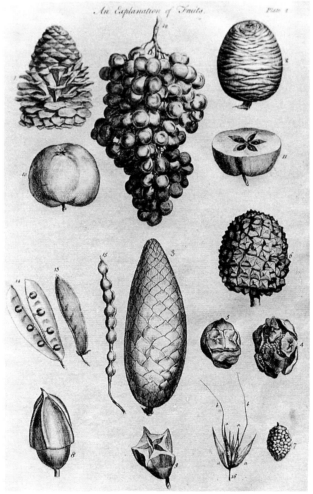

An explanation of fruits [pl. 2, GD]

His legal mind jumped quickly to the defence of Miller, 'a man of truth and veracity' over the Guernsey Lily affair. John Hill had queried Miller's description and had published his views in *Eden, or a Complete Body of Gardening* (1759) and Justice retaliated in his *British Gardener's Calendar* (1759): 'I thought it my indispensable duty to give Mr. Miller his due, both from a love of truth and from a sense of gratitude to him for his public labours, as well as private friendship.'

Differences of opinion on nomenclature were rife at this time. Opinions were often presented as papers to the Royal Society, of which Philip Miller became a Fellow in 1730, proposed by Stephen Hales, William Rutty and Peter Collinson. Some of his lengthy dissertations will be considered in a later chapter (p. 101); short critical comments can be included here. A letter to Peter Davall Esqr. in the Temple, London, written 1753 and read a year later, points out that seeds exhibited at the Society did not fit the description of a particular species of *Bauhinia*. A note to William Watson suggests that there might be a case of mistaken identity in an abstract he presented from the *Flora Sibirica* on *Sphondylium vulgare hirsutum* [i.e. *Heracleum sphondylium*].

Miller's relations with the Royal Society were not always amicable. Although John Ellis, a botanical and zoological Fellow, had written to Linnaeus, 'Miller's Dictionary is the chief book that is read by gentlemen who study the art of gardening', there seems to have been little pleasant exchange between them. An argument arose over a paper by Miller on the dyeing properties of *Toxicodendron* (poison ivy), species of which occur both in North America and Japan, though represented in each by different sub-species. Made public, this became a display of petulance and obstinacy, from which Miller emerged the loser. In December 1757 he tried to excuse himself 'as my abode is at such distance from the place where the Royal Society hold their weekly meetings as to render it not only inconvenient, but unsafe for me to attend them in the winter season.' A month later Ellis countered with, 'I scarce think it possible that Mr. Miller should have no one friend in the Society to send him word and, indeed, I had told Rivington to tell Miller I would be glad to discuss the matter at Fulham, and Miller ignored it.' Obviously these two were at loggerheads. Come what may, Miller would listen to no counsel, not even his loyal publisher. After three years of wrangling, the matter was dropped, though Miller does in the eighth edition of the *Dictionary* admit that he made a mistake in former publications.

There remains one last letter dated September 1767 amongst those examined for this chapter. In spite of advancing years, disability and lack of prestige with the Royal Society, Miller's handwriting is still meticulous, his manner courteous and his behaviour diligent. Although there is no addressee, it appears to be written to the Secretary of the Society:

I was favoured with your letter and should have been glad to embrace this opportunity of sending a packet of seeds to Dr. Manetti of Florence, but the season has been so cold that but few of them have ripened as yet, but if the next month proves favourable, I hope to send him some in November, if you have any opportunity to convey them. I have been confined almost a year by the dislocation of one of the ankle-bones of my leg, so have not been able to get as far as the Society House, but have enclosed the shilling you was so kind as to pay for a letter from Monsieur du Hamel. I shall be obliged to you if you will be so good as to let the bearer have my copy of the last year's Transactions, in which you will greatly oblige, Sir, your most humble servant, Philip Miller.

This letter is included in a *Historical and Topographical Description of Chelsea* (1829) by William Faulkner, owner of a small bookshop in Paradise Row, close by the Physic Garden, to which he devotes some pages. On the science of botany he comments that 'the lucid order and systematical arrangement of plants was not fully completed until a very recent period, when a Swede first gave lessons and then laws in this interesting science.' This reference to Linnaeus leads on to exchange between Chelsea and Europe.

Different Structures of flowers.

6 European Exchange

In the Preface of the Octavo *Dictionary* (1724), Philip Miller remarked that before the beginning of the century this country's preoccupation with trade had allowed the Italians, French and Dutch to outstrip it in horticulture. However, in 1733 he described a new trend:

> But it is very lately that the truly magnificent taste in gardening has flourished in these northern parts of Europe, for although in King Charles the Second's reign there was great spirit amongst the nobility and gentry of England for planting and gardening, which spirit was greatly heighten'd in King William's reign, during which time most of the large gardens of England were laid out and planted, yet we find the taste at that time extended little farther than to small pieces of box-wood, finish'd parterres and clipp'd greens, all of which are now generally banished out of the gardens of the most Polite Persons of this age, who justly prefer the more extended rural designs of gardens which approach the nearest to nature.

This concept of the extended garden, one which fell in line so well with our undulating country and expanses of fine grass, was to dominate horticultural thinking in the eighteenth century and a mutual exchange of thoughts and plants continually crossed the Channel.

There are constant references to Europe in the *Dictionary*, particularly to the Dutch knowledge of horticulture. Miller respected Holland's expertise and in the *Dictionary* stressed plant rarity with the qualification: 'there being very few in the Dutch gardens at present.' In 1727 he visited Holland and established a firm friendship with the celebrated Herman Boerhaave (1668–1738) at Leyden, the most important and esteemed teacher of medicine in Europe. As professor of medicine and botany Boerhaave took charge in 1709 of the university botanic gardens of Leyden (founded in 1587). In the following decade its collection of plants increased from about 3000 to nearly 6000, largely as a result of his correspondence with more than fifty botanists throughout the world. In 1720 Boerhaave produced an impressive catalogue of plants in the Leyden Garden, *Index alter Plantarum* (2 vols), and under *Protea* in the *Dictionary* Miller refers to this work (he also included it in the bibliography). Over twenty varieties of this Cape genus are, he says, well figured from drawings made there and of these he grew three at Chelsea: *Protea conifera*, *P. argentea* and *P. nitida*, although the last was lost.

Plate 1

LILIO-NARCISSUS Japonicus rutilo flore. Merj.

G. D. Ehret p. 1744.

Guernsey Lily, Nerine sarniensis *(L.) Herbert; drawing by G. D. Ehret. Native of*
South Africa.

Plate 2

Common Lilac, Syringa vulgaris L.; drawing by R. Lancake [pl. 163, FIGS]. Native of eastern Mediterranean region.

Dr Herman Boerhaave (1668–1738)
1710

Oud-Poelgeest, the country home of
Dr Boerhaave

In 1724 the University Garden needed more space and Boerhaave used his newly purchased country estate at nearby Oud-Poelgeest as an extension. In the following year he received 1416 parcels of seed from correspondents and collectors employed by him. William Sherard wrote to Richard Richardson about those searching for new plants in Austria, Hungary, Spain and Italy and added 'if you meet with any berries of *Juniperus alpinus*, pray gather some for him'. In a lecture on his retirement, caused by illness, in 1729 Boerhaave acknowledged contributions from William and James Sherard, Hans Sloane, Isaac Rand, Philip Miller and many others in Europe: 'You have enriched my collection with rare gifts from Bohemia, Transylvanis, Hungaria, the Danube plains, from Frejus, Carinthia, Styria and Illyria'.

Pieter van der Voort de la Court
(1664–173)

Such were the treasures to be seen when Philip Miller arrived at Oud-Poelgeest in 1727 and he reported on many rare shrubs and gathered seeds from curious plants. He also visited another important garden in the area, Meerburg, where the gardener kindly instructed him on the cultivation of pineapples — his employer, M. de la Court, was among the first to grow this fruit successfully in Europe. A wealthy Dutch merchant of English extraction, George Clifford, later patron of Linnaeus, gave Miller plants of the strawberry, *Fragaria chiloensis*, from his extensive grounds near Haarlem.

There was time for botanising in the Dutch countryside where Miller noticed *Acorus calamus*, sweet rush, in the ditches and on the banks of the Meuse growing to a height of 4 feet. He also saw *Juncus acutus* and

Meerburg, the house and garden of M. de la Court

J. filiformis and noted their use against erosion by water. He collected *Circaea alpina* in a wood near the Hague and brought it back to England, together with *Parietaria officinalis* and *Centaurea augustifolia*. He visited the vegetable markets, renowned in Europe, where he obtained seeds of celeriac, a vegetable new to England, and not readily accepted by London's market gardeners. He saw none of our usual green cucumbers for sale, the Dutch preferring a long, white, prickly variety, not as watery or so full of seeds. However, Miller praised the English cauliflower, originally from Cyprus, and commented that in France they rarely had them until near Michaelmas while Holland was generally supplied from England, and Germany had only recently started to cultivate them.

No visit to Holland would have been complete without a study of the important Dutch bulb industry and soon after his return Miller produced a paper, read at the Royal Society, on the practice of growing them in water. The culture of hyacinths and tulips is fully described in the *Dictionary*. He also studied – between Helvoetfluys and the Brill – the production of madder, *Rubia tinctorum*, used in dyeing and 'took some minutes of it down upon the spot.' In 1758 he published a comprehensive pamphlet on this

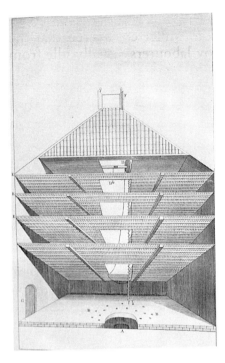

Production of Madder in the pounding house [GD]

Drying tower for Madder [GD]

industry, and when later reproduced in the *Dictionary* it occupied seven pages of text and a further seven of illustration. Miller considered that the cultivation of madder in England would employ labourers, usually idle from the end of harvest until spring, and thus parishes would be eased of the Poor's Rate, 'a consideration worthy of public attention'.

Undoubtedly this visit promoted further exchange between Chelsea and Leyden. Boerhaave sent seeds of *Cleome viscosa*, originally from Ceylon, and R. van Royen, a later Professor of Botany at Leyden, contributed *Apocynum reticulatum* from India, and *Calendula fruticosa* and *Haemanthus carinatus*, both from the Cape of Good Hope. Another Dutch friend, Dr Job Baxter of Zirkzee, sent seeds of *Watsonia meriana*, *Ixia* and *Cluytia pulchella* from the Cape, all to bloom well at Chelsea in due course as, indeed, the Watsonia still does today. Through Miller plants from America found their way to Holland. For example, lily thorn, *Catesbaea*, was first discovered by Mark Catesby in the island of Providence in 1726. Unfortunately, in the severe winter of 1739 all the European specimens perished, but in 1760 Miller managed to obtain fresh seed for raising plants to pass to Holland.

Accounts of the Apothecaries show that the Clerk of the Company had provided Miller with £10 for his expenses on this trip to Holland. He spent £9.14.6., mostly on plants from Jacob von Haapens and Warner van de Blooms, probably nurserymen, and listed many more plants from Leyden, but these would almost certainly have been gifts. A further note shows that 13s. in customs dues was paid on plants imported.

While Miller seemed chiefly to glean knowledge on the cultivation of flowers and vegetables from Holland, he turned to Italy for information on fruit culture and here again he had many correspondents. He received recognition there by being made a honorary member of the Botanical Society of Florence, a body existing from 1718 to 1783. His name first

32 Filippo Miller Sopraintendente dell' Orto Medico di Chelsea a Londra

appeared in the record of a Society Meeting as No. 32 from the Catalogue of the Foreign Associates, or Honorary Members of the Academy: 'Filippo Miller Sopraintendente dell' Orto Medico di Chelsea a Londra'. In the following month his was amongst the names of twenty foreign professors to receive the Micheliano Catalogo and in 1758 he appeared on a list of those to receive a consignment of seeds. The Amhurst bibliography lists a *Discourse on the Irritability of Some Plants* as being translated from the Italian by Philip Miller, so his knowledge of the language must have been adequate.

Another good Italian friend was 'Chevalier Rathgeb, his Imperial Majesty's Minister at Venice', who sent seeds of persimmon and the Cantaleupe melon. He also presented a large collection of fig trees to Chelsea, from which Miller tested the fruit and listed fourteen varieties ripening from July to late September. Hitherto there had only been four or five types available in England. There was also an 'ingenious correspondent' with his own vineyard in Italy, whose letter, in reply to Miller's pertinent queries, is in the Royal Society records (X.44). He is fully quoted in the *Dictionary* on Chianti wines and different methods of cultivation. However, instruction was not entirely one way as Peter Collinson told John Bartram of an instance where Miller had advised a correspondent in Naples on apricot culture.

Miller maintained close contact with France, particularly in the exchange of beautiful flowers from the royal gardens. Diligent French missionaries, like Père Nicholas d'Incarville in the Far East and others in Canada and South America collected many plants, seeds of which were sent to Chelsea by Claude Richard, the King's Gardener. These included *Vitex chinensis* and *Gloriosa superba*, a climbing lily from Senegal and *Liquidambar orientalis* from the Levant.

The French family, de Jussieu, had a great interest in botany and of two wild tomatoes, named by Miller *Lycopersicon pimpinellifolium* and *L. peruvianum* he wrote in the *Dictionary*:

> The seeds of these two sorts were sent from Peru by Mr. Joseph de Jussieu to the Royal garden at Paris, part of which was sent me by his brother Bernard de Jussieu of the Royal Academy of Science'

These did not fruit well at Chelsea but by now the tomato, also known as the love-apple, had become well known in England (it had been introduced in the sixteenth century, when Gerard considered it of little value) and was much used in soups. Miller appropriately named it *L. esculentum*.

The *Dictionary* was available in northern Spain, though not used to advantage by the Spaniards. William Bowles, (1705–1780) an Irishman who became superintendent of mines in Spain, was dismayed by the lack of unusual plants in the area and wrote to Peter Collinson from Bilbao in 1733 asking for packets of seeds and bulbous plants and continued: 'There is a Miller's Dictionary in Town, so I would take some pains to give the Spaniards a taste ... you know what best to send'. On the back of the letter is a note, presumably of what was dispatched: peony, hellebore, lily, colchicum, iris, martagon, cyclamen and crown imperial.

William Sherard spent many years abroad (he was Consul at Smyrna from 1703–17) and enriched his brother James's garden at Eltham with treasures from the Near East, which Dillenius recorded in his beautifully illustrated *Hortus Elthamensis* (1732). Miller frequently mentions Sherard's contributions to Chelsea, among them *Phlomis orientalis*, Jerusalem sage, completely destroyed by the great frost of 1740 and *P. flavescens*, which managed to survive many years in a warm border. *Phlomis fruticosa*, now known as fern sage, was another contribution from Smyrna.

George Clifford, whom Miller met in Holland, had placed a brilliant young Swede, Carl Linnaeus in charge of his large garden and menagerie at De Hartekamp. He had no problems in stocking these from the Far East, India or the Cape with help from Dutch merchant-ship captains, but he wanted to obtain those North American novelties which he knew to be flourishing at Chelsea, so in July 1736 Linnaeus came to England with a letter of introduction from Boerhaave to Sir Hans Sloane. The meeting, however, was hardly amicable, the old naturalist was more than sceptical of the revolutionary ideas of the younger. At the Physic Garden Miller was equally brusque and Linnaeus found three days of tactful approach necessary to obtain the North American plants wanted for Clifford's garden. He next proceeded to Oxford where his initial reception was unenthusiastic, but with great patience Linnaeus expounded his method of classification and nomenclature to Dillenius, first occupant of the Chair of Botany, founded by William Sherard at the University. The Professor appeared impressed and asked Linnaeus to remain at Oxford and share his stipend. He did extend his stay, helped to arrange and classify the Sherard collection of plants, many obtained from Greece and Asia Minor, and found more in the Botanic Garden to take back to Holland.

Although first reactions to Linnaeus were usually unfavourable, on account of his egoistic nature, his visit helped to create an understanding on which goodwill and confidence were built, and his system of classification, based on the number of sexual parts in the flowers, became generally accepted within the next thirty years. (see Chapter 20 by William Stearn).

Linnaeus respected Miller's work and corresponded with him after his return to Europe; there are ten letters from Chelsea in the Linnaean collection covering the period from 1752 to 1768. The first five are in Latin, but Miller, realising his limitations, wrote in August 1763, 'I have taken the liberty of writing to you in English, being informed that you can either read it yourself, or have some persons who can translate it for you'. These letters (see also Chapter 20) throw some light on Miller's last decade. He continued to cooperate in the exchange of books, plants and seeds and he contributed specimens from Chelsea for Linnaeus's son, who was forming an ambitious herbarium. In the final letter, written in 1768, when he was in his late seventies and obviously under some stress he complains about the lack of co-operation from Solander and Ellis. There is no doubt that he was being obstinate and suspicious, but his competence had been proved by his latest publication. He maintained he had never received replies to letters or acknowledgement of seeds but the dispatch of the eighth edition of the

Dictionary (April 1768) awaited direction and then, with an unusually personal note, he excuses himself, '... having had the misfortune to dislocate the ankelbone of my leg above a year and a half since gone ... confinement and want of usual exercise has brought many maladies upon me, but I am in hope of proper remedies to prolong life a little longer.'

Twenty years earlier, when in more robust health, Miller received another Swedish visitor at the Physic Garden. Pehr Kalm had been a student of Linnaeus, to whom he wrote in March 1747 saying that he had collected a great many seeds from the Essex garden of Richard Warner, a special friend of Miller, who promised an introduction and that he intended 'taking up my quarters a little way from Chelsea garden to be always with him'. Kalm was an excellent observer, a meticulous recorder and made the most of his time at the Physic Garden, which he judged to rival those of Paris and Leyden at the time, and believed it to 'overgo them in North American plants'. He was interested to see Ray's collection, presented to Samuel Dale just before he died, who later passed them on to Chelsea. The plants had been sown with cotton into a large book which, he was told, probably somewhat testily by Miller, William Sherard had borrowed and from which he had extracted some desirable specimens to incorporate them into his herbarium, bequeathed to Oxford University.

Kalm was very impressed by the stoves at Chelsea, 'all arranged in the way discribed in Dictionary', and he learned from Miller that two orangeries in England had been burnt by tan overheating (the fermenting bark of the oak and a by-product from the tanning industry). At Chelsea they burned coal in winter as it tended to give an even heat, whereas wood burned too quickly and peat had a strong smell. Kalm noted that the spent tan was afterwards spread in the garden as manure and that nothing was laid on pots in the summer, compared with Moscow where he had seen sawdust used to keep them moist. They had a long discussion on the longevity of seeds and no doubt Kalm delighted in the *Dictionary* and later set out in his Diary a splendid commendation:

> I have asked several of the greatest and best horticulturists, both in England and America, what author and what book they had found and believed to be the best in horticulture ... they have all answered with one mouth, Miller's *Garden Dictionary*. Either in folio or the abstract in octavo was best of all ... The same answer I have got from several distinguished persons who had themselves had a particular pleasure in planting trees and plants with their own hands. If any of the Lords or great 'Herren' in England wished to lay out an new garden or remake an old one, Mr. Miller would always show them how it ought to be done. When the greatest lords drove out to their estates, he often drove out with them in the same carriage. In a word the principal people in the land set a particular value on this man.

7 Some Noble Estates

Thomas Knowlton (1691–1781), a gardener employed first by William Sherard and then by the Earl of Burlington, wrote to Samuel Brewer in 1741*, 'as to Miller he does not look at poor men, only a lord or a duke is company for him'. This rather uncharitable remark possibly arose out of jealousy as Miller certainly did not give all his attention to the gentry, although, as Kalm said, the aristocracy did seek his advice. One who set great store by Miller was young Lord Petre (1713–42) whose plants Miller managed at Ingatestone in Essex. In 1732 Lord Petre moved to Thorndon Hall, also in Essex, where he created one of the most ambitious estates in the country.

It is apparent that he followed Miller's advice on the establishment of lawns and walks. The lawn to the south of the house, shown on a plan by Bourginion, the French surveyor employed to redesign the garden, corresponds almost exactly with the description given in the second edition (1733) of the *Dictionary*, where Miller insists on frequent mowing and rolling to keep the grass in good order. He no doubt approved of Lord Petre's great roller for the park, usually drawn by two horses on account of its weight of 11,750 lbs.

In 1736 Miller prepared a catalogue† of the contents of the Thorndon garden. This octavo volume of 310 pages, with plants arranged under 696 genera, proves his intimate knowledge of the estate. Peter Collinson (1694–1768), a Quaker clothing merchant with strong horticultural interests, had organised a syndicate, which included Lord Petre and Philip Miller, to finance an American plant collector, John Bartram. In 1741 Collinson reported to him on the miraculous achievement at Thorndon:

> The trees and shrubs raised from thy first seeds are grown to great maturity. Last year Lord Petre planted out about ten thousand Americans which, being at the same time mixed with about twenty thousand Europeans, and some Asians, make a very beautiful appearance, great art and skill being shown in consulting everyone's particular growth and the well blending of the greens ... His nursery being fully stocked with flowering shrubs, of all sorts that can be

---

* See Henrey, Blanche. *No ordinary gardener Thomas Knowlton 1691–1781* p. 197. London 1986

† MS in Passmore Edwards Museum, Stratford, Newham. Microfilm in Essex Record Office (T/A 671)

pictured, with these he borders the outskirts of all his plantations and he continues, annually, raising from seed and layering, budding, grafting, that twenty thousand trees are hardly to be missed out of his nurseries. When I walk amongst them, one cannot well help thinking he is in North American thickets, there are such quantities.

Garden flowers received little attention at Thorndon, although asters were raised from seeds sent by Bartram. In the Octagon, an area specifically set aside for plant-raising, were exotics, reckoned to number 218, 925 in 1742. These would have claimed much of Miller's attention, but his expertise would have been in great demand over the cultivation of rare fruits. Lord Petre's stoves were among the largest in the world and their produce was unrivalled as Collinson continued:

> But to be at his table, one would think South America were really there, to see a servant come in every day with ten or a dozen pine apples, as much as he can carry. I am lately come from thence quite cloyed with them. Thee will not think I talk figuratively when I tell thee that his pine apple stove is sixty feet long, twenty feet wide and height proportionable. And if I tell thee that his Guavas, Pawpaws, Ginger and Lime are in such plenty that yearly he makes abundance of wet sweetmeats, of his own growth that serves his table and makes presents to his friends. Finer I never saw or tasted from Barbados or better cured. But these trees grow in beds of earth in houses, some twenty, some thirty feet high.

John Martyn's 1732 translation of Tournefort's *Histoire des Plants qui naissent aux Environs de Paris* (1698, 1725) was dedicated to Lord Petre and Martyn remarked on his surprise to see in the noble stoves

> ... plants wholly new to me which your Lordship first brought to England and which you have as generously communicated for the publick benefit. I have now, through your lordship's favour, the satisfaction of seeing them cultivated in my neighbourhood, by the skilful hand of my friend, Mr. Miller, and shall take the first opportunity of describing and engraving them that the public may see how much they are indebted to your lordship.

Perhaps choice specimens found their way to the Chelsea Physic Garden in exchange for invaluable advice on their cultivation at Thorndon. Miller described *Datura arborea*, from Chile, as one of the greatest ornaments to be found in the gardens, where the scent was almost overpowering. He told of two or three being raised at Thorndon and two more at Chelsea, where one flowered although no seeds were produced. The *Camellia* first flowered in this country at Thorndon, where many of the curious journeyed to see it as well as trellises backing the stoves covered with 'all sorts of passion-flowers, clematis's of all kinds that could be procured and Creeping Cereus.' Suddenly in the summer of 1742 a fatal attack of smallpox arrested progress at Thorndon with the death of the young Lord Petre, 'ornament and delight of the age he lived in'. Great was the loss of one who Peter Collinson lamented 'spared no pains in his building, gardening, farming, nurserys, stoves, to add new improvement and useful experiments for the benefit of his country.' Later he was to advise the next Lord Petre on planting around a proposed new home and again he wrote to Bartram for plants. The American replied that he was glad to find that botanical taste had been inherited and reported that a pear tree, grown from a seed sent to him by Lady Petre, had produced the finest fruits in Pennsylvania.

In 1742 the vast Thorndon collections were dispersed amongst other estates. The Duke of Bedford sent Philip Miller to value the thousands of rare trees and to purchase those he thought suitable for Woburn. At this time Miller was acting in an advisory capacity, as recorded in the *Memoranda Book of John, Fourth Duke of Bedford* (Woburn Mss HMC 62, extract above): 'March 13 1740/1 agreed with Mr. Miller to pay him Twenty

Guineas a year for inspecting my Gardens hot houses, pruning the trees, etc. and to come to Woburn at least twice a year and oftner if wanted, to be paid at Lady Day yearly.' Payments terminated on 31 May 1753, but evidently no ill feeling marred the end of Miller's contract as a few years later he dedicated to the Duke the beautiful *Figures of Plants* (2 vols.) which had been published in parts from 1755–60. Maybe by then Miller had more than enough work to do at Chelsea; no comment on the matter occurs in the Minutes of the Apothecaries' Garden Committee and this was probably a private arrangement between the Duke and the Chelsea Gardener.

Collinson also acted as intermediary in obtaining seeds from America, particularly those which gave rise to an extensive plantation of evergreens in the park, a principal feature of Woburn at the time. Miller mentions some of the trees in the *Dictionary*: *Abies balsamea*, Balsam fir, first grown in this country in the Bishop of London's garden at Fulham, but states, 'the only place they have made any figure is at Woburn'. He also commented on *Pinus rigida*, pitch or Virginian pine, reaching great height in its native country, and there were many at Woburn, 'twenty feet high, though not of many years standing and keep pace with the other kinds of Pines and Firs in the same plantation'. When Kalm visited Miller, they discussed cultivation of trees, particularly conifers, and he was told that at Woburn larches had been planted 'some in good soil, some in meagre' and the latter 'looked very lively, while the former looked quite drooping, as though they were obliged reluctantly to force themselves to grow'.

There was correspondence with Woburn over the construction of a shelter for orange trees, to be added to an existing wall, with a moveable roof erected every autumn. The glass for this could, Miller suggested, be of inferior quality for the top, but the front should be 'glaz'd with new Castle Glass'. Miller was conscious of economy and recognised that from an aesthetic viewpoint the Duke must be gratified, but felt that good use could be made of cheaper material elsewhere.

During the eighteenth century the second and third Dukes of Richmond planted many trees at Goodwood, their country estate near Chichester in Sussex. The elder Duke (1701–1750) was one of the original subscribers to John Bartram's collecting expeditions and Collinson wrote to Philadelphia in 1743: 'Only Philip Miller and the Duke of Richmond, who love new things, continue to contribute.' It was said of the younger Duke (1733–1806) that he intended to cover all the surrounding hills with evergreen woods, and many of the finest hardy exotic trees in this country were to be found in the park. All these were recorded by Philip Miller in his *Dictionary*.

He admired the fine *Bombax*, the silk cotton tree, raised from seed sent from the East Indies and *Pistacia vera*, the turpentine tree, able to survive several winters without protection. This, according to Miller was used to produce all the common turpentine in the shops, until a substitute from

American Bull Bay, Magnolia grandiflora *L.; drawing by G. D. Ehret*

cone-bearing trees had replaced it. He recalled that a large *Cupressus lusitanica* (known as Cedar of Goa, though from Mexico) had flourished at Goodwood until 1740, when frost killed it. On the other hand, two large specimens of *Pinus halepensis*, the Aleppo pine, had escaped because, he imagined, they had been transplanted the previous year making no shoots that summer, thus faring better than other plants with tender new growth. A *Magnolia grandiflora*, 'one of the most beautiful of evergreen trees yet known', produced flowers for several years at Goodwood, but again the severe winter of 1740 destroyed it. However, the collection of this variety must have been considerable: Collinson noted on the back of a print of the *Magnolia grandiflora* flower in his copy of Catesby's *Natural History of Carolina*, that there were twenty-nine of these trees at Goodwood in 1759, two of them twenty feet high.

There is a copy of Miller's *Gardeners Dictionary* (third edition, 1737) in the private library at Goodwood today, in two folio volumes. Just as great family bibles were used to record births and other family events, so the Dukes used the *Dictionary* to preserve for posterity dates of important plantings at Goodwood. There are MS records on the title page of a collection of evergreens planted on the bowling green in the 1730s; of Tulip trees and 'Virginia Oakes' (the American evergreen oak) on the Arbor Vitae Grove in 1739; and an important note of the planting of 1000 cedars, procured from a butcher at Barnes (for £70.16s) giving their exact distribution over the estate in 1760. Under the frontispiece is another note concerning a new wall built and a plantation of cedar of Lebanon and pines made along it in 1761. There are no MS notes in the actual text of this copy of the Dictionary. Miller was also interested in the fruit garden at Goodwood and reported on trials carried out with various walls to see if a circular construction might be beneficial, but he came to the conclusion that nothing would thrive in a constant draught of air.

Philip Miller much respected Hugh Percy (1715–1786) the second Earl, and later first Duke, of Northumberland, to whom he dedicated the sixth, seventh and eighth editions of the *Dictionary*, referring to many improvements to his estates and particularly to his plantations in 'a Country almost destitute of Timber'. He would have been well acquainted with the Northumberland gardens at Sion House by the Thames (originally laid out by the Duke of Somerset in the sixteenth century) and supported an application by William Forsyth, one of his most promising pupils at Chelsea, for the appointment as head gardener there. But it is Northumberland's curious garden an Stanwick on the Yorkshire-Durham border, where he lived before moving to Alnwick in the 1750s, about which we hear more from Miller.

Stoves and heated walls were essential in the north of England to cosset rarities sought by most ambitious gardeners and Miller warmly commended the Earl's generosity in his distribution of these treasures. For example, he recorded that cones of *Larix chinensis* had been successfully grown at Stanwick and seeds had been passed to Chelsea, where they also flourished. The seed of *Hypericum monogynum*, also from China, was raised successfully at both gardens and '*Morus papyreia*' (i.e. *Broussonetia papyrifera*, the paper–mulberry) from Japan, was another successful novelty to thrive well in the open at Chelsea as, in fact, did many mountain subjects. Another plant to reach Chelsea from Stanwick was the North American *Ascyrum crux-andrae*, St Andrews Cross – a plant of little beauty, Miller said, and seldom cultivated, but one grown in botanical gardens for the sake of variety. By bestowing the name *Piercea* in 1759 on a West Indian plant, Miller honoured his noble friend, 'not only a great encourager of botanical skills, but greatly skilled in the science itself'. The name *Piercea* is, however,

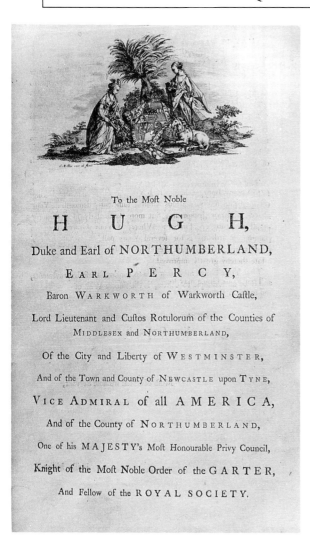

To the Moſt Noble

H U G H,

Duke and Earl of NORTHUMBERLAND,

E A R L P E R C Y,

Baron WARKWORTH of Warkworth Caſtle,

Lord Lieutenant and Cuſtos Rotulorum of the Counties of
MIDDLESEX and NORTHUMBERLAND,

Of the City and Liberty of WESTMINSTER,

And of the Town and County of NEWCASTLE upon TYNE,

VICE ADMIRAL of all A M E R I C A,

And of the County of NORTHUMBERLAND,

One of his MAJESTY's Moſt Honourable Privy Council,

Knight of the Moſt Noble Order of the GARTER,

And Fellow of the ROYAL SOCIETY.

MAY IT PLEASE YOUR GRACE,

YOUR Grace's kind Acceptance of two former
Editions of this Work, has emboldened me to
lay this at Your Grace's Feet, as a public Acknowledgment of the many uſeful Obſervations
and Inſtruΰions, which Your Grace has at ſeveral
Times communicated to me for its Improvement.
If I have been ſo happy as to employ them in ſuch manner, as to
merit Your Grace's Approbation, I ſhall have leſs Reaſon to doubt
that of the Public; ſince the moſt ſkilful Perſons in this uſeful Branch
of Science, pay the higheſt Regard to Your Grace's Judgment.

The many Improvements which Your Grace is annually making
ſo happily upon Your various Eſtates, ſufficiently demonſtrate Your
Grace's ſuperior Judgment; but more particularly in a Country
almoſt deſtitute of Timber: Where, if Your Grace continues
planting, ſo ardently as for ſeveral Years paſt, the whole Face of
the Country will be much altered for the better, and Your Grace's
Eſtate thereby greatly improved.

That Your Grace may long live to continue theſe Improvements,
and to be an Example to others, is the ſincere Wiſh of

Your GRACE's

Moſt obedient humble Servant,

CHELSEA,
March 1, 1768.

Philip Miller.

Dedication from the Gardeners Dictionary *to Hugh Percy, Duke of Northumberland*

now treated as a synonym of *Rivina*. The juice of the berries from these
West Indian plants produced a bright red dye, and by standing stalks of
flowers such as tuberose and narcissus in a solution of the dye over night, he
obtained some blooms 'finely variegated with red'.

Ten miles west of London, near Hounslow, Archibald Campbell (1682–
1761), the 3rd Duke of Argyll, established his garden at Whitton. Work
commenced in 1723 and by the time Pehr Kalm saw it, over twenty years
later, a large collection of trees had become well established. He noted many
cedar of Lebanon and small groves of North American trees, including
pines, firs, cypresses and thuyas. The Duke told him he had given the trees
priority over the house because they took longer to become established, but

Kalm drily commented in his diary that his wealth was such that he could have built 'a most handsome castle in one year or less'. He had also converted the poor heathland soil of the area into most fruitful land, a point stressed by the observant Kalm.

Philip Miller could visit Whitton easily from Chelsea, travelling by boat to Twickenham and he seems to have known the garden well, often commenting on North American plants. *Kalmia augustifolia* had spread rapidly, being left undisturbed to sucker, a method of propagation he considered better than by seed; a *Cephalanthus occidentalis*, the largest he had seen, 'liked the situation well enough' and *Itea virginica* was 'in the greatest vigour'. He particularly admired the beautiful white spikes of *Itea* and recommended it for late flowering, a quality which also applied to *Clethra alnifolia*. Here, too, fruit of the citron, *Citrus medica* 'were as large and perfectly ripe as they are in Italy and Spain'. This was achieved by training the plants against a south wall, with flues and glass covers for the winter.

Firs and pines flourished at Whitton and Miller made a special note of *Abies canadensis*, i.e. *Picea glauca*, the white spruce from America. The white pine, *Pinus strobus*, also from America and known in this country as the Weymouth Pine, impressed Miller both for its beauty and utility. Being tall, straight and pliant it was much in demand for ship masts, 'therefore the legislature thought proper to pass a law for the preservation and increase of these trees in America'. However, by the mid-eighteenth century this pine was being raised in this country by Lord Weymouth, Sir Wyndham Knatchbull in Kent and by the Duke of Argyll at Whitton, where large quantities of cones were produced annually, 'which his Grace did most generously distributte to all the curious.' On the death of the Duke in 1761, many of the beautiful trees at Whitton were bought for Princess Augusta's garden at Kew by her botanical adviser, Lord Bute.

Other noteworthy plantings were mentioned by Miller: the Duke of Norfolk had, at Worksop, the greatest number of *Magnolia glauca* then growing in England; while in Sir John Collinson's garden at Exeter, he had seen the largest *Magnolia grandiflora* in the country. At 'Badington' the Duchess of Beaufort grew *Cestrum nocturnum*, a native of the West Indies, and this was distributed on the continent, known there as the 'Badington Jasmine'. *Tulipifera liriodendron* (i.e. *Liriodendron tulipifera*) known in England as the tulip tree and as a 'poplar' by settlers in America, first flowered in this country in the Earl of Peterborough's garden at Parsons Green where it had been planted, according to Miller, in a wilderness with other trees allowed to overhang it for protection. This was a misguided precaution because, in fact, it was stifled and destroyed. The Marquis of Rockingham at Wentworth Hall in Yorkshire was successful in producing flowers of *Cereus compressus*, the beautiful American torch thistle, which James Gordon had triumphantly raised from seed at Mile End (See opp.).

Plate 3

Campanula; Canariensis; Atriplicis folio, tuberosa radice Tourn

Linn: Sp: Pl: 168.

Canary Bell-flower, Canarina canariensis (L.) Vatke; drawing by G. D. Ehret.
Native of Canary Islands.

Plate 4

WATSONIA.

Watsonia meriana *(L.) Miller; drawing by J. S. Miller [pl. 276,* FIGS*]. Native of South Africa.*

Miller had also known this to flower at Hampton Court, although more than once he speaks with some disparagement of inefficient gardeners at this Palace. Their *Phyllanthus epiphyllanthus* from the West Indies had been lost but he had seen one in the physic garden at Amsterdam where, with proper management, it was in great vigour. He also expressed regret at not being able to see *Elaeagnus latifolia* from India and Ceylon, and 'pretty rare in English gardens', when it had flowered at Hampton Court. It would seem that Miller cannot have been on amicable terms with the gardeners there, otherwise he would have made a point of a visit then. He mentions *Teucrium marum* growing in the warm borders of Kensington Palace Gardens in the early part of the century, clipped to conical forms three feet high, but there is little else to be found about eighteenth century Palace gardens in the *Dictionary*.

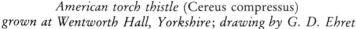

American torch thistle (Cereus compressus)
grown at Wentworth Hall, Yorkshire; drawing by G. D. Ehret

8 Collinson, Bartram and Fothergill

Although Philip Miller received seeds and specimens through various channels from America, Peter Collinson can be considered the chief link between Chelsea and the New World. Through his diligent direction a collector was found, transport organised and distribution arranged amongst those in this country best fitted to propagate and redistribute these rarities from the West. His occupation as a City merchant and his great interest in horticulture gave him an advantageous position amongst a wide circle of friends, both at home and abroad.

Collinson's first garden at Peckham was a modest one, but from there he took nosegays and potted flowers to grace his City window, and when Kalm visited him in 1748 he remarked on the many rare American plants already established there. In that year Collinson inherited from his father-in-law Ridgeway House, Mill Hill, now the site of Mill Hill school. Before the move he had already been planting exotics in the sheltered garden with a slope to the south-west; an ideal situation for the rare trees he collected over the next twenty years. His reference book was the *Gardeners Dictionary* and its author he held in high esteem, writing much later,

> Mr. Miller of the Physic Garden, Chelsea, has made his great abilities well known by his works, as well as his skill in every part of gardening and his success in raising seeds procured by a large correspondence. He has raised the reputation of the Chelsea Garden so much that it excels all the gardens of Europe for its amazing variety of plants of all orders and classes and from all climates, as I survey with wonder and delight, this 19th July, 1764.

In 1752 he prepared a catalogue of the contents of his Mill Hill garden and later had this bound with the seventh edition of the *Dictionary* where he made his own marginal notes on items of interest, including remarkable first flowerings in Britain. It would seem that this book was his constant companion and the title page of his copy of the eighth edition, published in the year of his death , 1768, was inscribed 'The Gift of my old friend, the author'.

Collinson was also instrumental in promoting the *Dictionary* abroad and, having become an agent for the Library Company of Philadelphia, he presented them in 1732, with Sir Isaac Newton's *Philosophy* and Philip Miller's *Gardeners Dictionary*. These were the first volumes to be received by the library from overseas and it is significant to note that after two centuries many of the original books remain on the shelves and Miller's *Dictionary* is still is use. Collinson had told John Bartram to consult this work in the library before sending him a personal copy in 1737 and two years later wrote to the American collector:

> Lord Petre has sent thee a present of Philip Miller's second part of his Dictionary in return for the specimens sent him. Thou will see a cut in (it) of a Polygala which is a reputed specific for pleurisy.

Polygala senega, *from* Gardeners Dictionary *(1768); engraving by G. D. Ehret*

Colonel John Custis of Williamsburg, a wealthy Virginian planter, was also advised by Collinson to purchase a copy of the *Dictionary*, a 'work of the greatest use' and one which 'no lover of gardening ought to be without'.

It was to be found in the libraries of other leading Virginians: Lord Botetourt, Thos. Lord Fairfax, John Herbert, Peter Thornton, Colonel W. Fleming, Councillor Robert Carter and John Randolph Jr. The latter (1727–1784) used his copy extensively in preparing his own *Treatise on Gardening*. Lady Skipwith of Prestwould, another Miller devotée, often quoted the *Dictionary* in her garden records, sometimes making a detailed note of species ('Miller's first or second sort') or applying 'not in Miller' to wild-flowers in her garden collection. But the most eminent of all the *Dictionary* possessors in Virginia was Thomas Jefferson, in whose *Garden Book* (1766–1824) are many references to his 1768 edition, particularly regarding the trees and vegetables at Monticello his high country home overlooking Charlottesville. He also had a copy of the French Edition (1885).

In a pamphlet, now in the British Museum, Collinson tells how he came to employ John Bartram. Although his business brought him into contact with many American settlers, he had received little co-operation in the collection of plants 'for what was common with them (but rare with us) they did not think worth sending'. John Bartram was recommended: 'being a native of Pensilvania with a numerous family, the profits arising from gathering seeds would enable him to support it. At first it was not thought that sending over would prove a trade, but with the demand the price was fixed at £5.5.0. a box.' At the end of the pamphlet some seventy subscribers stretching over thirty years are listed, headed by Lord Petre, the Dukes of Norfolk, Richmond and Bedford and Philip Miller. Collinson was meticulous in his careful distribution of plants and seeds always including instructions on growing them in a manner approximating to their native conditions, as carefully described by John Bartram.

Great credit must be given to this largely self-educated farmer who, often alone, trudged many thousands of miles in the Eastern States, searching for new trees, shrubs, plants and seeds to send to Collinson. Their happy relationship flourished for forty years and led to about two hundred plants being introduced into Europe from America.

John Bartram lost his parents while still young and lived with his grandparents who had emigrated to America with William Penn in 1682. In 1728 he established a farm at Kingsessing near Philadelphia, with six acres sloping away to the river in the south-west for a garden and where horticultural work in due course supplanted his pursuit of agriculture. This was not a botanic garden in the modern sense of the word, but an area in which Bartram grew and propagated his comprehensive collection of current American ornamental plants for which he had arduously searched in un-explored country. His garden became the pivot of plant exchange between America and Europe during the eighteenth century.

Thomas Meehan, one-time caretaker of the Bartram Garden, stressed his early dedication, 'So earnest was John Bartram in the pursuit of learning that he could scarcely spare time to eat and might often have been seen with food in one hand and a book in the other. While ploughing or sowing his field, he was still pushing his enquiries into the operations of nature. He regarded with scrutinizing curiosity the infinite varieties of plants unknown and undescribed.' By middle age Bartram has so educated himself in the classics, sciences, medicines and above all, botany, that he was regarded as one of the intellectuals of his time. He was indeed fortunate in his local friends who recognised his 'propensity to Botanicks' (Benjamin Franklin, *Pennsylvania Gazette*, 1742), encouraged expeditions and subscribed 'to induce him and enable him wholly to spend his time and exert himself on these employments'. Franklin also introduced him, through correspondence, to J. F. Gronovius of Holland, a friend of Linnaeus, from whom he received a copy of the *Systema Naturae* by Linnaeus in 1740. James Logan, William Penn's secretary, obtained for him from England Parkinson's herbal, probably his *Theatrum botanicum* (1640) and made it 'a present to a person worthier of a heavier purse than fortune has yet allowed him'. These works, along with Miller's *Dictionary*, provided the theoretical background for practical expeditions.

In 1738 Bartram journeyed to Williamsburg in Virginia with a letter of introduction from Collinson to John Custis: 'In the vegetable kingdom perhaps you will find him more knowing in that science than any you have met with. He is employed by a Sett of Noble Men (by my recommendation) to collect seeds and specimens of rare plants'. Custis endorsed this in a reply, '... he is the most takeing faceitious man I have ever met with and I never was so much delighted with a stranger in all my life'. Equally enthusiastic was Pehr Kalm, who arrived at Kingsessing three days after he had reached Philadelphia in 1748, also with a letter of introduction from Collinson.

Bartram usually made his expeditions in the autumn when farm work diminished and when seeds in the wild would be ripe for collection and specimens best transplanted. These journeys took him to the furthest extent of the colonies, from Lake Ontario to Virginia and into the Carolinas and Florida. He described one journey to the source of the James River in 1738 in a letter to Collinson, '... over and between the mountains in many very crooked turnings and windings; in which I travelled 1,100 miles in five weeks, having rested but one day in all that time ... I gathered abundance of kinds of seeds in perfection.' Two accounts of his travels were published: *Observations on the Inhabitants, Climate, Soil, River, Production; from Pennsylvania to Onondaga, Oswego and the Lake Ontario* (London 1751) and *An Account of East Florida, with a Journal* (London 1767); these covered every aspect of natural history in the regions.

Linnaeus considered the American collector to be 'the best natural botanist in the world' and was no doubt instrumental in securing his election to the

Royal Swedish Academy of Sciences in 1768. Apart from a silver cup sent by Sir Hans Sloane in 1742, with which John Bartram was 'well pleased that thy name is engraved upon it at large, so that when my friends drink out of it, they may see who was my benefactor' and a gold medal from a Society of Gentlemen in Edinburgh, tangible appreciation was slow to cross the Atlantic. A further twenty-three laborious years were to elapse before official recognition of his services to Britain was given. In April 1765 Collinson wrote, 'I have the pleasure to inform my good friend that my repeated solicitations have not been in vain, for this day I received certain intelligence from our gracious King that he has appointed thee his Botanist with a salary of fifty pounds a year.' This position of American Botanist to the King of England Bartram held until the outbreak of the Revolution, supplying the boxes of plants and seeds for which, Collinson remarked, 'the honour of giving is sufficient, but there is no notice taken of the freight and other charges'. He is justly recognised by the American Philosophical Society, in whose annals his name stands second only to that of Benjamin Franklin.

Perhaps for Bartram the greatest satisfaction came from his correspondence with leading botanists and horticulturists in Europe and his valuable exchange with Philip Miller has yet to be considered (see pp. 81–89). There is no doubt that he owed much to Peter Collinson for various introductions and was especially grateful for one who assisted with his son William's career. This was another Quaker, John Fothergill (1712–1780), who wrote to Linnaeus in 1774: 'Our Collinson taught me to love flowers and who that shared his comradeship could do no other than cultivate plants'.

Fothergill was a doctor and in 1740 he set up a practice in White Hart Street very near the Collinson establishment and flowers from Peckham might well have adorned yet another house in the City. At that time Fothergill had, as he explained in a letter to Bartram, 1744, little chance to pursue the practical study of plants as he would wish, but he did, now and then take a walk to Peckham or Chelsea. In those gardens he would, no doubt, have noted new plants from America and how best to grow them in this country.

By 1762 his profitable practice enabled Fothergill to purchase Ham House in Upton with about thirty acres of land and to embark on the creation of an outstanding garden. He corresponded with Humphry Marshall, a cousin of John Bartram, another enthusiastic transatlantic botanist and author of *Arbustum Americanum*, the first account of native trees and shrubs to be published by an American. From his botanic garden in Pennsylvania he supplied Fothergill with a number of plants, including the ferns and polypodiums particularly requested. The doctor had intended to reciprocate with a copy of the *Dictionary* ('I know not whether anything would be more acceptable to a botanist'), but on finding it out of print, sent a copy of the

Swamp Pink, Helonias bullata L.; *drawing by W. Bartram* [pl. 272, FIGS]

Abridgement 'not long since published' (fifth edition, 1767).

Within a decade, Fothergill was able to give Marshall a descriptive account of the flourishing Upton garden acknowledged, he said, 'by the ablest botanists we have, that there is not a richer bit of ground in curious American plants in Great Britain; and for many of the most curious I am obliged to thy diligence and care.' He explained how, in order to achieve such success, he had appreciated the importance of providing these treasures with conditions similar to their native habitat and ensuring their protection from frost – lessons well learned from his visits to the gardens of Collinson and Miller during his busy 'doctoring' days.

Collinson had been told by John Bartram of his son's artistic talent: 'Botany and drawing are his darling delight ... I'm afraid he can't settle to any business else'. Knowing of Fothergill's interest in natural history generally, Collinson invited him to breakfast at Mill Hill and showed him a diversity of William's drawings. The doctor agreed that 'so fine a pencil is worthy of encouragement.' In his last letter to Bartram, Collinson passed on this welcome news. Generous sponsorship was amply justified: William

Bartram's *Travels through North and South Carolina, Georgia, East and West Florida*, with charming illustrations, was published in Philadelphia, London and Dublin. He proved also to be an able writer, many of his descriptive passages, pleasing readers such as Wordsworth and Coleridge, were echoed in their own writing. A collection of William Bartram's drawings is now in the Department of Botany, British Museum (Natural History), South Kensington and has been published in J. Ewan's handsome volume *William Bartram's botanical and zoological Drawings'* (1969).

Quotations from the writings of these three garden-lovers summarise different aspects appealing to them. From an entry in one of his interesting *Commonplace Books*, Collinson's deep appreciation of trees is apparent:

Everyone that would beautifully imitate nature should well consider the diversity of trees, the size and shape of leaves and the many shades of green. To know properly to mix them in planting is another matter of painting with living pencils, for greens properly disposed throw in a mixture of contrasts of lights and shades which wonderfully enliven the pictures and which insensibly strike the senses with wonder and delight. The effects must be charming, to see the dark green elm with the lighter shades of the lime and beech or the yellowish green planes with the silver-leaved abele, the Chestnut, the poplar, the acacia, the horse-chestnut, *cum multis aliis*, when fanned by a gentle breeze, then how beautiful the contrast, how delightfully the light and shade fall in to diversify the sylvan scene.

Flowers, accurately depicted by his son, were described by John Bartram with a deep feeling for their beauty:

What charming colours appear in the various tribes. What a glow is enkindled in some. What a gloss shines in others. With what a masterly skill is everyone of the varying tints displayed. Here they seem to be thrown on with an easy freedom, there they are adjusted with the nicest touches. Some are intersected with elegant stripes or studded with radiant spots; others affect to be genteelly powdered or neatly fringed. Some are arrayed in purple; some charm with a virgin's white; others are dashed with crimson, while others are robed in scarlet. Some glitter like silver lace, others shine as if embroidered with gold.

Finally, Fothergill's preference is well epitomised by Linnaeus suitably giving the name of *Fothergilla* to a shrub of brilliant autumn foliage. He told Humphry Marshall about his favourite 'Americans':

My garden is well sheltered; the soil is good and I endeavour to mend it as occasion requires. I have an Umbrella Tree, above twenty feet high, that flowers with me abundantly, every spring. The small magnolia, likewise flowers with me finely. I have a little wilderness, which, when I bought the premises, was full of yew trees, laurels and weeds. I had it cleared, well dug and took up many trees, but left others standing for shelter. Among these I have planted Kalmias, Azaleas, all the Magnolias and most other hardy

American shrubs. It is not quite eight years since I made a beginning; so that my plants must be considered as young ones. They are, however, extremely flourishing. The great magnolia has not yet flowered with me, but grows exceedingly fast. I shelter his top in winter; he gains from half a yard to two feet in height every summer and will, ere long, I doubt not, repay my care with his beauty and fragrance.

Botany is in debt to these three enthusiasts of the eighteenth century; all friends of Philip Miller and, in their turn, indebted to him. With their aesthetic appreciation and practical execution, they furthered knowledge of the multitude of new plants arriving in this country from overseas.

A Cedar of Lebanon flourished in
Collinson's garden at Mill Hill;
drawing by G. D. Ehret

9 Hazards of Transport

In an era when many months might elapse between the collection of plants and seeds from abroad and their arrival in Britain, care over their packing and transport was essential. Botanists and horticulturists depended upon the good services of British sea captains to carry plants from the West Indies and North America. Others were brought to the West by European ships from the East Indies and the Cape of Good Hope, while in the Far East French missionaries collected on their travels and sent their discoveries overland by various stages to Paris. This was long before Nathaniel Ward (1791–1868) invented the invaluable closed Wardian case and there existed no means to guarantee the survival of living plants removed from their native habitat.

At home coaches were sometimes used to convey perishable goods: Alexander Pope sent two precious pineapples from his Twickenham hot-houses to his friend, Ralph Allen at Prior Park, near Bath, using the coach from Turnham Green. Gilbert White was proud of his early cucumbers, cutting the first of 1753 on 5th April to take to his brother in London and when he discovered they were priced two shillings apiece in Town, arranged for a further thirteen to be conveyed on the coach from Selborne. Carriage by water was used where practicable, taking produce into the City from market gardens alongside the Thames. Philip Miller used the east coast sea route to send seeds, shrubs and trees to Patrick Blair in Boston, Lincolnshire, loading them at Cotton's Wharf, and also to Alston in Edinburgh, though in 1757 he queried the safety of this method during the war with the French.

Carriers provided more general means of conveying plants and in 1697 the London/Bradford service brought Richard Richardson a box of July-flowers from Robert Uvedale (1642–1722). This master of Enfield Grammar School neglected scholastic responsibility somewhat in favour of his extensive hothouses filled with exotic plants and his letter to Richardson recounted a need for restocking after a disastrous winter. This shows the extent of seed movement across land and sea at that time. He had, he said, received little of 'Affricans', except a small parcel from Petrus Hotton of Leyden, who had in turn received them from Denmark, 'one of their ships touching last year at the Cape'. Additionally, William Sherard had sent seeds from Rome and others had come from the Oxford Garden and from Scotland. In March 1704 Sherard told Richardson, 'We sent a vessel over this week to Calais to exchange some prisoners of war. I have there a large collection of dried

The olive, Olea europea *L.*

plants and a pacquet of seeds, which I hope for before the end of April.' Five years later, the Reverend Adam Buddle (*c.*1660–1715), Reader at Gray's Inn and an enthusiastic botanist, after whom Buddleja is named, welcomed an offer from Richardson to send seeds and roots from Yorkshire to him and to the Chelsea Garden 'which is now putting into very good order ... we design to cultivate all the rare English plants we can get to grow there.' He hoped, he said, that peace might bring an end to difficult communication.

By the time Philip Miller came to Chelsea thirteen years later, attention was turning towards imports arriving from the East as well as the West. Captain Quick brought a *Mangifera*, mango, and *Nycanthes*, Arabian jasmine, from India and both flourished at Chelsea. Enthusiasm for botanical discovery took Captain Hutchinson of the *Godolphin* some miles inland at the

Cape of Good Hope, drawn, Miller reports, by the fragrance of beautiful flowers. For Richard Warner, this sailor also brought from India a *Cycas circinalis*, unfortunately to be decapitated by crossfire from the French when nearly home. However, it became established at Woodford and through Warner's generosity offshoots were distributed, as were many other rarities raised by him from seeds brought in from the Far East. Gardening owed much to these cooperative captains; the two mentioned above faithfully observed Miller's directions for the transport of plants, set out at length in the *Dictionary*.

The first consideration was seasonal: from a hot country plants should be sent in spring in order to recover before winter, while those from a colder clime would travel best through winter, when they would not shoot unduly on the voyage. Secondly, packing should be in strong boxes, with handles for ease of movement and a hole in the base, covered with tiles or oyster shells for good drainage. Specimens should be planted as closely as possible two or three weeks before being taken on board and then kept on deck, covered in bad weather with a tarpaulin against salt spray, a precaution made unnecessary after the invention of the Wardian case.

Sedums and other succulents need not be planted, but should be placed in a box wrapped in dry moss, with hay or straw placed between layers and small holes pierced in the box. If stowed in a dry place, where there was no danger from rats, they would grow 'though they be two, three or four months on their passage and will be less liable to suffer than if planted in earth, because the sailors generally kill these plants by overwatering them.'

Transport of trees presented no problem: packed in chests with moss about their roots they could be kept out of ground two or three months, provided it was a dormant season. Miller pointed out that 'Oranges, jesmines, capers, olives and pomegranites ... are annually brought from Italy and, if skilfully managed, very few of them miscarry, notwithstanding they are many times three or four months out of the ground.'

The greatest problem with seeds was to keep them dry and free from rats. Miller quoted Mark Catesby, who always packed dry seeds in paper and sealed them in a dry guord shell. Seeds arrived at Chelsea from a diversity of sources: for example, species of *Aster*: *A. grandiflorus*, found by Catesby in Virginia, *A. nervosus* from Pennsylvania; *A. chinensis* (now *Callistephus chinensis*, the China Aster) sent to France by missionaries and thence to Chelsea and of this species, a double white from 'my worthy friend, Dr. Job Baxter of Zirkzee, Holland'; and finally *A. amantus* and *A. procumbens* from William Houstoun in Vera Cruz.

In his *Directions for Taking up Plants and Shrubs and Conveying Them by Sea*, John Fothergill suggested placing seeds among specimens in boxes, some of which might succeed if the plants failed. On domestic hazards, he advocated nets over the boxes to prevent dogs and cats scratching in the

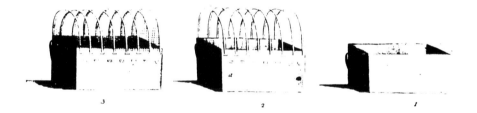

DIRECTIONS *for taking up* PLANTS *and* SHRUBS, *and Conveying Them by* SEA.

IN Order to take up the Plants advantageously, each Ship should be furnished with a Mattock and a Spade; with the Mattock a small Trench should be opened round the Plant intended to be taken up; the Spade should then be put under the Root, which must be lifted up with a very large Ball of Earth surrounding it; the Ball may afterward be pared carefully with a Knife, and reduced as small as can be done without wounding any of the larger Roots.

Of each Kind the youngest Plants of Shrubs and Trees that can be found should be taken; none of them should be above a Foot high; as young Plants are found by Experience to bear removing much better than old ones.

The most convenient kind of Boxes for the Conveyance of Plants in long Voyages are made about Four Feet long, Two broad, and Two deep; these, when half filled with Earth, can be conveniently carried by two Men holding the Rope Handles fixed to their Ends.

These should be filled about half full of Mould, with a few rotten Sticks or Leaves at the Bottom, and the Plants intended to be sent, planted in it. as soon after the Ship's Arrival as possible. When the Ship is about to sail, and they are sent on board, Hoops are to be nailed to the Sides of the Box in such a Manner, that, arching over it, they may cover the Highest of the Plants; small Ropes are to be twisted between these in the Form of a Net to prevent the Dogs or Cats from getting at them, and scratching them up, on Account of the fresh Mould.

For each Box so hooped and netted, provide a Canvas Cover, which may when put on entirely protect it; and to prevent this Cover from being lost or mislaid, nail it to one Side, and fix Loops or Hooks to the other, by which it may occasionally be fastened down.

The Captain who takes Charge of them, must be particularly informed that the chief Danger Plants are liable to in Sea Voyages is occasioned by the minute Particles of Salt Water with which the Air is charged, whenever the Waves have white frothy Curls upon them; these Particles fall upon the Plants, and, quickly evaporating, leave the Salt behind, which choaking up the Pores prevents Perspiration, and effectually kills the Plant; he therefore should never let the Covers be off, except on Days when the Wind is not sufficiently high, to beat the Water up into what the Seamen call White Caps; he must not keep them always shut up during the Voyage: for if he does they will mould and perish by the Stagnation of the Air under the Covers; and if at any Time, by Accident or Necessity, they should have been exposed to the Wind, when the Waves have White Caps, he must be desired to water them well with fresh Water, sprinkling all the Leaves with it, to wash off the Salt Drops which cover them. In this Manner Plants may be brought from almost any Distance; many come from *China* every Year in a flourishing State.

If it is convenient to the Captain to give up a small Part of the Great Cabbin to the Plants, this is certainly by far the best Station for them, nor are they much in the Way; as the Place which suits them best is close to the Stern Windows: in this Case they need not be furnished with their Canvas Covers, and they may frequently have Air, by opening the Windows when the Weather is quite moderate.

Ripe Seeds of all Kinds should also be brought Home; and it will be proper to sow in the Boxes of Earth, between the growing Plants, as many Sorts as possible, some of which may succeed in Case of Failure of the Plants.

And if very small Bits of broken Glass are mixed with the Earth, or thrown plentifully over its Surface, in the Boxes, it may prevent Mice or Rats from burrowing in it, and destroying the tender Roots of the Plants and growing Seeds.

Fig. 1. Represents the Form of the Box.
—— 2. The same, with Hoops and Loops, *a---a* for securing the Canvas.
—— 3. The same, netted.

FOTHERGILL'S INSTRUCTIONS FOR COLLECTORS
(date probably 1771).
Copy in Linnaeus's correspondence at the Linnean Society.

earth and small pieces of broken glass scattered in it to deter burrowing by rats and mice. But chiefly he stresses the danger of salt spray, 'Never let the covers be off, except on days when the wind is not sufficiently high to beat the water into what the seamen call white caps.' If they suffered in this way, they had to be sprayed with fresh water. With care and following Fothergill's instructions many plants arrived yearly from China in splendid condition.

John Ellis, basically a trader like Peter Collinson, found his position as Agent for West Florida and Dominica helpful in furthering his interest in botany. He published *Directions for Bringing over Seeds and Plants from the East Indies and other Distant Countries in a State of Vegetation* (1770) and one method he favoured was to coat seeds in wax to protect them from extreme temperatures.

As has been seen, the most diligent organiser of plant transport from the West was Peter Collinson and much relevant correspondence will be found in William Darlington's *The memorials of John Bartram and Humphry Marshall* (1849) where the author considered sea captains of such importance as to merit a special index. Forty-eight are listed: Buddle, Falconer, Savage, Richmond and Wright being the most frequently mentioned, the latter twenty-two times in the short space of seven years. Wright and Richmond were recommended by Collinson to Bartram as being the most reliable, and were sometimes asked to convey zoological cargo; live squirrels, red-birds and terrapins for Lord Petre or insects mounted in a cork-lined box for Dr Fothergill.

Initial collection needed the greatest care and early in his correspondence with Bartram, Collinson expressed disappointment because plants of *Cypripedium*, ladies slipper, had not survived transport for want of proper attention at the outset. He suggested using watertight ox bladders as containers; in them, tied to the saddle, plants could be kept fresh for a long time. Fothergill wrote to Marshall, advocating William Young's method of packing: plants safely wrapped up in moss and packed very tightly in a box. He also advised that seeds be sent in a vegetating condition, packed in layers of damp sphagnum moss. Thus acorns succeeded extremely well, and Fothergill's splendid collection of 'Americans' at Upton justified his emphasis on proper care in transport.

Once collected and properly packaged, these precious cargoes had to survive long voyages, often in the intimate care of the ship's captain. In January 1735 Collinson reported back to Bartram, '... how well the little case of plants came, being put under the captain's bed and saw no light till I sent for it. But then Captain Warner had a very quick passage and it was put on board in the right month ... The warmth of the ship and want of air had occasioned the skunk-weed to put forth two fine blossoms, very beautiful ...' On another occasion, things did not go so well, 'for at each corner of each box they [rats] had made a proper hole for access and in each box was a warm nest of straw and the leaves and stalks of the shrubs. It grieved me to see how they had stripped the great Rhododendron and the lesser Kalmias.' There was also a chance that plants might be stolen and Collinson reported in January 1751, '... to my great loss, some prying, knowing people looked into the cases and out of that numbered 2 took the three roots of Chamaerhododendron, honey laurel, root of silver-leaved arum and the *Spirea alni folio* ... I fancy some of the sailors, having relatives gardeners, seeing these plants so carefully boxed up, took them for rarities; so were tempted to steal them and give them to their friends.'

However, these inroads by man and beast on board were light when compared with losses at sea, due to storm or war, when whole shipments might be lost. The wars with France and Spain during the eighteenth century stretched over many years and disrupted plant exchange as did the American War of Independence in 1775. Bartram seemed particularly grieved when, in 1744, he learned that a letter about one of his journeys to Lake Ontario might be lost with

> ... a particular account of the soil, productions, mountains and lakes which I observed in my journey thither ... but I have lately heard that Reeves is taken by the French. I conclude that which I took so much pains about will never come to thy hands.

The following year he sent to Gronovius in Holland 'many curiosities' via Collinson, hoping they may not be intercepted by the French and Spaniards, as the year before. Yet he added a generous Quakerly note:

> If I could know that they fell into the hands of men of learning and curiosity, I should be more easy about them. Though they are what is commonly called our enemies, yet, if they make proper use of what I have laboured for, let them enjoy it with the blessing of God.

Loss of manuscripts or illustrations seem to cause him the greatest concern. Ten years later he wondered

> ... if there should be a war with France, how shall I send my descriptions of trees or Billy's drawings, without falling into ignorant people's hands, that will not take any notice of them or maybe, throw them away? Suppose I should direct them (under the cover) to Mr. Dalibard, Buffon or Jussieu, or Dr. Gronovius. If the French should take them and see them directed to such noted men, they might take care to send them to them.

Collinson agreed with this proposition:

> In case of war, I approve thy plan of directing all to Mr. Buffon's at the Royal Garden Paris and then, underneath direct to me. Then I should have it one time or another. But our affairs are so surprisingly situated that none knows, yet, whether it will be war or peace. We continue taking the French ships, but

they take none of ours. So reconcile this piece of French policy, if thou can, and foretell its consequences.

Miller wrote to Bartram in January 1758:

The specimens you were so good as to send to me by Captain Lyon would have been a treasure had they arrived safe; but his ship was taken by the French, so those were all lost, which is a great misfortune at this time, when they would have been of great service to me, in ascertaining the names of some plants which remain doubtful.

In 1763 Collinson told Bartram of his concern for the *Carolina*:

Captain Friend being taken by the Spaniards and carried into Bilboa, but as she was taken eleven or twelve days after the treaty was signed, she has been claimed and, I hear, this day, she will be delivered. I presume all our seed boxes are on board, but, as it is customary, all letters were thrown overboard, so shall be at a great loss to find things. So pray write by the very first and send to our friend Alex Colden, postmaster at New York, to go by the first mail from thence which sails every month.

Finally Benjamin Franklin, writing to Bartram from Paris in May, 1777 expressed his concern and willingness to help:

The communication between Britain and North America being cut off, the French botanists cannot, in that channel, be supplied as formerly with American seeds, etc. If you or one of your sons incline to continue that business you may, I believe, send the same number of boxes here, that you used to send to England; because England will then send here, for what it wants in that way. Inclosed is a list of the sorts wished for here. If you consign them to me, I will take care of the sale and returns for you. There will be no difficulty in the importation, as the matter is countenanced by the Ministry, from whom I received the list.

Such were the difficulties facing collectors and transporters of plants in the eighteenth century. With unbounded patience they sought and sent plants, wrote requests and provided information, waited months for replies and maybe tried again, eventually to receive those novelties to be propagated in nurseries and distributed to gardens on either side of the Atlantic. To this end the sea captains contributed considerably.

Plate 5

*Evening Primrose: Fig. 1, Oenothera parviflora L.; Fig. 2, Oenothera biennis L.;
drawing by J. S. Miller [pl. 189, FIGS]. Native of North America.*

Plate 6

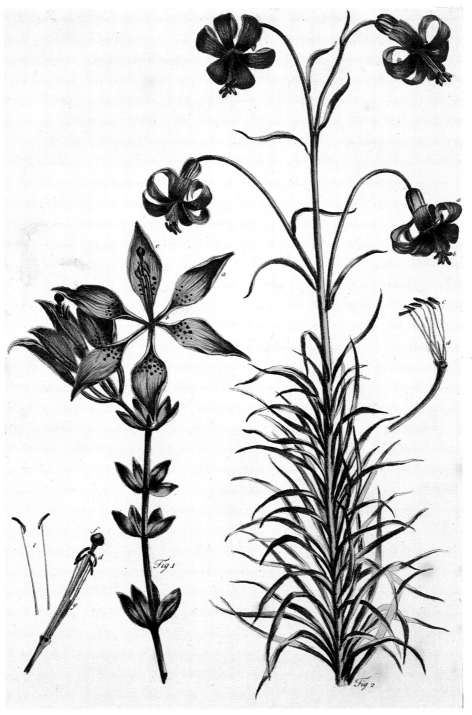

Lilies: Fig. 1, Orange cup Lily, Lilium philadelphicum *L., native of eastern North America; Fig 2, Pompon Lily*, Lilium pomponium *L., native of southern Europe; drawing by R. Lancake [pl. 165,* FIGS*].*

10 Transatlantic Collaboration

An excellent example of perseverance and a rewarding exchange of information and plants can be found in correspondence between Philip Miller and John Bartram, although it covers only five years between 1755–1760. Before they were in direct contact, Collinson had acted as a go-between although Bartram was thoroughly conversant with Miller as an author. With a present of tulip bulbs, offsets and seeds for his garden came the directive from Collinson 'Consult Miller on their culture'. Again, in 1747, when reporting back on germination, Collinson referred Bartram to the *Dictionary*:

> Of the seeds thou sent, the Rose Laurel are some come up, and are very thriving, Red Cedar by thousands, White Cedar, a few, Black Haws, none, thou must send a young tree, two, three or four ... White Pine, some; Sassafras, a few, Sugar Maple, a few, Allspice, a few, Witch Hazel, one. What they belong to I cannot say. Make these queries to Dr. Dillenius. Hast thee consulted Miller – the last being new, he may know nothing of.

Collinson procured from 'my knowing friend Philip Miller' sixty-nine sorts of seed to send to Bartram. These included some of the plums, nectarines and apricots successfully coaxed by Miller to produce early fruit at Chelsea. At the same time came a request for 'a handful or two of white cedar cones for Philip Miller, for in separating the seeds, by accident he had none.' A note from Bartram in 1745 seems to imply a slight difference of opinion as his account of some American pines had been questioned: 'But as I have great opinion of Miller's learning and judgement, I am engaged in duty and friendship to inform him the best I can.'

Of the existing dozen letters passed between Chelsea and Kingsessing, 1755–1760, nine are published in William Darlington's *Memorials of John Bartram and Humphry Marshall* (1849, 1967) and three are held by American Libraries. Of these eight are from Miller and they give an insight into the work of the Chelsea Gardener when he had probably reached the peak of his career. The Physic Garden had become so well stocked with rarities as to rival any other garden in Europe. Through his worldwide correspondence Miller had gained tangible results and rare commendation from the Apothecaries. The *Dictionary* had reached its sixth edition and Miller was working on the seventh, revising it to incorporate the Linnaean system of classification. His *Figures of Plants* were appearing periodically to amplify and embellish his writing, the very successful Abridgement had reached its fourth edition and the *Garden Kalender* its tenth. Bartram's *Observations on the Inhabitants, Climate, Soil, River, Production: from Pennsylvania to Onodaga, Oswego and the Lake Ontario* had been published in London (1751), and for the past twenty years he had dispatched his boxes of seeds and plants to be disseminated amongst owners of noteworthy gardens who acknowledged his industry. Certainly these two had made their mark on the ever-widening fields of botany and horticulture when John Bartram wrote his first letter to Philip Miller on 20 April 1755:

> I have received thy kind letter of February the 19th 1755, which gave me much satisfaction: and some uneasiness, that so many years have elapsed wherein we might have reciprocally communicated our observations to each other; and although thee had incomparably the advantage over me, yet, notwithstanding, I love to peep into the abstruse operations of nature. Perhaps I might, by thy familiar instruction have made some remarks that might have been satisfactory. But, for the time to come, I hope we may double our diligence, if the war with France do not obstruct our endeavours ... for time is so far spent, past our meridian, that the affair calls for diligence.

Bartram then told Miller about his method of collecting specimens of pines; when they are in flower and the young cone just impregnated, and asked whether European pines set their cones on the same spring's shoot, 'or the second year's wood, as by your draught, the Scotch Pine doth?' Miller had evidently criticised Bartram's long descriptions because he replied:

> ... I am obliged to thee, for thy good advice, to contract my descriptions. I own, the leaves, acorns, and especially the cups, are very material in ascertaining the different species of our Oaks; yet the description of the bark, and form of growth, are useful helps, in our mature Oaks. I can often discover our different species of Oaks, one from another, by their form of growth, half or a whole mile distance; and I am sure he must be very sharp-sighted that can know them, at half that distance, by their leaves, acorns, and cups, all together.

Bartram expressed gratitude for Miller's offer to assist him in understanding Linnaeus's system and commented on the Swedish naturalist's publication of all the North American plants observed by Kalm on his visit (i.e. *Species Plantarum*, 2 vols. 1753) adding, 'I long to see these books – to see if they have done me justice, as Kalm promised me.' The letter ends with Bartram's eager anticipation for some *Figures of Plants* and a promise of assistance 'with any new plant, or shrub – either dead or alive – in substance or a particular description.'

The next letter from Miller, dated 2 February 1756, acknowledged three from Bartram and two boxes of plants and he added 'To the first of your letters, I returned an answer in September last, but for fear it may miscarry,

Gladiolus floribundus *Jacquin* [pl. 40, FIGS]

I beg leave to repeat the substance of that here.' Then, in reply to Bartram's initial regret about their correspondence, Miller continues:

I am sorry so many years passed without our having an intercourse by letters, as I am sensible how many observations I have lost which must have fallen in your way to have made. As I seek after truth, so shall I always be glad to receive any information from my friends, even if they should contradict what I may have published, yet I shall never think it derogatory to my character to own my mistakes, and rectify them.

Bartram's query regarding Kalm's American observations was dealt with: Miller had not seen whether Linnaeus had included them in his Species of Plants, but mentioned that Kalm had published them himself; 'in the Swedish language; but as I do not understand it, so I have not been curious enough to send for the book*, nor do I hear any good character of it.'

But sixteen days later, on 18 February 1756, Miller quickly wrote to apologise for giving the wrong name of the ship by which he had sent seeds, roses and cedar cones, and also to thank Bartram for his letter of 9 December in which he mentioned he would like the Norway Maple. This could easily be sent because a large tree in the garden seeded in all the borders and cuttings rooted easily, like willows. Thoughtfully, Miller sent a list of items he wanted; taken out of the *Flora Virginica*, a book he supposed Bartram would have. [This work by J. F. Gronovius (1793) included material from another American botanical collector, John Clayton.] Some of these plants had arrived in the last box, but in a bad condition and, moreover, unnamed.

Miller next wrote on 15 February 1757 reporting that he had just received a letter from Bartram, written at the beginning of November, with the 'disagreeable account that neither of my letters, wrote last summer' had arrived and thus some of his important queries had not been considered. This was particularly annoying as he had wanted particulars of *Gale asplenii folio* [i.e. *Comptonia peregrina* var *aspleniifolia*] for the revised seventh edition of the *Dictionary*. Bartram had insisted that this differed from the candleberry, *Myrica cerifera*, while Miller had found other authors ranging it with the Liquidambar, 'so I shall be much obliged to you, if you can send me a perfect specimen, that I may determine its proper genus.' Then came a question on the size of the Balm of Gilead Fir in America and which sort of soil suited it best, 'for there is but one place, in England, where the trees live more than ten or twelve years.' – a reference to the Duke of Bedford's estate at Woburn.

Less than a month later, at the beginning of March 1757, Miller wrote a letter, now held by the Historical Society of Pennsylvania, reporting that promised specimens of *Crataegus* had not arrived and could not be included in the current edition of the Dictionary; he repeated his request for *Gale asplenii-folio* and for all sorts of lilies and *Andromeda*. He had been much taken with a small low-growing *Kalmia* at Whitton – from Pennsylvania so the Duke of Argyll had told him – but did not specifically request it.

On 20 June 1757, Bartram acknowledged the February letter, together with six cedar cones, parts of the *Dictionary* and *Figures*, and confirmed that

* This was Kalm's *Resa till Norra America* (3 vols. 1753–1761) of which an English translation was published in 1770–1771. It was also translated into German, French and Dutch, so eager were Europeans to get first hand information about North America.

Crataegus crus-galli *L. [pl. 178*, FIGS]

he had sent the *Gale* which he believed to be a new genus; in this he was right, for L'Heritier later founded the genus *Comptonia* upon it. The basket of Norway Maples and roses he had shared with his friend, Dr Bond.

Part of Miller's next letter, 12 January 1758, has already been quoted (p. 80) with regard to loss of specimens at sea and this was regrettable as his *Hortus siccus* contained nearly ten thousand specimens and he wished to make it as complete as possible. He continued

I am afraid the cutting of the great *Toxicodendron* [poison ivy] is perished; for it lay at the bottom of the box, where there had been wet. I am very desirous to get all the species of this genus which I can, and am making observations on their flowers and fruit: for Doctor Linnaeus has joined these to his genus of *Rhus* [sumach], with which all the species of *Toxicodendron*, which I have yet examined, will by no means agree; for these are either male and female in distinct plants, or have male flowers in separate parts from the fruit on the same plant, which, according to his own system, must remove them to a great distance from the *Rhus*.

There was some cheerful news from Miller regarding the plant named *Bartramia* about to flower in Chelsea's stove. He promised to forward a specimen when it was dry but went on to say 'the flowers are so small as not to be discerned, by my eyes, without a glass'. He requested a Mountain Magnolia, not yet in the Garden, and ended on a rare personal note: 'But you complain of age too soon. I am now entering on my sixty-fourth[?] year; and bless God, I am still hearty and well ... I sincerely wish you health and happiness.'

Irregularity of mails is emphasised in John Bartram's letter of 16 June 1758. The last quoted had arrived with one dated the previous 26 August (1757) and many of the *Dictionary* and *Figures*, in parts, had miscarried. He enclosed an account of the most troublesome weeds in Pennsylvania, most of them 'imported' from Europe, including the Scotch Thistle, believed to have been spread from mattress stuffing. Within ten weeks, in August 1758, Miller replied promising to replace the lost *Figures* and reported the find of a 'sort of Crataegus' in a clod of earth. This had flowered and fruited and, although too late to be included in the *Dictionary* it might be brought into a later supplement because several new plants had been omitted once their initial letter had been passed in the main work.

This letter is incomplete in the Darlington collection, but it obviously contained much of use to Bartram whose draft reply (in the Library of the American Philosophical Society) dated February 1759 stated that had the postage been three times more he would not have missed it. He was pleased to know that the New England *Crataegus* from West Jersey grew well at Chelsea; with him the fine juicy fruit had been stripped by birds one September day. He reported diligent perusal of the *Dictionary* and *Figures* and believed them to be the 'compleatest work of that kind extant', but expressed his regret that many American plants had been omitted: he hoped to remedy this by sending specimens of growing plants within the next few years. He believed he had found a good humoured gentleman in Holland who would send him plants, but was critical of him for overheating his stoves. He concluded by asking Miller for one little root of *Ixia*, or other bulbous plant from the Cape.

A second letter in the Library of the Historical Society of Pennsylvania is dated 30 May 1759, and in this Miller seemed irritated that plants had arrived unnamed and seeds mixed. He complained that there was no root of *Veratrum* to replace one lost nor of the various martagons which he had found so slow to mature from seed in England. He said he would like a plant or two of *Gale* with spleenwort leaves (i.e. *Comptonia peregrina* var. *aspleniifolia*) and dried specimens of the male and female plants, having only seen the former. Ladies Slipper, Evergreen Pyrola, *Tetragonotheca* (a type of dwarf sunflower, rare in England) and any variety of *Polygala* and *Gerardia* were also requested. For his part, Miller said he would send the plants Bartram desired from Chelsea seeds, the remainder of the *Gardeners Dictionary*, now finished and the missing *Figures*.

With this letter were two lists of plants for Miller and Collinson, both headed 'sent by Budden, 1759' and Miller's assortment seems largely to tie up with requests made in the above letter. It included *Gale*, evergreen *Veratrum* with flowering buds, dark green and striped-leaved Pyrola and a pretty *Lycopodium*. A blue cloth bag contained roots of Yellow-Root (see below) with several kinds of Orchis and in a white bag were various Martagons. Both Collinson and Miller received a root of Bartram's dwarf black plum and Collinson had five grafted Newton pippins, together with a Laurel, a pretty striped Orchis and roots of single Ranunculus wrapped in a white woollen cloth.

The last and incomplete letter from Miller in the Darlington collection, dated 10 November 1769, carried a wish for plants from Bartram's garden, because he believed there to be new genera amongst them, but specimens had been 'so much compressed as to render the distinguishing characters very doubtful'. He reported success with Yellow-root (i.e. *Hydrastis canadensis*) as it had 'flowered and ripened seeds in our garden, two years past, from some roots which were sent me from the inland parts of your country. It is a new genus. I have figured and described it, by the title of *Warneria*.' (This was to honour, after many years of botanical friendship, Richard Warner of Woodford, but *Hydrastis* is now the accepted name.) Miller believed Bartram's Dwarf Cherry to be the same as he had figured; he had received the stones via Paris and Canada and, easily propagated, it was now common in gardens.

This sample of correspondence shows that a great many plants were introduced into England by John Bartram. He was collecting for over forty years and, as Miller was a regular recipient of Bartram's shipments, it can be assumed that 'a large proportion of plants credited to Miller as introducer consisted of collections by Bartram and if this is true he was probably responsible for the first appearance in the gardens of England of between one hundred and fifty and two hundred plants' (John Hendley Barnhart, 'Significance of John Bartram's Work to Botanical and Horticultural Knowledge', *Bartonia* Special Issue, 1931).

Yellow-root, Hydrastis canadensis *L. [pl. 285,* FIGS]

Miller only credited Bartram with a few plants in the Dictionary: *Lilium philadelphum*, 'at present very rare in English gardens', *Toxicodendron serratum*, 'not yet flowered' and *Veratrum americanum*, another rarity which had in a good season both flowered and seeded in this country. *Magnolia acuminata* received more precise acknowledgment: '... there are but very few plants at present here, nor is it very common in the habitable parts of America. Some of these trees have been discovered by Mr. John Bartram, growing on the north branch of the Susquehannah River.' However, it must not be forgotten that Miller's expertise in the propagation and care of these newcomers, together with detailed advice on their cultivation in the *Dictionary*, undoubtedly played an important part in the availability and

Fig. *1, Double European Cherry,* Prunus avium *L. 'Plena';*
Fig. *2, Dwarf American Cherry,* Prunus pumila *L.; drawing by R. Lancake [pl. 89,* FIGS]

successful growing of hitherto unknown plants. Also through him many others from Europe and countries further East were introduced to gardeners on the other side of the Atlantic.

The letters between Miller and Bartram show what could be achieved by patience and forbearance two hundred years ago. Delay was anticipated, loss accepted, requests repeated lest they miscarry and appreciation re-stressed lest it appear forgotten. Questions were put, answers sent, roots and seed dispatched, flowers and fruit cultivated, nomenclature discussed and through this comprehensive exchange between two great gardeners working beside the Thames and the Schuylkill, botany and horticulture have bene-fited the world over.

II *The Gardeners Dictionary and its Abridgement*

References by Miller's contemporaries to his *Gardeners Dictionary* already mentioned have shown how widely it was used and appreciated both in Britain and abroad during the eighteenth century. However, its contents have not yet been revealed in any detail, neither has the valuable *Abridgement* been considered. Closer investigation shows the extraordinary extent of Miller's theoretical knowledge of and practical expertise with an enormous diversity of matters.

The two-volume octavo work of 1724, known as *The Gardeners and Florists Dictionary*, is omitted from the enumeration of editions, the folio work of 1731 being classed as the first. On 27 May of that year, John Martyn read to the Royal Society an account of a book entitled *The Gardeners Dictionary*, introducing it as follows:

> A general system of gardening founded on experience is a work of which the public has long stood in need. The almost incessant labour which that art requires leaves so little time for study that one can hardly find any person of sufficient experience capable of writing. On the other side, men of letters have so few opportunities of applying themselves to the general practice that the rules they lay down, however plausible they may seem in the closet, would often ruin the honest gardener who should venture to follow them. We might still have laboured under these difficulties if our author, who has added a considerable stock of reading to many years experience, had not entered upon the task.

He then gave a resumé of the practical contents; directions for the kitchen garden, with vegetables through the seasons; the fruit garden, where some erroneous methods of pruning were corrected; the flower garden, where both exotic and domestic blooms might be raised and, finally, the wilderness, where the correct choice of shrubs and trees and particularly their size and shape was all-important. On this last, a comparatively new concept, he added, 'Were the rules that Mr. Miller has laid down under this article widely pursued, we should reap a much greater satisfaction from this principal ornament of a fine garden.'

He commended the author for his exact instructions regarding the building of greenhouses and stoves, each of which was illustrated to show improvements he had made in these aspects of horticulture. Equally instructive was the section on vineyards and wines, the result of much correspondence with France and Italy. Martyn referred to Miller's use of works by those better versed in scientific aspects of gardening, to whom due acknowledgment is given, and concluded with an appreciation of the author's own industry: 'As to the practical part, he has given us hardly anything but from his own knowledge and of the great number of plants mentioned in his book there are scarce any which he has not cultivated with his own hands.' Thus the *Dictionary*, dedicated to Sir Hans Sloane, was launched by one of the author's neighbours in Chelsea.

Amongst four hundred subscribers listed at the beinning of this *Dictionary* John Martyn was one of the sixty to order large paper copies. The names provide comprehensive evidence of support for the project, both from the academic and practical viewpoint. Among many eminent subscribers were the Duchess of Gainsborough, the Duke of Queensborough, the Lord High Chancellor and the Resident of the King of Prussia. Lord Petre ordered one for himself, another in the name of his gardener, James Hunt, while a dozen more were bespoke on behalf on those who tended the great gardens; James Hoyland for the Earl of Carlisle at Castle Howard and Rice Lewis for the Earl of Burlington at Chiswick, for example. Men with widely differing occupations like the Collector of the King's Customs at Plymouth, a Lord Commissioner of the Admiralty, the Treasurer of St Bartholomew's Hospital and a Chief Clerk of Session in Scotland all shared a common interest in the *Gardeners Dictionary*.

Academic subscribers included Edmund Halley, Astronomer Royal, the Professor of Modern History at Oxford, the Provost of Oriel, Professors of Botany at both Dublin and Edinburgh Universities and the Vice-Master of Trinity, expressly for use in the Library of that Cambridge College. Abroad, Boerhaave at Leyden, the merchants George Clifford at Amsterdam and Daniel Gould at Leghorn wanted copies and two names came from across the Atlantic: the Governor of South Carolina, H. E. James Johnson and a Mr John James of Boston.

At home many keen gardeners amongst the clergy subscribed, for example, the Dean of Rochester and the Rev. Mr Elisha Smith, Rector of 'Tid St Gyles' in the Isle of Ely. The list also included Fellows of the Royal Society, apothecaries and physicians interested in the scientific aspect of the publication. Leading nurserymen sought practical advice: subscriptions came from Christopher Gray at Fulham, Henry Woodham at Strand-on-the-Green, John Tilford at York and, for two copies, John Perfect at Pontefract. One seedsman is listed, Nicholas Sayers in Pall Mall. Quite apart from all these individual subscribers were those wishing to promote the work. Up and down the country, sixteen booksellers from John Waghorn in Durham to Benjamin Smythurst in Plymouth, from William Eaton in Yarmouth to Samuel Lobb in Bath, were interested and Thomas Howard in York invested in three copies.

Pineapple, Ananas comosus *(L.) Merr.; drawing by G. D. Ehret*

Such wide and varied support guaranteed the success of the *Dictionary* and a further five editions followed in the next twenty years. Thomas Martyn, son of John Martyn and who succeeded his father as Professor of Botany at Cambridge, summarised these in the Preface of his revised edition of the *Dictionary*, published in 1807. He dismissed the small 1724 work as 'merely a germ of those which succeeded in folio' and quotes Pulteney's assessment of the 1731 edition as 'the most complete body of gardening extant'. The second edition followed two years later and a third, with corrections and the inclusion of a garden calendar, in 1737. This provided information on the cultivation of *Ananas* (pineapple) and on the management of stoves and hot walls, and in an addendum many new plants were introduced. There was a catalogue of hardy deciduous trees and shrubs, and three elegant plates from drawings by Ehret (see p. 99). The fourth and fifth editions followed in 1741 and 1747, although Thomas Martyn confessed never to have seen a copy of the latter. The sixth, published in 1752 and dedicated to the Earl of Northumberland, had an elaborate frontispiece (hitherto it had been just a large formal garden with a plantation in the distance) etched and engraved by Edward Rooker (1711–74), after a drawing by Samuel Wade of an allegorical group showing Britannia receiving the fruits of the earth. In this preface Miller apologised for alterations and additions which would render previous editions of inferior value. He had, he said, originally planned to keep improvements apart, but had now been forced to combine them on account of a 'piratical' edition, published in Dublin, producing everything under one cover, and therefore he had been obliged to do the same.

The seventh edition, in 1759 'revised and altered according to the latest system of Botany', included many new plants from overseas and, as Miller emphasised in the Preface, their descriptions had not been copied from books, but taken from nature: 'the far greater number are from growing plants which the author has under his care, and the others are from dried samples which are well preserved; of which he has, perhaps, as large a collection as can be found in the possession of any private person.' Miller also pointed out that although his book was a dictionary for gardeners, all branches of agriculture were included, as well as timber production and cultivation of products by settlers overseas.

Nine years elapsed before Miller produced his eighth and final edition, the one studied in depth for this book. For those who have never seen or handled one of the Miller Dictionaries, it is perhaps worth mentioning that the eighth edition (1768) weighs $17\frac{1}{2}$ lbs (c.8kg), contains 333 folio sheets and measures 430 × 90 mm (666 sides of text). In comparison, the first edition (1731) contained 215 sheets and in Miller's estimation the number of plants cultivated in the country since that date had doubled. This was in no small measure due to his industry, both in correspondence overseas and practical work in the Chelsea Garden.

As John Martyn had emphasised nearly forty years earlier, Philip Miller wrote this conviction from his own trials in cultivation and propagation. With this remarkable period of intensive work behind him, Miller again stressed in the Preface that he had not advanced anything but what he had found fully convincing in his own experience. He mentioned that he sought advice from 'the masters' for particularly scientific sections, and Boerhaave, Boyle, Blair, Grew, Halley, Hales and Newton are all acknowledged in the text. Communication was the basis of his work; he invited contributions from those with particular expertise and these he collated with his own experience in the most comprehensive form to present a reliable work of reference.

Between the Preface and the actual text of the *Dictionary* is an explanation of botanical terminology, with three pages of illustration showing the different parts of plants, various fruits and the structure of flowers. A fourth plate illustrates the system of Linnaeus, 'who classes the plants by the number of stamina in the flowers'. The bibliography, with abbreviations used in the text, is comprehensive and covers one hundred and twenty works ranging from the second edition of the commentaries on Dioscorides's *Materia medica* by Pierandrea Mattioli, printed in Venice in 1558, to the second edition of Linnaeus's *Species Plantarum*, published in Stockholm in 1765.

The text covers almost every corner of the world: plants from the Alps, the Pyrenees, Bohemia, the Levant, Egypt, Siberia, North and South America, the East and West Indies, China and Japan are included. The only part of the globe not mentioned is the Antipodes, for Joseph Banks and Daniel Solander had not yet returned from their voyage with Captain Cook in the *Endeavour* and plants from Australia, New Zealand and the Pacific Islands had yet to be described. However, although the *Dictionary* is principally filled with accounts of genera and their cultivated species, from *Abies alba* of Europe to *Zygophyllum fulvum* of South Africa, there is also comprehensive practical advice on cultivation.

Thus Miller dealt with arculation (propagation by layering), grafting, hoeing, inarching, innoculating, layering, planting, ploughing and pruning. He advised on avenues, borders, edges, groves, hedges, hotbeds, manures and pastures. With the help of others, he expounded on the hazards of frost, fire, ice, rain, snow, water and wind. He warned against more unpleasant aspects: blights, mildews, 'pernicious' caterpillars and 'troublesome vermin', e.g. earwigs. With great patience and no doubt a certain amount of pride, for here he was expert, he minutely described the cultivation of pineapples, melons and oranges in stoves and greenhouses, cucumbers on hot beds and of early fruits, wall-forced, for which he had a special reputation. This is merely a random selection to demonstrate the encyclopaedic nature of the work.

The indexes, in Latin and English, are followed by seven practical lists, similar to those in the catalogues of many leading nurserymen today and they can still be consulted to advantage. The author directs attention to the all-important consideration of scale: 'We often see some of the smallest growing shrubs placed where the largest trees should have been planted.' The first list deals with hardy, deciduous trees and shrubs thriving in this country without shelter and has a key to their height, flowers and scent. Miller liked his ground cover to be permanent and he has not included 'any of the undershrubs, which are of short duration, such as Southernwood, Rosemary, Lavender, Lavender Cotton, etc. because whenever these decay, they occasion gaps in the plantation.' Next he grouped the climbing,

The different Parts of Plants

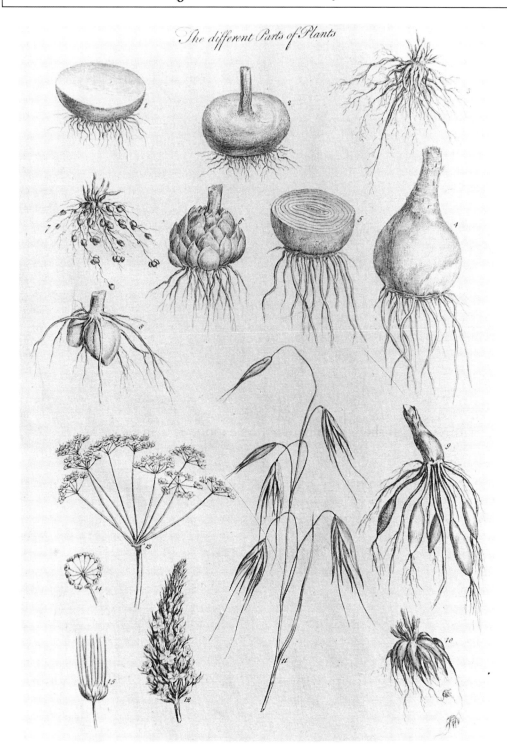

Different parts of plants [*pl. 1*, GD]

A Catalogue of hardy evergreen trees and shrubs.

Those marked with A are such as grow more than forty feet high; those with B are such as grow from twenty to forty feet high; those with C grow from ten to twenty feet; and those marked with D are low shrubs.

ABIES, 1, 2, 3, 4, 5. Fir-tree, A 6, 7, 8, 9. B
Alaternus, 1, 2, 3, 4. C
Arbutus, 1, 2. Strawberry, C
Bupleurum, 6. Hare's-ear, D
Buxus, 1, 2. Box, C 3. D
Celastrus, 1. Staff-tree, D
Cistus, 1, 2, 3, 4, 5, 6, 7, 8, 9, 12, 13, 14, 15, 16. Rock-rose, D
Cneorum, Widow-wail, D
Cupressus, 1, 2. Cypress, B 3. C 5. D
Cytisus, 6. Trefoil-tree, D
Daphne, 1, 4. Mezereon, D

Euonymus, 3. Spindle-tree, D
Hedera, Ivy, D
Hypericum, 3, 4, 6. St. John's-wort, D
Ilex, 1. Holly, B 2, 3. C
Juniperus, 1, 10, 11. Juniper, D 2, 3, 4, 5, 6. C 7, 8, 12, 13. B
Kalmia, 1, 2, 3. Rose-laurel, D
Larix, 3. Cedar of Libanus, A
Laurus, 1, 2. Bay-tree, B
Ligustrum, 2. Privet, C
Magnolia, 2. Laurel-leaved Tulip-tree, C

Medica, 8. Moon Trefoil, D
Mespilus 6. Pyracantha, C
Padus, 4, 5, 6. Laurel, C
Periclymenum, 1, 8. Honeysuckle, D
Phillyrea, 1, 2, 3. C 4, 5, 6, 7. D
Pinus, 1, 3, 5, 10, 13. Pine-tree, A 2, 4, 6, 7, 11. B 8, 9, 14. C
Quercus, 3, 16. Oak, A 17, 20. B 19. C 18
Rosa, 8, 9. Rose, D
Taxus, Yew, B
Thuya, 1, 2. Tree of Life, C
Viburnum, 5, 6. Laurus Tinus, D

List of hardy evergreen trees and shrubs [GD]

shrubby plants needing support or fastening and these are followed by hardy evergreen trees and shrubs. Perennials for open borders are classed as 'proper furniture for the flower garden', with shade-lovers advocated for the wilderness. There is a long list of greenhouse plants in no need of artificial heat and an even greater number of those which do, with an indication as to whether they require a very hot stove or moderate warmth.

Some four hundred medicinal plants 'hardy enough to bear the open air' are listed and for those found in the fields, 'generally termed as Weeds', typical habitat is given to assist those 'inclinable to cultivate them'. Their names were 'such as have been adopted by the Dispensaries' and species are related to numbers given in the *Dictionary*. Lastly, there is a 'Catalogue of large Trees which are admitted in the London Dispensary, but generally grow too large to be admitted into small gardens'. These two lists make a fitting *finis* for a work emanating from the Garden of the Apothecaries.

The *Gardeners Dictionary* was not confined to English readers; it was first translated into Dutch in 1745, an indication of the author's close association with Holland. German translations followed in 1750–58 and 1769–76, with a French edition in 1785–90. English copies would have been available in Europe and mention of distribution in the new American Colonies has been made, so it was an internationally known work by the latter part of the eighteenth century.

Because of its size and cost, copies in folio were of necessity confined to persons of substantial means. These graced stately homes, were used in libraries and by those with a specific academic interest in botany or horticulture. Philip Miller, always conscious of economy, recognised that a

Plate 7

Trumpet-vine, Campsis radicans *(L.) Seemann; drawing by R. Lancake [pl. 65,* FIGS]. *Native of eastern North America.*

Plate 8

Fig. *1*, Turnera ulmifolia *L. var.* angustifolia *(Miller) Willd.; Fig. 2,* Turnera ulmifolia *L. var.* ulmifolia; *drawing by J. S. Miller [pl. 269,* FIGS*]. Native of tropical America.*

concise, cheaper form would find a ready sale with the average gardener. He was also 'hastened by an advertisement that an abridgement was nearly finished in other hands.' In 1735, four years after the first folio edition, an octavo abridgement appeared in two volumes, with plates reduced, but containing the whole of the practical part and species included in the folio. Etymologies, explanations of words, philosophical articles and the Kalendar were omitted, but some new articles were included. A second *Abridgement* was published in 1741 and others followed in 1748 and 1754, all consisting of three octavo volumes.

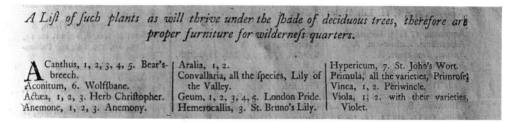

List of plants thriving in shade [GD]

Of these 'Abridgements', the 1754 edition is nomenclaturally the most important (see William Stearn, Chapter 20) and is, therefore, the one considered here. Miller dedicated it to the Earl of Macclesfield, then President of the Royal Society and to the Fellows 'for the improving of natural knowledge'. Once again the Preface provides a useful commentary by the author on his previous works and the reason for promoting the current one. He pointed out that as the three former impressions had sold out and as there had lately been a new edition of the main *Dictionary*, (the sixth, 1752), with many alterations, he judged it proper to include them in a new abridgement. However, economy being of prime importance, he included, he said, nothing inessential to the art of gardening that might increase the size and price (eighteen shillings), but neither had he omitted any advice which might be deemed useful to the profession, 'so that upon the whole the work is rendered as complete a system of practical gardening as present knowledge of vegetation can supply'.

Miller stressed the point that former writers had not had the opportunity of seeing the flower or fruit of new exotics cultivated in English gardens, but by this time many had and details of others had been 'communicated by persons of skill from abroad' and 'so the ranging of plants under their proper heads is now better understood and the science of botany rendered more complete'. He then proceeded tactfully to admonish the theorists of botany in order to protect the practitioners of gardening.

As there are many persons of distinction in England who are pleased to honour the art of gardening by making it a considerable part of their amusement and have been greatly assisting in the introducing of large numbers of new plants, shrubs and trees into the English gardens and as some of these noble persons have studied the science of botany and are well acquainted with the characters and true names of the plants ... their example will render it necessary for the Professors of Gardening at least to know the plants they cultivate by their proper titles ...

Two further editions of the *Abridgement* were warranted, in 1763 and 1771, the year of Miller's death, the last containing some articles not included in the 1768 *Dictionary*.

The number of editions of these two publications, eight of the *Dictionary* and six of its *Abridgement* in Miller's lifetime provides clear evidence of Kalm's sweeping statement that this was the most sought after book on horticulture. But it may not be appreciated that Miller's work provided the foundation for later encyclopaedic horticultural works (see William Stearn, Chapter 20) and the 'bright beam of gardening', of which John Rogers wrote in 1839, has continued to shine for two centuries.

12 Miller's other Works

The Gardener's and Florist's Dictionary of 1724 can be regarded as Philip Miller's first contribution to garden literature. Although, as we have seen (p. 31), it was more than likely a joint production of leading London nursery-men, they undoubtedly recognised Miller's ability and, with their support, Miller began his career as a horticultural writer. The dedication to Sir Hans Sloane (see p. 27) was equally a dedication of himself to botany and horticulture. The Preface sets a note of confidence, 'We have grounds to hope, notwithstanding the inclemency of our seasons ... England though a Northern Climate, will be able to vye with those of a more southerly situation, even to Italy itself, which some have styled the Garden of the World.' This hope was to be realised within the next three decades.

Although Miller stated that he had collected most of the information from well-known authors and always acknowledged them, there are instances when the first person indicated his own contributions. For example, on almond trees: 'I find them to be trees making a good hedge in a short time ... look well round a little wilderness quarters planted with flowering shrubs in a small garden.' Two appendices, 'Forcing Fruits to have them Early' and 'Building a Greenhouse', both subjects of importance to Miller were also probably by him. This work established a firm foundation of respect on which he was to build, with experience, over the next forty-five years.

Although the Society of Gardeners gave their name to the *Catalogus Plantarum* (Catalogue of Trees and Shrubs both Exotick and Domestic that are Hardy enough to Bear the Cold of our Climate in the Open Air and are Propagated for Sale in the Gardens near London) 1730, Philip Miller and Thomas Fairchild are thought to have been its chief promoters. Both had previous publications, Fairchild's *City Gardener* needed updating and Miller had specialised knowledge of this aspect of gardening. The following extract from the Preface of the *Catalogus* appears to have been written by one who had sound knowledge of the Chelsea Garden – almost certainly Philip Miller.

> We cannot in justice omit to mention the establishing of the Publick Botanick Garden at Chelsea by the Worshipful Company of the Apothecaries of London, not only for the instruction of such as should be employed in the compounding of medicines, in the particular simples therein used (which alone is a very laudable design) but also for introducing still a greater variety of trees

and plants, which although their virtues or uses are not at present known, yet may hereinafter be found of excellent use for many purposes in life.

The wise prognosis was confirmed by W. T. Stearn in his address on the occasion of the Garden's tercentenary in 1973 (see p. 188). The opportunity afforded for exchange of knowledge and practical study – Miller's basic principles – are emphasised and due credit is respectfully given to the Apothecaries.

However, the main purpose of this publication was to protect the nurserymen, to establish recognition through text and illustration of many new plants on sale in this country. The Preface further explains that there had recently been many books published by amateurs, 'mere plagiarists', who had confused names and caused trouble, not only to customers, but also to the growers. Quite frequently a certain plant was reordered under a different name from the correct one and consequently the nurseryman, who honestly believed he was fulfilling the order, was dubbed a 'knave or a blockhead', whereas the fault lay with 'too much dependence upon careless naming by an unexperienced author'. Additionally, the Society gave an assurance that all trees and plants described in their publication were available in their nurseries and were not just those displayed in botanic gardens, or owned by curious gentlemen.

Thus the Preface of the *Catalogus Plantarum* emphasised correct identification as a prime factor for success both in the nursery and the garden, and the text of the work presented a practical guide, suggesting the best uses for the new trees and shrubs with which there had been little experience. In this respect it was good sales promotion, a catalogue of positive persuasion as the following quotation shows:

> In all we promise the publick to be as careful as possible not to lead them into mistakes, nor will we mention any particular tree, plant, flower or fruit which is not in our own garden ... we do not propose to mention many different species of trees and plants that are either in the Public Botanick Garden, nor that may be in the possession of some curious gentlemen, but only such as are actually in the nurseries of persons belonging to this Society and from where any Gentleman may be furnished with any of the particulars here treated of by directing their letters for the Society of Gardeners at Newhall's Coffee House in Chelsea, Nr. London, at the easiest rates and may be ascertained of the right kinds.

The Society of Gardeners originally planned to cover all aspects of horticulture in one large work. However, the cost of painting so many large plates proved too expensive so plans were made to issue five sections: trees and shrubs, greenhouse plants, exotics, flowers and fruits; all with plates of the most unusual varieties. Only the first was achieved before the collapse of the Society and it was left to Philip Miller to carry on with instruction through his *Dictionary*. According to John Rogers, who knew Miller, a serious difference of opinion over the publication of some of the Society's proceedings caused the break-up and, he says, 'the opponents of the publication demanded their papers from Miller, who immediately gave them up, having, however, with his usual foresight, taken a copy of each, otherwise their valuable contents would most likely have been lost to the world.' Undoubtedly some of this information was to be incorporated in his own *Dictionary*.

That Miller was known outside the gardening fraternity at the time is evidenced by the fact that his expertise was sought by Nathan Bailey for his *Dictionarum Britannicum or a more Compleat Etymological English Dictionary*, 1730. This, 'collected by several hands' gave acknowledgment on the title page to 'the Mathematical part by G. Gordon and the Botanical by P. Miller'. A glance at the Chelsea Gardener's relevant entries shows them to be concisely informative.

In 1730 Miller edited a list of the medicinal plants at Chelsea, published as *Catalogus Plantarum Officinalium suae in Horto Botanico Chelseano aluntur*. This led to a certain amount of friction between the Gardener (Hortulanus) and the Keeper of the Garden (Praefectus Horti), Isaac Rand, who, in accordance with his office, published in the same year *Index Plantarum officinalium quae in Horto Chelseiano*. In compliance with the rules laid down by Sir Hans Sloane's original deed of conveyance (see p. 22), dried and labelled specimens of fifty species grown in the Garden had to be sent each year to the Royal Society. Lists of these were regularly published in the *Philosophical Transactions* and it is highly probable that Miller, when he was well established at Chelsea, was involved in the selection of these.

Four of Miller's papers were read at the Royal Society. Two are of particular interest: one described how to cultivate the coconut (see p. 39) and other seeds considered impossible to grow in this country (*Phil. Trans.* **135**: 485–488, 1728); and the other how bulbs of tulips, narcissi and hyacinths might be grown in vases filled with water, a method recently devised by a Swede, Martin Triewald (*Phil. Trans.* **137**: 80–84, 1733). In 1758, 'roused by its enormous price' Miller wrote a pamphlet on madder, *Rubia tinctorum* (p. 102), as produced by the Dutch in Zeeland where, as we have seen (pp 51–53) he had personally studied their methods. The paper was 'embellished with drafts of the building and kilns erected for that purpose', and these were reproduced in the *Dictionary*. This paper was probably circulated amongst those interested and Miller's advice followed, as the *Register of Premiums and Bounties* of the Royal Society of Arts contains many awards for the cultivation of madder, particularly in East Anglia and Kent, during the years 1755–67.

Miller's *Gardener's Kalendar*, published in fifteen editions between 1732 and 1765, catered for the modest gardener who needed practical advice and

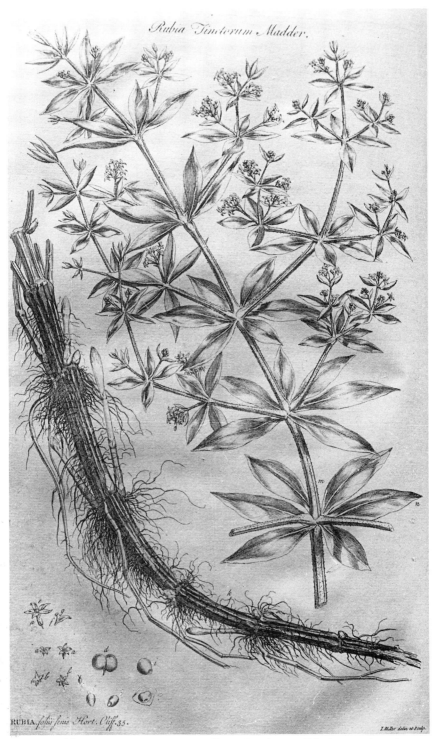

Madder, Rubia tinctorum *L., from* Gardeners Dictionary *(1768)*

the Preface again contains some personal comment, rarely apparent even in his correspondence. Since work to be undertaken in respective months in the kitchen, fruit and flower gardens was noted in the *Dictionary*, it might be thought that a *Kalendar* was superfluous, but Miller explains that at the request of particular friends he had produced a work not only portable, but also at a price to suit those who could not afford a larger book. At four shillings a copy it came within the purse of most and indeed was judged to be 'a manual to the whole kingdom'. Its aim was to bring into 'one easy and concise view' what might be of use to those 'hindered by other avocations from bestowing much time in the study of this delightful and innocent work'. Miller explained that lack of space prevented directions on specific culture of plants, but where necessary, he had referred the reader to the *Dictionary*.

While Miller was preparing the *Kalendar*, he was told of the 'ungenerous intention' of others to use *Dictionary* information for the same purpose, 'upon which I was the more intent to have it published before such a design could be accomplished by any other hand, which was not very difficult for me to do, having a complete Diary of my own, so that I had little more to do than to transcribe my loose papers and dispose them into the method wherein they are here presented to the world.' This is the only mention found of Miller's diary, without doubt one diligently kept at the end of every long day, and it is indeed regrettable that this meticulous record of his day-to-day activities and achievements at the Chelsea Physic Garden has not survived.

John Martyn considered this publication of enough importance to warrant his presenting another account to the Royal Society, only six months after his dissertation on the *Dictionary*. He emphasised the importance of the *Kalendar* – to show in 'short compass' what had come before – and outlined the contents. Under each month could be found directions for work to be done in the kitchen garden with notes on its produce, the pleasure or flower garden with plants then in flower, and the greenhouse and stove with their plants in bloom. There were also details of hardy trees and shrubs. It was in fact, 'by no means a bare collection of what was scattered in the former ... but a performance so well designed and so well executed, ... very acceptable to all who make gardening either their profession or diversion.'

Rivingtons, Miller's publishers, placed advertisements in the back of the 1732 *Kalendar* for current works: the *Dictionary* of the year before, the *Catalogus Plantarum*, John Martyn's translation of Tournefort's *Tabulae Synopticae Officinalium* and his *First Lecture on a Course of Botany*. The tenth edition of the *Kalendar* in 1754, contained a write-up of the sixth edition of the *Dictionary* (1752) and on its title page was notice of the fact that it had been 'adapted to the new style, with a list of medicinal plants which may be gathered in each month for use'. This was two years before the Linnaean system of classification was used in the seventh edition of the *Dictionary* (1756–59) and, probably, Miller's first public acknowledgment of it. The 1760 *Kalendar* included 'A Short Introduction to the Knowledge of the Science of Botany', with some plates to illustrate the Linnaean system. Regarding medicinal plants, Miller took care to indicate the most appropriate times for collection: when flowers were fit to gather for distillation, roots in an efficacious state of dormancy and seeds fully ripe for harvesting. This was a sensible and useful method of reference; one which would have been invaluable to the gatherers of simples, who must have been grateful to find the information in a reasonably priced book.

This 1760 *Kalendar* advertised the recently completed *Figures of Plants*: at twelve guineas coloured and six guineas 'plain'. They could also be bought in parts, usually containing six plates and one printed sheet describing them, for 5s coloured and 2/6d plain. Miller's beautiful *Figures* will be discussed more fully in the next chapter. However, here he was at pains to point out that 'although this work was intended for an appendix to the Gardeners Dictionary, yet it may be reckoned a complete performance in itself independent to that'. Classification encompassed the methods of Ray, Tournefort and Linnaeus, titles used by botanic writers and bibliographic details were included and mention made of the country of origin. Botanical description was detailed, but there was no attempt to give instruction on cultivation or propagation. It was a work designed to catch the eye, to tempt the curious and to help with the identification of rarities. If readers of the *Figures* wished successfully to grow the delectable assortment presented by Miller, they had but to turn to his *Dictionary* for all the practical advice gleaned over half a century's gardening and, if that proved too expensive, then there was the *Abridgement* or the *Kalendar*. Contrary to Knowlton's suggestion (see p. 57), Miller's thoughts and works were not entirely directed towards the wealthy. He was anxious to offer his advice, reasonably and concisely, to the 'generality' so that the average small gardener and even the collector of herbs might all have their 'Miller'.

13 *Illustrators at Chelsea*

Before the camera provided an instantaneous record of new plants in their native habitats, collectors had faithfully to record their discoveries with pencil and brush. Sir Hans Sloane employed a local artist in Jamaica, while others delayed their journeys in order to draw plants which might not survive lengthy and hazardous transport. William Houstoun went to the trouble of making drawings in the West Indies, which he bequeathed to Philip Miller and from these Sir Joseph Banks published the engravings as *Reliquiae Houstounianae* (1781). When botanising abroad Mark Catesby also appreciated the value of records made while on expeditions, and he drew much in the field for his *Natural History of Carolina, Florida and the Bahama Islands* (1730–47). On his return to England he found the cost of engraving his plates far beyond his means and so he learned the art and later produced this beautiful book, which brought in enough income to support his family after his death in 1749. Philip Miller refers in the *Dictionary* to *Mimosa circinalis*, brought from the Bahamas by Catesby in 1726. The seeds, he says 'are flat and one half of a beautiful red colour and the other half of a deep black ... the flowers have not yet appeared in England, but from a painting done from the plant in the country, they seem to be very beautiful.'

The Chelsea Garden, a centre for the receipt, cultivation and redistribution of rare plants, provided much to attract the botanical artist. Jacobus van Huysum (*c*.1687–1740) brother of the famous Dutch flower painter, Jan (1682–1749), lived at Chelsea from 1720 to 1740 and worked in the Physic Garden to provide some of the illustrations for John Martyn's *Historia Plantarum Rariorum* (1728–37). This included American plants from Lord Petre's garden in Essex and West Indian plants received by Miller from Houstoun. Van Huysum's was the 'able hand' chosen by the Society of Gardeners to illustrate their *Catalogus Plantarum*. Twenty pages of his illustrations, engraved or etched by Kirkhall and Fletcher, included trees and shrubs from Carolina, some grown from seeds sent to Miller by Catesby. *Wisteria frutescens*, a climbing shrub known as the Carolina kidney bean tree and *Ascryum hypericoides*, St Peterswort, were both depicted, also *Myrica cerifera*, fully described in Catesby's book, and *Fraxinus caroliniana*, seeds of which Miller had received from him in 1724. Other plants illustrated from diverse regions were the Bermudan Cedar, Lord Weymouth's Pine, a Long Con'd Cornish Fir and the Scarlet Horse Chestnut from America.

One of the greatest botanical artists of the period, Georg Dionysius Ehret (1708–1770), was related to the Millers by marriage. He worked closely with Philip, one raising rarities and the other capturing them with pencil and brush at the moment of their greatest beauty. Ehret was born in Heidelberg where his father, like Miller's, was a gardener. Ehret senior possessed some artistic skill and he encouraged his son in both pursuits, urging him to travel. In 1731 a friend, Ambrosius Beurer, introduced young Ehret to the celebrated Dr Christopher Jacob Trew of Nürnberg, another physician-botanist, whose encouragement enabled Ehret to develop into one of the foremost botanical illustrators of the eighteenth century. He next went to Paris and was persuaded by Bernard de Jussieu to visit London, where he met Sir Hans Sloane and Philip Miller and made a number of drawings in the Physic Garden before proceeding to Holland in 1736. There he brought himself to the notice of George Clifford, the wealthy Amsterdam banker and horticulturist (see p. 50), who had engaged young Linnaeus as his personal physician and as recorder of his garden plants. Twenty of Ehret's illustrations were included in the sumptuous *Hortus Cliffortanianus* (1738). Later Ehret made many coloured drawings of Chelsea garden plants for his other patron and a selection of these was published in Trew's *Plantae Selectae* (1750–91). The originals are in the university library at Erlangen, Germany.

Ehret returned to London later in 1736 and England became his permanent home. Two years later in 1738 he married Mrs Miller's sister, Susanna Kennet, linking himself securely to the Chelsea circle. He enjoyed success with the aristocracy, was commissioned by the King's Physician to paint some two hundred rare plants and turned to tutoring in the London Season. Among his illustrious pupils were the Dukes of Norfolk and Leeds, who rewarded him generously, and instruction often proved far more remunerative than the sale of his pictures. He visited stately homes in the summer and was often at Bulstrode, where the Duchess of Portland pursued her great interest in botany.

Ehret's enthusiasm over rare blooms was such as to prompt a daily walk from Chelsea to Parsons Green to watch the progress of *Magnolia grandiflora* in Sir Charles Wager's garden. He recorded a visit of several days to Thorndon, Lord Petre's estate, where he collected many rare specimens and must have been delighted by the tapestry of exotic climbers woven through trellises at the back of the stoves (see p. 58). John Ellis wrote to Linnaeus in 1758 to say that he, with Collinson and Ehret, had been to Richard Warner's garden at Woodford to see his rare plant, 'like a Jasmine, with a large double white flower, very odoriferous'. This was the first gardenia to flower in this country. In Fothergill's garden he found *Arbutus andrachne*, raised from seeds sent by Russell from Aleppo in 1754 and to flower at Upton in 1766.

For a short while in 1750–51 Ehret was officially employed as head

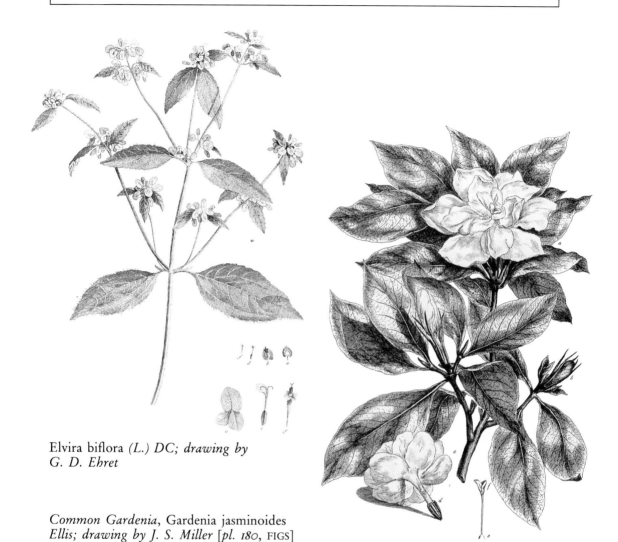

Elvira biflora *(L.) DC; drawing by*
G. D. Ehret

Common Gardenia, Gardenia jasminoides
Ellis; drawing by J. S. Miller [*pl. 180*, FIGS]

gardener at the Oxford Botanic Garden, but a difference of opinion with
the successor of Dillenius, the autocratic professor, Humphrey Sibthorp,
brought about his resignation. He stayed at Oxford as a private teacher
of botany and flower painting until 1755, when he returned to London
to the friends and patrons who appreciated his great talent. From the
Newfoundland and Labrador collections of Joseph Banks, he painted twenty-
three plants, five of which later appeared in Aiton's *Hortus Kewensis*.

Although the *Dictionary* had comparatively few botanical illustrations, its
text was augmented with more technical diagrams for the practical horticulturist such as those of melon frames and wine presses. There is, however,
an engraving by Ehret of *Polygala senega* from Virginia (see p. 67). The root
of this species, Miller explained, had:

been long used by the Seneka Indians to cure the bite of the rattle-snake which, if taken in time, is an infallible remedy. And of late years it has been used by the inhabitants of Virginia in many disorders, which are occasioned by thick, sizy blood; so that the root of this plant, when its virtues are fully known, may become one of the most useful medicines yet discovered.

Here he obviously considered the pharmaceutical value of this plant important enough to include an illustration, and he felt the economic significance of *Rubia tinctorum*, madder, warranted an engraving by John Sebastian Miller, from *Hortus Cliffortianus*.

John Müeller had come to London from Nürnberg, had changed his name to Miller and settled down to work in close collaboration with Philip Miller at Chelsea. The four full page introductory plates in the *Dictionary* of fruits, flowers and parts of plants were drawn and engraved by him in meticulous detail. In 1771, Miller's successor, William Forsyth, reported to the Garden Committee that Mr Miller, an engraver, desired to view and take plants 'as may be of use in the work he is now engaged on'. This was probably John Sebastian's son, John Frederick, who followed the profession and accompanied Joseph Banks on an expedition to Iceland in 1772. Later he presented the Company with his catalogue of the plants in the Chelsea Garden.

Elizabeth Blackwell (née Blachrie) was another artist who painted at the Chelsea Garden. She had to come to London from Aberdeen with her husband Alexander, a doctor turned printer. However, resentment from those who had learned the trade through the proper apprenticeship forced him into a debtors' prison in 1738. Elizabeth included Sir Hans Sloane among her friends and, on learning that an illustrated book on medicinal plants was needed, decided to produce one and use the money acquired to get her husband out of prison.

Sloane introduced her to Isaac Rand, the Demonstrator of Plants at the Physic Garden, who advised her to live near it where she would find the plants needed and where she would certainly have met Miller and Ehret. Encouraged by several physicians and apothecaries, including Rand, Douglas, Sherard and Mead, and aided by her spouse who contributed to the text from prison, she produced in 1737–8 *A curious Herbal, containing 500 Cuts of the most Useful Plants now used in the Practice of Physic*. Her work was brought to the notice of Dr Trew, who produced an enlarged edition under the name *Herbarium Blackwelliarum* (5 vols. 1750–56) with five hundred hand-coloured etchings. The success of his wife's industry ended her husband's two years in prison. In 1742 he went to Sweden without her and became an esteemed agricultural adviser, but was executed in 1747 for alleged political activities. His gifted wife died at Chelsea in 1758.

Plants from the Physic Garden were copied by the gifted collage artist, Mrs Delaney, and fourteen were faithfully reproduced in her delicate paper mosaic work, some of which may be seen in the British Museum today. She

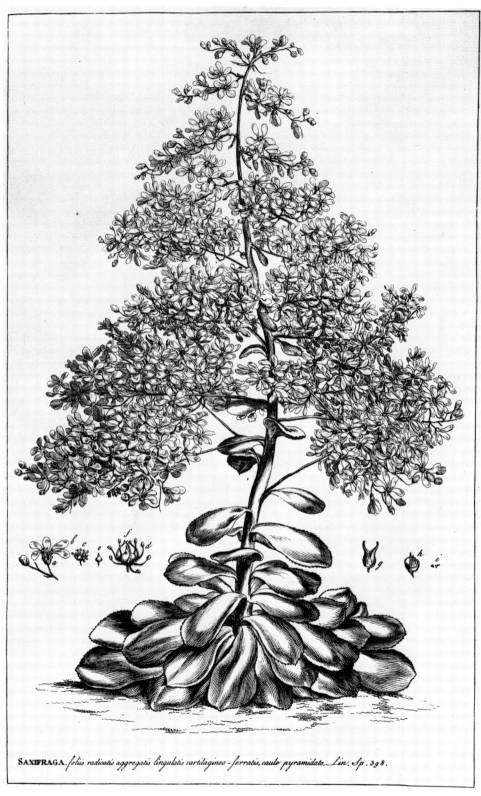

SAXIFRAGA, *foliis radicatis aggregatis lingulatis cartilagineo-serratis, caule pyramidato. Lin. Sp. 398.*

Saxifraga cotyledon *L.; drawing by J. S. Miller [pl. 243,* FIGS]

was a close friend of the Duchess of Portland and, when staying with her at Bulstrode in Buckinghamshire, December 1753, reported that Philip Miller had been working in the library and, on another occasion when they met, she commented on his reticence.

The *Figures of Plants*, dedicated to the Duke of Bedford, contained the 'most beautiful, useful and uncommon plants described in the *Gardener's Dictionary*, exhibited on 300 copper plates'. They appeared in parts over five years from March 1755 to June 1760 and eventually made two folio volumes. The original concept, as Miller set out in the Preface, was 'to exhibit the figures of one or more species of all the known genera of plants'. However, it was considered that this would make it too expensive for the 'generality of purchasers' and it was confined to 'those plants only which are either curious in themselves or may be useful in trades, medicines, etc. including the figures of such new plants as have not been noticed by any former botanists.' Judging by the many Figures covered by the first letter of the alphabet – fifty-eight at the beginning – it can be appreciated that Miller had been justly advised; such expansion throughout the work would have priced it far outside the purse of the 'generality' if, indeed, it could have been completed in his lifetime.

The plates are not entirely in alphabetical order. For instance, half a dozen *A's* are included much later because as Miller explained varieties of Aloe and Agave had only recently flowered in the Chelsea Garden for the first time and could not have appeared before. Miller's *Vinca rosea* (now *Catharanthus roseus*) had been brought forward: 'as this plant is a great novelty in Europe ... the Figure of the Plant has not yet been seen by any living person' and of *Gardenia capense*, called by him *Jasminium*, he wrote, 'Could we have procured a good drawing in proper time it would have been in its proper place, but as this is so curious and being an undescribed plant, we hope our purchasers will not be displeased with insertion here.'

Miller stressed the importance of accuracy in illustration; each plant had to be drawn from nature at its best stage of flowering, with the fruit and seeds to be added later on ripening. If an artist fell short of the standard, he was replaced. Most of the illustrations were drawn by Lancake (forty-eight of the first hundred), J. S. Miller both drew and engraved a considerable number, while Mynde and Jeffreys appear most frequently amongst engravers. Ehret contributed sixteen plates, including various *Acacia* and *Mesembryanthemum* (illust. rg. p. 111) and one of *Ricinus palma christi*, the castor oil plant (now *Ricinus communis*) which he also engraved. Of this Miller writes, 'It grows naturally in the West Indies, whence the late Mr. Robert Miller sent me the seeds', and it would seem likely that Ehret's specimen had been raised at Chelsea.

An interesting inclusion is *Veratrum americanum*, by 'J. Bartram'. It was, in fact, the work of his son, William, and Miller comments 'I was first

Fig. 1, LYCIUM *folus linear longioribus, tub, florum longiore, segmento crasso.*
Fig. 2, LYCIUM *folus linear brevioribus, tub, florum breviore, segmento er oblivio patentissimis.*

Fig. 1, MESEMBRYANTHEMUM *annulo folis subteretibus connatis floribus octagynis .Lin sp pl 481*
Fig. 2, MESEMBRYANTHEMUM *folis dolabraformibus Hort Cliff 219*
Fig. 3, MESEMBRYANTHEMUM *caule hispido folis cylindricis deflexio .Lin sp plant 482*

Fig. 1, Lycium afrum *L.; Fig 2*, Lycium italicum *Miller; drawings by R. Lancake* [*pl. 172* FIGS]

Fig. 1, Cylindrophyllum calamiforme *(L.) Schwantes; Fig. 2*, Rhombophyllum dolabriforme *(L.) Schwantes; Fig. 3*, Drosanthemum hispidum *L.; drawings by G. D. Ehret* [*pl. 175*, FIGS]

favoured by this sort by Mr. Peter Collinson, FRS and afterwards received a plant with a drawing of it made in the country where it grows, by Mr. John Bartram, JR, and have since been furnished with more plants by Dr. Benzel of Germantown in Philadelphia, who found it growing plentifully in shady, moist places.' Miller must have sent word to Bartram that *Figures of Plants* would be coming, as, in April 1755, only one month after initial publication, John Bartram wrote to express grateful anticipation. In February 1756 reference is made to four illustrations 'sent some time since by our friend, Mr. Collinson' and Miller said he would have sent others except for the fact that he had been waiting for better colourists. There was further trouble with production, as just over two weeks later Miller hoped to send some better done, having changed his engraver. On checking artists' names appended it appears that up to 1756 Jeffreys did most of the engraving for

Figures of Plants but thereafter his name disappears except for the odd plate, which may well have been made earlier. As this date coincides with the time of Miller's comment, it seems that he was the incompetent engraver.

For a glowing appraisal of the *Figures of Plants*, when considering Philip Miller's many works in the Preface of his revised edition of the *Dictionary* in 1807, Thomas Martyn chose an earlier quotation from Richard Pulteney (see p. 149):

> Whether we consider the rarity of the subjects, the speciousness of those he selected for his purpose, or the general production of the whole, England had not before produced any work, except the *Hortus Elthamensis* or Catesby's *Carolina*, so superb and extensive, and in one respect Miller's had an advantage, as they exhibited much more perfectly the separate figures of parts of fructification.

Plate enamelled in colour, Chelsea c.1755–58.
Acanthus spinosus *copied from Miller,* Figures, *pl. 7; engraved 29 April 1755*

Some of these illustrations were perpetuated in another medium. Their publication coincided with the Red Anchor period of the Chelsea porcelain factory in the mid 1750s, when many beautiful floral paintings decorated plates and other pieces. These came to be known as 'Hans Sloane plants', although he died before their reproduction. The use of his name and his connection with the area, particularly with the Physic Garden and also his

Plate 9

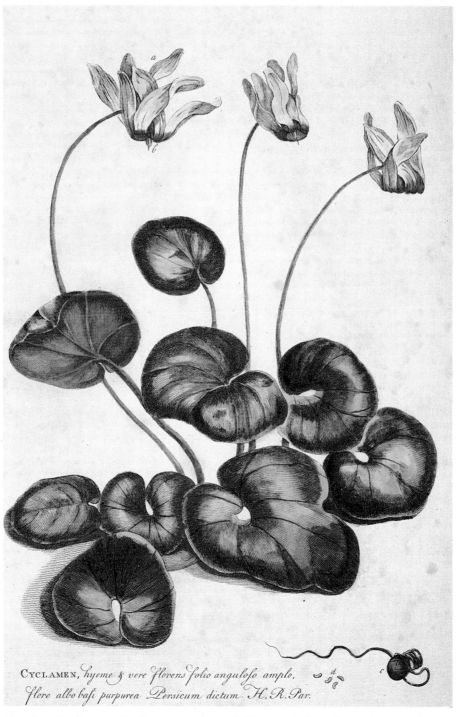

CYCLAMEN, *hyeme & vere florens folio angulofo amplo,*
flore albo bafi purpurea Persicum dictum H.R.Par.

Persian Cyclamen, Cyclamen persicum *Miller, excluding fruit; drawing by R.*
Lancake [pl. 115, FIGS]. Native of eastern Mediterranean region.

Plate 10

Gazania rigens *(L.) Moench; drawing by R. Lancake [pl. 49,* FIGS*]. Native of South Africa.*

Acacia cornigera (L.) *Willd; drawing by G. D. Ehret* [pl. 6, FIGS]

reputation abroad, lent an air of authority to these pieces of china – as no doubt Mr Sprimont, the astute manager of the factory appreciated.

Two distinct types of botanical embellishment were used: some showed dissected plants and were obviously copied from engraved plates in authoritative works, while others were taken from live plants. Some designs have been traced to illustrations in Miller's *Figures*, although they had to be adapted to fit the curved surfaces of porcelain pieces. It is noteworthy that the majority are of plants starting with the letter 'A' which, as has been explained, proportionately outnumbered the other letters in the *Figures*. *Abies, Abrotanum humile, Acacia, Acanthus spinosus, Anonis, Anthemis* and *Antholyza* were all used and in some instances butterflies and insects were added. Ehret was responsible for three of these designs and is the only artist to whom any of the originals have so far been traced. An almost exact reproduction of *Bocconia*, which appeared as Plate IV of Trew's *Plantae*

Selectae, is featured on a plate now on display in the Victoria and Albert Museum, and from *Plantae et Papiliones rariores*, two more Ehret illustrations were used: *Iris* and *Alcine* (VI) and *Convolvulus* (VII). It is fair conjecture that the Chelsea porcelain painters working from live plants sought subjects from the nearby Physic Garden, where they might find many impressive exotics flowering for the first time in this country. Rare elegance would enhance the products from a London porcelain factory competing with the current fine ware from Germany.

No edition of Miller's *Dictionary* included illustrations on a lavish scale and, although Thomas Martyn recognised that his was an age of 'sumptuous plates and ornamental publications', he included in his revised edition of 1807 'nothing beyond utility ... to render the book really useful to botanists and gardeners.' Miller provided a wealth of elegant ornamental plants in the *Figures* for those appreciating beauty in botany and included many others on account of their usefulness or rarity. They remain botanically important because some were cited by Linnaeus and other botanists and because they graphically record plants in cultivation at that time.

Alba Rose, Rosa alba *L.; drawing by Elizabeth Blackwell*

14 Miller's Most Valued Flowering Shrub

Miller's partiality for flowering shrubs is evident throughout his writing and among them perhaps the versatile roses offered him greatest scope: he appreciated the many aspects of this genus and he understood how they might be best displayed. In the eighteenth century the majority of garden roses flowered for only about six weeks from the middle of June until the end of July. Exceptions included some earlier species and *Rosa virginiana*, with smooth purple young stems pleasing Miller's perceptive eye before its late summer flowering. *Rosa moschata*, the old Musk Rose, produced umbels of sweetly scented flowers in August to 'continue in succession until the frost stops them'. Reference to pre-Chelsea days are rare, but Miller described in the *Dictionary* how he grew Monthly Roses (the Autumn Damask) in his original Southwark Nursery; under glass against a warm wall, 'using dung placed against its backside, as practised by raising early fruits', to produce roses in February, for which there must have been a ready market.

The Gardener's and Florists's Dictionary of 1724 stated that there was a greater variety of roses propagated by gardeners than of any other tree or shrub and listed twenty-nine available in the nurseries. The Duchess of Beaufort is also mentioned as having additional rare sorts in her garden at Badminton. Six years later the *Catalogus Plantarum* listed forty-three roses and stressed the importance of growing them informally because 'being intermix't with flowering trees and shrubs in small wilderness quarters [they] afford the most agreeable prospect of any of the Flowering Trees and the great variety of Sorts do continue flowering at least three months. They are all very hardy and may be planted in the openest places.' Musk Roses, however, had weak branches and needed wall support and flowered the better without being pruned. (Later advice in the *Dictionary* suggested budding on the robust Frankfurt Rose for greater strength.) Plate 18 of the *Catalogus* shows five brightly coloured roses: Red Provence, Austrian Rose, Moss Provence, Double Yellow and Double Velvet.

Miller's *Catalogue of Plants at the Physic Garden* (1730) listed *alba*, *canina*, *damascena* and *rubra* – a quartet also to appear in the *Dictionary's* Catalogue of Medicinal Plants – and in this respect the last was the most important. He called it the Common Red Rose and described it as having 'flowers not very double, open wide', indicating that this must have been

Roses, pl. 18 Catalogus Plantarum *(1730)*

Red Gallica Rose, Rosa gallica *L. var.; drawing by Elizabeth Blackwell*

Rosa gallica officinalis or the Apothecary's Rose. This had evolved from the ancient single red *R. gallica* and had long been used in medicine. In the ninth century a German monk, Walahfrid Strabo wrote: 'No man can say, no man remember, how many uses there are for Oil of Roses as a cure for mankind's ailments.' In his *Herball* of 1597 John Gerard drew attention to the use of distilled water of roses for strengthening the 'heart, liver, kidnies and other weak entrails', while Nicholas Culpeper advised a 'decoction of Red Roses made with Wine' for 'the Headach and pains in the Eyes, Ears, Throat and Gums' (*The English Physitian Enlarged*, 1652). There can, therefore, be little doubt that this rose was brought to the attention of the Apprentices during their studies in the Physic Garden. Miller also makes a point of mentioning that the fruit of the wild Dog Rose was made into a conserve for medicinal use in his time.

The *Garden Kalendar* did justice to the use of roses in the garden, mentioning them in nine months of the year. By April the single Virgin Rose would be in flower and others were listed to bloom throughout the following five months. June was the time for 'innoculation' (budding) and the best stocks to use were Frankfurt and Damask roses, these being the 'freest shooters'. October was the month to 'plant out suckers of lilacs, roses and such other flowering trees and shrubs which are propagated in this way' and the gardener was advised to leave them to gain strength for two years in the nursery before placing them in a permanent position. This was also the time to lay 'haws, hips and holly berries in a trench' for a year, while November and February were the best months for transplanting.

Plate CCXXI of the *Figures of Plants* shows two roses: the variegated Damask, or York and Lancaster, had long been known and to his descriptive account of this Miller added a note on Mrs Hart's Rose, probably a sport, with its more distinctly striped petals than the other's rather blotched red and white ones. Of the second here illustrated, the Moss Provence, Miller said that it had not long been known in London and the first time he saw it 'was in 1727 in the garden of Dr Boerhaave near Leyden who was so good as to give me one of the plants, but from where it came I could not learn. It was probably a variety which was obtained by seeds from some other roses … the flowers are the same shape and colour as the provence Roses and have the like agreeable odour.' The variation was in the so-called 'moss' on sepals, calyx and flower stalk; a unique characteristic and source of the name.

The Provence seems to have been Miller's favourite type of rose; he frequently stressed its outstanding fragrance, an important consideration in the flower garden, and said that by the mid-eighteenth century it had become the most widely propagated of any kind. In the *Abridgement* of 1754, Miller listed fifty-one roses and said that at least three variations of the Provence were sold 'promiscuously' by the nurserymen. One, seldom more than three feet high and called by Ray the Dwarf Red Rose, had small flowers and rounded buds which before opening appeared 'as if they had been clipp'd with Scissars'. He criticized sellers of the single Yellow Rose, *Rosa lutea*, 'esteemed for their colour, but as these flowers have no scent and are of short duration, they do not merit the price they are generally sold at.'

In the first edition of the *Dictionary* Miller listed forty-six roses as species, but in the eighth, where his descriptive and practical text covers four full pages, he split them into species and garden varieties. Although some of the former have been reclassified today, it is interesting to see what were listed in the mid-eighteenth century: *Rosa canina, spinosissima, villosa, eglanteria, scotica, inermis, hispanica, scandens, sempervirens, virginiana, lutea, punicea, moschata, centifolia, damascena, alba, belgica, provincialis, incarnata, gallica, cinnamomea* and *muscosa*.

Fig. 1, RO SA *rubra plena, spinosissima, pedunculo muscoso Boerh. Ind. alt. 2. 252.*

Fig. 2, RO SA *prænestina, variegata plena Hort. Ey.*

Fig. 1, Moss Rose, Rosa centifolia L. 'Muscosa'; Fig. 2, Damask Rose, Rosa damascena Miller 'York and Lancaster'; drawings by J. S. Miller [pl. 221, FIGS]

As throughout the *Dictionary*, each species is fully described and Miller added notes of interest, especially to those from overseas. *Rosa scandens*, 'a wild, woody, climbing rose, with a shining evergreen Myrtle leaf, a white sweet-scented flower and small, round prickly fruit', was, he said, found in woods near Florence by Signor Micheli who sent it to Dr Boerhaave of Leyden, 'in whose curious garden I saw it growing in the year 1727.' Seeds of both *R. sempervirens*, 'evergreen rose with an oval germina, whose foot-stalks are prickly', and *R. hispanica*, 'with leaves hairy on both sides, the small leaves of the empalement sharply sawed and a smooth fruit' were sent to Miller by Robert Moore Esq. from Spain, where he had found them growing in the wild. *R. scotica* was noted by Miller as the 'Burnet-leaved rose with a livid red flower' and, having had dried specimens of *R. alpina* sent to him from Italy, he found them to be exactly the same. This little rose was seldom more than a foot in height and bore deep purple hips, 'inclining to black when ripe'. Another observation on rose fruits, given under *R. villosa*, tells of its large, round hips, with a pleasant acid pulp surrounding the seeds, being 'made into a sweetmeat and served up in deserts to the table.'

The second group Miller referred to as

> a great variety of double roses now cultivated in English gardens. Most of them have been accidentally obtained from seeds so they must not be esteemed as different species, therefore I shall only insert their common names by which they are known in gardens, that those who are inclined to collect all the varieties may be at no loss for their titles.

Among them were three Velvet Roses; single, double and Royal, all, Miller said, raised by himself from seeds of the pale Provence Rose. Six Damasks were included and Rosa Mundi as a variety of the Red Rose. Three varieties of the common Sweet Briar, *R. eglanteria*, found growing naturally in some parts of Kent, were listed as double, evergreen and double blush, and the Double Yellow is classed as a variety of the single, *Rosa lutea*.

More than once Miller emphasised that roses, being natives of northern countries or from the cold mountains of warmer ones, relish their freedom. Some of them did not flower too well in confined conditions and others, like the Double Yellow, proved intolerant of London's smoke. A rich, moist soil and an open situation he considered ideal for producing the best blooms. He also stressed that flowering times and scale of roses should be taken into account when they are planted informally. Only comparatively recently have roses been grown again in their own right as flowering shrubs (as opposed to being massed in beds for maximum display) and therefore the *Dictionary's* comments are pertinent today.

> ... [first] to flower in the open air is the Cinnamon which is immediately followed by the Damask Rose, then the Blush, York and Lancaster come;

21. Rosa (*Cinnamomea*) germinibus globofis pedunculifque glabris, caule aculeis ftipularibus, petiolis fubinermibus. Lin. Sp. 703. *Rofe with a fmooth globular fruit, prickly branches, and fmooth foot-ftalks to the leaves.* Rofa odore cinnamomi, flore pleno. C. B. P. 483. *The double Cinnamon Rofe.*

22. Rosa (*Mufcofa*) caule petiolifque aculeatis, pedunculis calycibufque pilofiffimis. *Rofe with armed ftalks, the foot-ftalks of the leaves and the empalements of the flower very hairy.* Rofa rubra plena, ipinofiffima, pedunculo mufcofo. Boerh. Ind. alt. 2. p. 252. *The moft thorny, double, Red Rofe, with a moffy foot-ftalk, commonly called Mofs Provence Rofe.*

There are a great variety of double Rofes now cultivated in the Englifh gardens; moft of them have been accidentally obtained from feeds, fo that they muft not be efteemed as diftinct fpecies, therefore I fhall only infert their common names, by which they are known in the gardens, that thofe who are inclined to collect all the varieties, may be at no lofs for their titles. The forts before enumerated, I believe, are diftinct fpecies, as their fpecific characters are different, though it is difficult to determine which of them are really fo; therefore I do not pofitively affert they are diftinct fpecies, though I have great reafon to believe they are fo.

The varieties of Garden Rofes which are not before mentioned:

The Monthly Rofe,
The ftriped Monthly Rofe,   } Thefe are all fuppof-
The York and Lancafter Rofe,   } ed to be varieties of
Mrs. Hart's Rofe,   } the Damafk Rofe.

The red Belgick Rofe is fuppofed a variety of the Blufh Belgick.

The fingle Velvet Rofe,   } Thefe three are all varieties;
The double Velvet Rofe,   } the laft I raifed from the feeds
The Royal Velvet,   } of the pale Provence Rofe.

The Childing Rofe,   } Thefe three have great af-
The Marbled Rofe,   } finity with each other.
The double Virgin Rofe,   }

The Cabbage Provence is only a variety of the Common Provence.

The Blufh or Pale Provence is a variety of the Red Provence.

Part of the Rosa *entry* Gardeners Dictionary *(1768)*

after which the Provence, Dutch Hundred-leaved, White and most other sorts of Roses follow; and the latest sorts are the Virginia and Musk roses which, if planted in a shady situation, seldom flower until September; and if the autumn proves mild will continue often until the middle of October

The lowest shrub of all the sorts here mentioned is the Scotch Rose which rarely grows above a foot high, so that this must be placed among other shrubs of the same growth, which should have a moist soil and a shady situation. The Red Rose and the Rosa Mundi commonly grow from three to four feet high, but seldom exceed that; but the Damask, Provence and Frankfurt Roses grow to the height of seven or eight feet, so that in planting them, great care should be taken to place their several kinds, according to their various growth, amongst other shrubs, that they may appear beautiful to the eye.

Roses were well represented in the lists of plants for varying situations to be found at the end of the *Dictionary*. 'All the sorts' were included with hardy trees and shrubs able to thrive unsheltered in open air. *Rosa scandens* and *R. sempervirens* were classed as 'climbing shrubby plants' alongside ceanothus and jasmine, as well as with 'hardy greens' like holly, phillyrea and viburnum. Miller advocated planting roses in wildernesses with honeysuckle and low flowering shrubs among deciduous trees, next to walks and openings where the passer-by might be regaled with their scent. He criticised those who 'planted them ... under the dropping and shade of large trees, where they seldom thrive and if they do, the pleasure of them is lost, because they are excluded from sight.' These directives could have been intended for the landscape gardeners, whose services were much in demand at this time and who used roses in their extensive planting schemes to provide unanticipated colour and fragrance for those taking a walk in wilderness greenery. For pleasure grounds at Kirklington and the wilderness at Petworth, 'Capability' Brown listed roses specifically mentioned by Miller to associate with other shrubs, along with quantities of Sweet Briar, probably used for hedging.

Cultivators of roses were given the usual careful guidance. Propagation could be achieved from suckers, by budding or pruning (i.e. cuttings). However, Miller only advised budding for less vigorous roses or where more than one variety was required on the same plant and then a compatible growth habit was essential. Suckers should be grown on when young, producing better roots than when taken off in early autumn. He himself always adhered to the layering method, as set out in his first publication, the smaller *Dictionary* of 1724: 'In the Spring prick a great many Holes with an Awl about a Joint that will be in the earth and cover it would a good Mound to peg it down.' When rooted by the autumn and replanted this would, in due course, become a fine bush and one superior to those budded or grafted because its suckers would be of the same kind. With regard to pruning, Miller advised removal of dead wood in the autumn, shortening of over-luxuriant branches and exposure of all parts of the plant to maximum light and air.

In earlier editions of the *Dictionary* the Sweet Briar warranted comment on its scent and 'though a wild rose in some parts of England, yet is preserved in most curious gardens for the extreme sweetness of its leaves, which perfumes the circumambient Air in the Spring of the Year, especially after a shower of Rain.' Occasionally we may catch a glimpse of Miller's interest in flower arrangement and he continued, 'The flowers being single are not valued, but the branches of the Shrubs are cut to intermix with Flowers to place in Basons to adorn Halls, Parlours, etc. in the Spring of the Year, the scent of this plant being agreeable to most persons.'

Miller included twelve roses in his final *Catalogue of Plants in the Garden*

(1770), of which six are recorded among the plants received by the Royal Society under the conditions laid down by Sir Hans Sloane. *Rosa sempervirens* and *R. centifolia muscosa* were despatched in 1735, *R. pimpinellifolia* and *R. palustria* (from America and also known as the Marsh or Swamp Rose) in 1739. *Rosa sylvestris pomifera nostras* (probably the old *R. villosa* and 'greater apple-bearing rose' of the *Dictionary*) followed six years later and, finally in 1764, *R. pendulina*, not listed in the 1768 Dictionary, although *R. pendulis* appeared in the 1770 Catalogue. The other six in the Physic Garden at that time were *RR. alpina, alba, eglanteria, cinnamomea, gallica* and *canina*.

List of roses from Miller's final Catalogue of Plants in the Garden (1770)

From this brief survey it will be seen that Miller's judgment was not confined to, nor his expertise solely directed towards, blooms of roses; rather he considered them as shrubs, studying their form of growth and additional bonus of foliage and fruit. His guidance on mixed planting should appeal to those who prefer to grow their roses informally today. Philip

Miller's appreciation was summed up in the *Abridgement* of 1754, where he considered roses to have

> the most beautiful and fragrant flowers of any kind of shrub yet known. This together with their long continuance in flower, has justly render'd them the most valuable of all the sorts of flowering shrubs ... the great Variety of different Sorts of Roses make a collection of Flowers, either for Basons or in the Garden, without any other additional mixture and their Scent, being the most inoffensive Sweet, is generally esteemed.

Common Provence Rose, Rosa centifolia *L.; drawing by G. D. Ehret*

15 Collection in the Countryside

Botanising, or 'simpling' as it was often called by the Apothecaries, was carefully practised by Philip Miller in his early travels and, as he referred to 'going a-herborising by water' in July 1724, these expeditions continued after his Chelsea appointment. The Dictionary gives few date references for discoveries of plants in this country – unlike the careful record of the introduction of exotics – but from Miller's notes of their history and original habitat, we can see that, by the eighteenth century, most areas of Britain had been searched for plants to be cultivated for useful or decorative purposes.

In Miller's day there was no need to travel far from London to make botanical discoveries: a mile alongside the Thames, a tramp on Putney Heath or a search in Wimbledon Wood might well result in collections worthy of garden cultivation. On the banks of the Thames, around Lambeth and Chelsea, Miller found what he calls Dr Plukenet's '*Sagitta aquatica omnium minima*', probably *Sagittaria sagittifolia*, and named least arrowhead he imagines, on account of it being found growing in the mud of tidal water which might stint the growth of the plants. *Anemone apennina*, both double and single, flowered in a Wimbledon wood, near a mansion there, where it had obviously been grown. Miller advocated transplanting these flowers to wildernesses in gardens, 'where they will greatly increase, if left undisturbed and in the spring, when trees are bare, cover the ground most effectively'.

Pepperwort, (*Lepidium petraeum*) grew on Putney Heath and there, in a bog, *Narthecium ossifragum*, had been discovered, known in Lancashire, Miller noted, as bog asphodel, the name commonly used throughout Britain today. *Scilla autumnalis* grew at Blackheath and was probably found by collectors of the local gravel, believed to be the best in the country; 'the smooth pebbles of which, if mixed with loam, will bind like a rock and never be injured by weather'. This gravel would have been used in town gardens where *Saxifraga granulata*, originally found wild by Joseph Blind, a gardener at Barnes, was 'commonly planted in pots to adorn courtyards in the spring'.

On expeditions north of London early in the year, Miller frequently saw *Adoxa moschatellina* (with varied names of hollow root, musk crowfoot, town hall clock or moschatel) 'on the top of Hampstead among the bushes near the wood' and considered it unattractive. However, it was often used by those who placed 'common species below their shrubs as ground cover'.

Fig. 1, Common Solomon's-seal,
Polygonatum multiflorum *(L.) Allioni*
Fig. 2, May Lily, Maiamthemum bifolium
(L.) F. W. Schmidt drawings by
R. Lancake [pl. 101, FIGS]

Once lily of the valley, *Convallaria majalis*, had grown plentifully on Hampstead Heath but, Miller explained, since all the trees had been destroyed, they no longer flourished, and while wild 'hawthorn' had grown abundantly in Cave Wood, it had latterly only been found in Hertfordshire. The large fruit of this tree, when ripe and brown in autumn if kept until as soft as ripe medlars, had an agreeable acid flavour and was sold in London markets. It is probable that this 'hawthorn' was in fact the wild service tree, *Sorbus torminalis*, whose brown fruits, according to Gerard, were used to settle colic 'when the belly is too soluble'. Bromfield in his *Flora Vectensis* (1856) says that the fruit was sold in the shops and markets of Sussex and the Isle of Wight, mainly to children. Miller also took roots of dwarf golden rod, *Solidago virgaurea*, from Hampstead to plant at Chelsea, where they continued to grow true for many years. He found another variety in woods near Dulwich and once, in July, he saw the lesser burdock, *Arctium minus*, growing in the road near the College.

Kent had proved a beneficial county for botanists through the years, and Miller recalls gathering *Aquilegia vulgaris* in woods near Bexley and also between Rochester and Maidstone. On the edge of the Medway below Rochester he found *Mentha verticillata* and on sandbanks between Sandwich and Deal, *Hippophae rhamnoides*, sea buckthorn. He noted in the Dictionary that *Dianthus armeria* grew in a particular meadow near Deptford, hence the title of 'Deptford Pink' and said that he had cultivated it for over forty years and had never found it to vary. Under the *Dianthus* entry, Miller pointed out that, 'Those which have narrow leaves were formerly entitled Sweet Johns by the gardeners and those with broad leaves were called Sweet Williams.' On the Isle of Thanet, canary grass, *Phalaris canariensis*, was grown profitably by those 'who are situated where they have water carriage for the London market, where there is a general demand for that commodity.' At Tunbridge Wells, *Myrica gale*, then known as Dutch myrtle and today as bog myrtle or sweet gale, was found; while on chalk hills near Northfleet, grew musk orchis, *Herminium monorchis* and man orchis, *Aceras anthropophorum*.

On the Sussex coast Miller collected chamomile, *Matricaria maritima*, and found it lasted only two years in the Chelsea environment. Rosebay willow herb, *Epilobium augustifolium* (*Chamaenerion augustifolium*) was considered unsuitable for gardens, smothering all neighbouring plants, but Miller advocated it for a low, moist place or very shaded area and thought it 'very proper to cut for basons to adorn chimneys [fireplaces] in the summer season.' In Miller's time it grew in Charlton Forest and several other woods in Sussex and although now common and widespread, this was formerly a very local plant (in 1696 John Ray knew of it only in a few places in the north of England). Miller considered *E. hirsutum*, the great willow herb, less beautiful and, found by ditches and rivers in many parts of the country, the rubbed leaves have a scent of cooked apples, hence the name of Codlins and Cream. From the shingly shores of Sussex and Dorset local people gathered *Crambe maritima*, sea kale, preferring it to any other of the 'cabbage kind' and Miller elaborated fully upon garden cultivation of this plant as a vegetable.

On his way through Surrey, possibly to Goodwood, Miller would pass Guildford, 'the nearest place to London where the marsh cinquefoil [*Potentilla palustris*] grew, although a few specimens had been transplanted to a bog in Hampstead.' He found field penny-cress, *Thlaspi arvense* thriving in meadows at Godalming, where light, sandy soil encouraged long root growth of liquorice *Glycyrrhiza glabra*, as at Pontefract in Yorkshire. An interesting comment on dairying appears in the Dictionary; should cows eat leaves or shoots of ash, all their butter will be rank and of no value 'which is always the quality of the butter which is made about Guildford, Godalming and other parts of Surrey where there are ash trees growing about all their pastures, so that it is very rare to meet with any butter in those places which is fit to eat, but in all the good dairy counties, they never suffer an ash tree to grow.' The box tree, *Buxus*, gave its name to a hill near Dorking once covered with very large specimens but, Miller stated, they had lately been destroyed; they have however grown again at Box Hill. The importation of mahogany and other woods almost banished the use of the walnut, *Juglans*, hitherto held in great esteem for furniture and fittings. Miller pointed out that large plantations of this tree on the Downs near Leatherhead, Godstone and Carshalton produced great quantities of nuts, 'to the great advantage of their owners, one of which, I have been told, farms the fruit of his trees to those who supply the markets, for £30 per annum.'

APARINE [this plant is so called, because it is very rough; it is called Philanthropon, of φιλέω, to love, and άνθρωπ℗, man; because if a person walks in uncultivated places, the plant not only applies itself to his garments, but it holds them, as if it had a mind to bind man with an amicable band:] Goose-grafs or Clivers.
The common sort grows wild almost every where, the seeds sticking to the cloaths of people that pass by where they grow: it is sometimes used in medicine, but it is too common a weed to be admitted into a garden.

Aparine *entry in* Gardeners Dictionary *(1768)*

Further west along the Portsmouth Road, Miller recounted gathering 'about Liphoeck in Hampshire' trailing goose grass with a blue flower which he named *Aparine pumila supina, flore caeruleo*, from Tournefort, now known as *Sherardia arvensis*, field madder. He visited Uppark, maybe to advise Sir Matthew Fortesque on planting trees on his estate, where he saw *Atropa belladonna* growing wild and told of *Daphne mezereum* being discovered in woods near Andover, 'from whence a great number of plants had been taken. It had long been cultivated in nursery gardens as a flowering shrub ... a very ornamental plant in gardens in early spring, before others make their appearance'.

Miller botanised north-east of London and into East Anglia. His friend, Richard Warner, thoroughly searched the Essex countryside to compile his *Plantae Woodfordienses* (1771). He dedicated this to the officials of the Company of Apothecaries, with gratitude for 'favours in the prosecution of his Botanical Amusements' and in the preface acknowledged help from twenty contemporaries including James Gordon, William Hudson and

Plate II

Madagascar Periwinkle, Catharanthus roseus *(L.) G. Don; drawing by R. Lancake*
[pl. 186, FIGS*]. Native of Madagascar.*

Plate 12

Iris orientalis *Miller, non Thunberg; drawing by R. Lancake [pl. 154,* FIGS*]. Native of eastern Mediterranean region.*

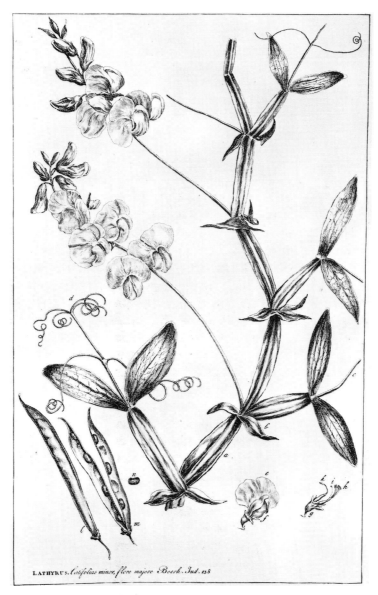

Broad-leaved Everlasting Pea,
Lathyrus latifolius *L.; drawing by R. Lancake [pl. 160, FIGS]*

Philip Miller. Chelsea's Gardener seemed to know this county well; by the side of the road between Bocking and Gosfield he found whorled mint, *Mentha gentilis*, with an unusual scent of basil. He noted that although the large-flowered hemp-nettle, *Galeopsis speciosa*, was chiefly found in northern counties, he had seen it here, within ten miles of London. Near Hockerel, in a site overrun by brambles, he was pleased to find a climbing vetch with hairy pods, *Lathyrus hirsuta*, today called hairy vetchling.

A reference in the *Dictionary* to a Suffolk plant shows the author's thoroughness in research. He classified *Lathyrus japonicus (L. maritimus)* as *Pisum maritimum* and remarked that this English sea-pea was 'first taken notice of

129

in 1555 between Orford and Aldborough, where it grew upon the heath where nothing, no not grass, was ever seen to grow and the poor people, being in distress by reason of the dearth of that year, gathered large quantities of these pease and so preserved themselves and their families.' The works from which Miller took this information were Camden's *Britannica* and Stowe's *Chronicle*. However, the practical gardener decided that both earlier authors were mistaken in imagining these peas to have made a timely appearance by miracle or shipwreck upon East Anglian shores as they were to be found in other parts of the country.

John Martyn, a somewhat itinerant Professor of Botany at Cambridge and doctor at Chelsea, published a Cambridge flora, *Methodus Plantarum circa Cantabridgiam nascentium* in 1727. Miller had, in all probability, botanised with him in the area as he was asked to go to Cambridge to advise on a proposed Botanic Garden. From Chelsea they would have travelled through Hertfordshire, pausing perhaps to look for the grass of Parnassus, *Parnassia palustris*, which, although plentiful in the north of England, grew no nearer to London than the low meadows by Cassioberry on the other side of Watford. Or, they may have searched for toothwort, *Dentaria bulbifera*, known to grow in moist shady woods near Harefield. Once on the East Anglian Heights, they would have found many of the plants in the Cambridge flora. On the distribution of the pasque flower, *Pulsatilla vulgaris*, Miller gave one of his most precise descriptions:

> It grows in great plenty on the Gogmagog Hills on the left-hand side of the highway leading from Cambridge to Haveril, just on the top of the hill, also about Hildersham, six miles from Cambridge and on Barnack Heath, not far from Stamford and on Southdrop Common adjoining thereto, also on mountainous and dry pastures just off Leadstone Hall, near Pontefract.

Horseshoe vetch, *Hippocrepis comosa*, also grew on the chalky Cambridge hills, while the smaller spiked speedwell, *Veronica spicata*, and small wild bugloss, *Lycopsis arvensis*, could both be found on Newmarket Heath and green hellebore, *Helleborus viridis*, at Ditton. Growing wild upon old walls at both Cambridge and Ely, Miller discovered the bastard tower mustard, *Arabis turrita*, a native of Hungary, Sicily and France, which he concluded had originated from gardens round about that area. Medicinal plants, water germander (*Teucrium scordium*) and hemp (*Cannabis sativa*), grew naturally in the Isle of Ely and other 'fenny' parts of England where, particularly in Lincolnshire, *Asparagus officinalis* was also found, its shoots 'no larger than straws'. Another herb, carroway, *Carum carvi*, much in demand for medicine and cookery grew in some rich meadows of Lincolnshire and Yorkshire.

Richard Richardson, Miller's chief correspondent in Yorkshire, collected

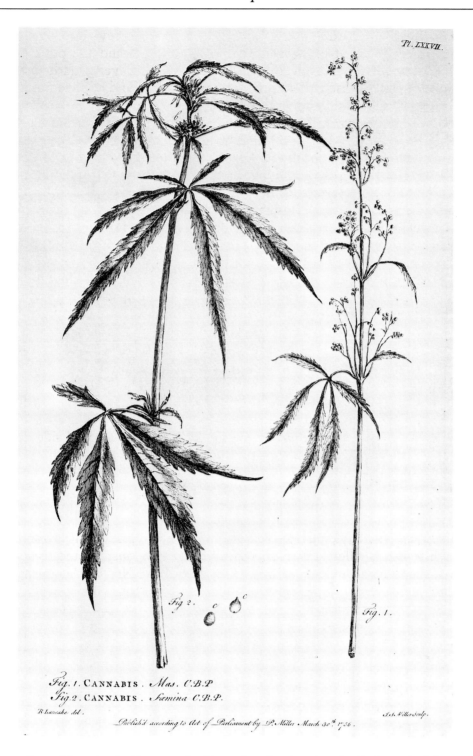

Hemp, Cannabis sativa *L. Fig. 1, male, Fig. 2, female; drawings by R. Lancake [pl. 77,* FIGS]

many of that county's plants for Chelsea and when on a visit Miller noticed the bird cherry, *Prunus avium*, growing naturally in hedges and remarked that this was propagated and sold as a flowering shrub in London nurseries. However, winter green, *Pyrola rotundifolia*, 'ordered by the College of Physicians to be used in medicine' – prolific on rocky hills, heaths and shady woods in Yorkshire – was very difficult to maintain in southern gardens. Near Ingleborough Miller found herb christopher, *Actaea spicata, Aquilegia vulgaris, Saxifraga oppositifolia* and Jacob's ladder, *Polemonium caeruleum*, at Malham Cove. Plants of the last could be easily grown from seed and, Miller wrote, 'transplanted into the borders of the flower garden at Michaelmas, where being intermixed with different sorts of flowers, they will make a beautiful appearance.' Our small wild bog rosemary, *Andromeda polifolia*, grew naturally in moss and bogs in Yorkshire, Cheshire and Lancashire, but disliked garden conditions.

Miller visited Robert Fenwick at Brough Hall in Lancashire, where he was excited to find growing in the park's shade, Ladies' slipper, *Cypripedium calceolus*, now alas, almost extinct in Britain through ruthless collecting. He gave precise directions for cultivation: 'in a situation where they must have the morning sun only'. In the same park he found globe flower, *Trollius europaeus*, growing freely; a pretty plant and easily grown in shady London gardens. This county gave its name to a prostrate pink-flowered variety of red cranesbill (*Geranium lancastrense*) now called *G. sanguineum* var. *striatum* and Miller also found yellow Welsh poppy, *Meconopsis cambrica*, growing near Kirby Lonsdale.

On the north-west route from Chelsea to Oxford, Miller collected through Berkshire and Buckinghamshire. In Windsor Forest, Chicheling vetch, probably *Vicia sativa*, grew well on moist meadows as did *Myrica gale*. Near Reading on the Cawsham (Caversham) Hills, he found orchids; musk again and *Orchis militaris*, which he called the man orchid, and it is probable that he used the correct Latin name and the wrong English one, as this very rare military orchid still grows today not far from Henley, where he also found pale toadflax, *Linaria repens*.

Hartwood, *Tordylium officinalis*, Miller explained, grew plentifully about Rome and Southern France and was 'mentioned in the last edition of Ray's *Synopsis* as an English plant, growing naturally in Oxfordshire, where I have seen it on the side of banks, but the seeds were sown there by Mr. Jacob Bobart, gardener at Oxford.' However, the Curator of the Oxford Botanic Garden had quite genuinely discovered a bramble with a white fruit, a variety of *Rubus fruticosus*, for which Miller gave him due credit.

He visited two more counties: Warwickshire, where he saw common meadow saffron, *Colchicum autumnale*, flowering in early September, and Nottinghamshire, to find hoary mullein, *Verbascum pulverulentum*. He mentioned difficulty in cultivating a 'dwarf honeysuckle', *Chamaeperi-*

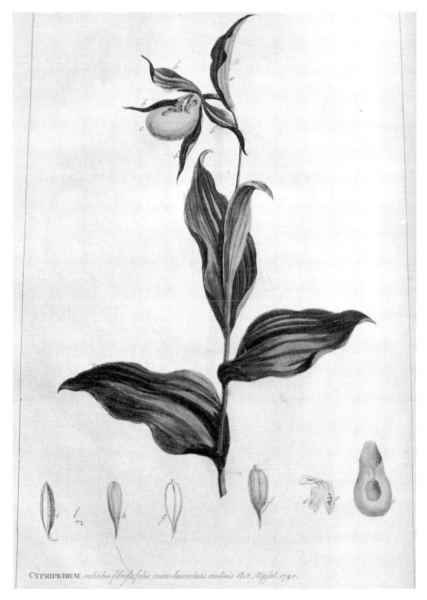

CYPRIPEDIUM. *radicibus fibrosis folus ovato-lanceolatis caulinis Act. Upsal. 1740.*

Ladies' slipper, Cypripedium calceolus *L.; drawing by J. S. Miller [pl. 242* FIGS]

clymenum suecicum, from Northumberland's Cheviot Hills, (the closely allied American species, *C. canadense*, is much easier). Miller made searches for hog's fennel, *Peucedanum officinale*, but penned a wistful note, 'said to grow naturally in England, but I have not been lucky enough to find it.' He tells of *P. minus* upon St Vincent's Rock in Bristol, where *Sedum forsterianum* and *Scilla autumnalis* were also found, while Cheddar pink, *Dianthus gratianopolitanus*, was found in Somerset's rocky gorge.

These extracts from the *Dictionary* illustrate the importance Miller attributed to careful searches for plants in the countryside and he was also watchful and critical over their collection and sale. Under *Vaccinium myrtillus*, common on heaths in the north, but intolerant of garden growth, he explained that the fruit, known as black whorts or bill-berries, were gathered by poor village inhabitants and taken to market towns where, eaten with cream or milk, they were much esteemed. Imported species from the continent, with larger fruit, were used by pastry-cooks in London for tarts during the winter season. Eyebright, *Euphrasia*, a medicinal plant found in fields and commons among grown heath, furze or other cover would not thrive in gardens and the markets relied on herb women to supply it. They also collected sea scurvy grass, *Cochlearia anglica*, from the tidal salt marshes of Kent and Essex and *Verbena officinalis* from roadsides and foot paths. The last was called 'Simpler's Joy' as 'wherever this plant is found growing, it is a sure token of a house being near'.

Rock samphire or sea fennel, *Crithmum maritimum*, found on rocks by the sea had long been recognised as a preventive against scurvy (and recent chemical investigation has demonstrated its high vitamin C content), but Miller said a species of Aster, called Golden Samphire, was often taken to markets in its stead. Another instance of deception was with dwarf elder, *Sambucus ebulus*, recommended for the treatment of dropsy, gout and scorbutic disorders, when young shoots of the common elder, *S. nigra*, were frequently offered in its place. Miller explained that they can be identified by the number and shape of lobes on each leaf: common elder seldom has more than five, being broad and short, while the dwarf variety has nine, eleven or thirteen which are long and narrow. The fruit of the blackberry-bearing alder or alder buckthorn, *Frangula alnus*, was often brought to London and sold as buckthorn berries, 'of which cheat all who make the syrup of Buckthorn should be particularly careful; they may be easily distinguished by breaking the berries and observing how many seeds are contained in each, the berries of this tree having two and those of Buckthorn generally four seeds in each berry and the juice of the latter dies paper of a green colour.'

Thus Miller tried hard to establish a correct code of commerce for botany and horticulture; believing that the patient searchers warranted proper promotion of their discoveries and the consumers reliable remedies. His sense of conscientious industry and careful economy was even more evident in his criticism of farmers.

16 Agriculture, Forestry and Specialised Husbandry

So far this survey of Philip Miller's work has considered the search for plants in Britain and overseas and of their propagation and use, with emphasis on botany and horticulture. However, other aspects of his industry deserve attention. The title page of the *Gardeners Dictionary*, 1768, pointed out that in addition to containing 'the best and newest methods of cultivating and improving the kitchen, fruit, flower garden and nursery' it was also for use in 'performing the practical parts of agriculture' and for 'progagating and improving from real practice and experience, all sorts of timber trees'. The management of vineyards and methods of wine making, as practised in Europe, are also included and even colonists in America and the West Indies receive a certain amount of straightforward advice from the Gardener at Chelsea. In forty odd years, the modest *Dictionary*, aimed to help those within reach of London nurserymen, had grown to a tome which might be consulted with confidence throughout the world.

Miller criticised farmers in Britain who were, he felt, far too conservative in their methods. He would not, he said in the Preface, comment without experience; his instructions 'are the result of more than twenty years practice in different parts of England, where the author has been permitted to superintend and direct the whole' and he had been 'very cautious in recommending any thing which he is not thoroughly convinced to be true.' Miller considered the adoption of the recently invented horse-hoe unlikely unless the garden farmers near London – 'undoubtedly the best husbandmen in Europe' introduced it, for the common farmers could never be persuaded to alter their old established methods. He referred those interested to a treatise written by Mr Jethro Tull, of Shelbourn in Berkshire, the inventor of the instrument.

Another point emphasised by the thrifty Gardener was the habit of extravagant seed sowing. Almost all people, he said, set their beans too close whereas better results could be obtained by the use of a drill plough to which a hopper was fixed for setting the beans. The drills should be three feet apart and the spring of the hopper set to scatter the beans three inches apart in the drills. In 1745, to prove this Miller persuaded a landowner in Berkshire to allow his Bailiff to set half of an eleven-acre field in the old-fashioned method, while he used his proposed economy for the remainder. When threshed out the yield was twenty-two bushels an acre for the Bailiff and near forty for Miller. The same sort of reduction was made for barley seed when a better result was obtained, and Miller quotes the finest field of wheat he ever saw, planted sparsely, yielding more than eleven quarters to an acre of land.

Reading of this last achievement today, an East Anglian farmer showed some incredulity. The figure was checked with the Science Museum, who confirmed that before 1800, 18 bushels per English acre was considered a poor crop, 30 bushels a fair average, 40 bushels a large yield on medium to good soils and from 38–55 bushels were occasionally obtained from prime soils under good management in a favourable year. The conclusion was that Miller's claim of 68 bushels to the acre was either exaggerated or based on too small a sample and should not be regarded as consistent achievement.

His observations on the price of corn are pertinent; he exposed the rising number of dealers in corn, who took advantage of farmers needing ready money, engrossing their corn to keep it for better markets, to the great prejudice of the raisers and consumers – a state of affairs requiring more public attention than had been given to it. Miller emphasised the point when commending the French for building public granaries to house corn of plentiful years for general use in times of scarcity.

On winter feed for domestic animals, Miller's advice was sought by the Society of Arts and in a long letter dated 17 May 1760 (*Guard Book* 5/7), he judged foreign grasses (grown from seeds sent to him by Linnaeus) to be inferior to our own common pastures. He considered however, that the long-lasting lucerne (alfafa), had no equal as feed for cattle, horses and sheep; in fact, most tame animals preferred it and one acre would maintain more than three of the best grass. He recommended therefore, that the Society should offer a premium to any person who might grow ten, twenty or thirty acres over one or two years, 'giving an account of its progress and the crop produced to the Society, it might occasion the plant being better known and thereby more generally cultivated.' Under this entry in the *Dictionary*, farmers are criticised for neglecting lucerne, known to improve milk production, even though it had been brought over from France in the mid-seventeenth century.

Miller's next suggestion was clover – the White Dutch variety, providing 'very sweet seed for most sorts of cattle and those who are curious to have good verdure on their lands.' However, as this generally had to be purchased from Flanders, it proved too expensive for the average farmer and he thought that if the Society would offer a premium for those who might save from one to four tons of seed, its price would be much reduced in this country. If farmers and gardeners could foretell hard winters, Miller continued, there might always be plenty of feed; savoys and caulworts he suggested were particularly useful for those who have ewes producing house lambs. Turnips had long been cultivated for winter use, but Miller believed

Rhubarb, Rheum compactum *L.; drawing by R. Lancake* [*pl. 218*, FIGS]

carrots to be three times more nourishing for horses, cattle, sheep, deer and hogs and, in a scarce year they would also 'provide great comfort for the poor'. He suggested offering a small premium for planting twenty to thirty acres of this root crop.

This letter was carefully considered and the Society of Arts accepted his advice, offering premiums for lucerne, white clover and carrots for the first time in 1761, thus recognising Miller's expertise in the agricultural as well as in the horticultural sphere. In 1760 they had also sought his judgment on identification of the true Rhubarb and he assured them (*Guard Book* 5/76) that it was the variety he had grown from seeds received from Petersburg.

The *Dictionary* covered every aspect of agriculture and practical advice was given, for example, on manures: 'Some lands abound too much in coldness, moisture and heaviness, others again are too light and dry and so, to answer this, some dungs are hot and light, as are those of sheep, horses, pigeons, etc. and others are fat and cooling, as of oxen, cows, hogs, etc.' However, Miller had found from experience that there was 'not any sort of manure equal to the cleansing of London Streets for all stubborn, clayey soils ... extremely worth procuring either for corn, grass or garden land.' His method of pest control was delightful: a sure method of destroying caterpillars attacking turnips in a dry autumn was to turn 'a large parcel of hungry poultry' into a field in early morning, when the crop might soon be cleared.

As far as the weather was concerned, Miller emphasised a real need for accurate forecasting to help both farmers and gardeners, 'The imaginary prognostications of almanack writers have been found to be a mere delusive cant or jargon. There is nothing more wanting than a just theory of the weather on mechanical principles'. He also advocated careful recording of winds and the weather brought by them. The effects of weather conditions were appraised and the hazard most feared in the eighteenth century was frost. Miller related detailed descriptions of the intensely cold winters of 1684, 1728/9 and 1739/40 – well worthy of study by any student of climatology. He counselled patience with affected shrubs and trees and advised leaving them for at least another season to allow for later revival.

Miller's appreciation of the importance of trees, both from aesthetic and utilitarian viewpoints, is apparent throughout his writing. Here again he was critical of mismanagement feeling that his lengthy discourse on timber was justified. He lamented the wholesale destruction of the oak, giving precise instructions on raising them from acorns to maturity and condemned the practice of spring felling for ease of bark-stripping, because ships built with this timber would last only a fraction of the time of those built from winter-cut wood. Again he praised the French, who wisely insisted that trees should be left another year or two before felling. Oaks were stripped to supply the tan or tanner's bark, essential in the dressing of skins and afterwards the coarsely ground material was used by gardeners in the construction of hot-beds and later, when well rotted, as manure for gardens. Miller explained how the first hot-beds in England had been used for raising orange trees at Blackheath towards the end of the seventeenth century. These had been made 'by two or three persons who had learned the use of them in Holland and Flanders.' However they were not widely seen in this country until the introduction of pineapples in 1719 and, half a century on, Miller believed that gardeners in England were better skilled in hot-bed practice than many in Europe. Certainly he used this by-product of the oak with great success in the cultivation of exotics at Chelsea.

Diverse Husbandry

In the mid-eighteenth century, the Society of Arts, aware of the shortage of timber for the Navy, offered medals and premiums for tree-planting, not only of oaks but of pines and lesser trees able to replace the use of oak in many domestic spheres. Miller was eager to stress the potential of secondary timber and almost certainly the *Dictionary* would be consulted by those wishing to gain a quick return from such plantings. Willow could be grown on moist, boggy ground, and the variety grown in ozier beds and used in basket-making could turn marshes 'to such good account as the best corn land'. Poplar wood, less likely to shrink than many others, was sought for house and wagon floors. Ash had great advantages economically because the underwood could be cut every seven or eight years, providing poles or hoops and still leaving timber for the wheelwright and cartwright. Box wood, being extremely hard made valuable utensils, while lighter lime was used by carvers, turners and architects for models of buildings. Rowan, white and smooth and easily polished, made husbandman's tools and holly, with the same properties, was used for furniture. Miller had seen a floor inlaid with holly and mahogany to produce a 'very pretty effect' and the common maple, full of knots, was also used by joiners for inlay work. Spindle, *Euonymus vulgaris*, often planted in gardens for display of its beautiful fruit, was used for musical instruments and smaller branches for toothpicks, skewers and spindles, hence the name.

Regarding conifers, Miller praised the potential of pines because they would grow on the most barren land and he gladly noted that legislation had been passed to encourage such plantations. He hoped that large landowners would plant for posterity, creating employment for the poor, whilst pointing out that these trees were a good economic proposition. Here he had practical experience, having supervised the planting of Scotch Pines on many acres of poor land, covered with heather and gorse and where in five years the trees had overcome the undergrowth. Apart from the cost of fencing the pines against cattle, hares and rabbits, there was little outlay except for the trimming of low branches – and here again the French are quoted as sharing these 'faggots' with those who cut them as payment for labour. They could be left fairly close together, Miller said, as they would then draw each other up to more than 70 feet 'as straight as walking cane' and from one tree he had known 'as many boards sawed as laid the floor of a room near twenty feet square'. These Scots pines were particularly encouraged by the Society of Arts and many large landowners in East Anglia planted them as wind breaks on their flat, sandy land for protection against erosion.

Another tree to flourish on poor soil was the Cedar of Lebanon, *Cedrus libani*, and Miller urged cultivation from seed as growth would be speedy and they might be 'a great ornament to barren, bleak mountains'. He related stories of this timber, quoting Lord Bacon's belief that the wood lasted a thousand years, and how it was supposed to produce the sawdust used in embalming and oil long used for preserving books and manuscripts.

From the detailed fifty-seven pages of the *Dictionary* devoted to the culture of the vine and to wine-making, with full page illustrations of presses, it is obvious that Miller was anxious to promote this industry. He listed seven varieties of grape which, with a little heat, would ripen in this country and advocated propagation from cuttings rather than from layers. In his opinion, use of a hot wall produced the best results, this being usually 10 feet high with trellis and glass in the front and ovens and flues behind, one oven heating 40 feet of wall. He showed surprise that gentlemen in the north of England did not use this method to grow all kinds of fruit, there being plentiful fuel in the area. As with other specialised subjects, Miller contacted the experts and included accounts of vineyards from Italy and France covering cultivation in the Chianti region, Burgundy and the area producing 'Champaign, of the colour of a partridge's eye ... this wine has a tartness, a headiness, a balsamickness or perfume, a quickness and a delicateness that exceeds all the most exquisite ones of Burgundy.'

On the scientific aspects of wine production, Miller quoted his Dutch friend, Boerhaave, on how best to meliorate muddy and tawny clarets or to amend the taste and scent of Malaga wine. Other authorities were quoted and Miller related an instance of being able to help an Italian correspondent over difficulty with fermentation after consulting Stephen Hales (1677–1761), the clergyman-physiologist.

The Society of Arts had again approached Philip Miller, this time for advice on growing Mediterranean grapes in the colonies. In January 1760, Miller apologised for his delay in replying; he had been in Buckinghamshire and afterwards had been indisposed with a severe cold. He related (*Guard Book* 4/92) that at one time the Corinthian grape, grown in the Islands of the Morea, had been cultivated at Chelsea, but had been destroyed when the new greenhouse was built. However, some nurserymen still had this grape and he advised that for successful growth in Carolina, it should be planted inland on rising ground, otherwise a moist coastal climate would cause the skins to burst.

Philip Miller had many connections with the American colonies and the West Indies, through correspondents, collectors and callers at Chelsea. From the early days of Mark Catesby's travels through to John Bartram's expeditions, there was no lack of contact at Chelsea with cultivators in the New World. However, on reading the *Dictionary*, one is hard put to find any praise for the average transatlantic settler. Rather they are criticised for lack of practical application in husbandry which Miller believed could have resulted in an advantageous two-way economy. For example, *Gossypium hirsutum*, a native cotton from both the East and West Indies, was cultivated successfully by Miller in his hotbeds of tanner's bark at Chelsea and he obtained seed pods of a size comparable to those from abroad. This variety

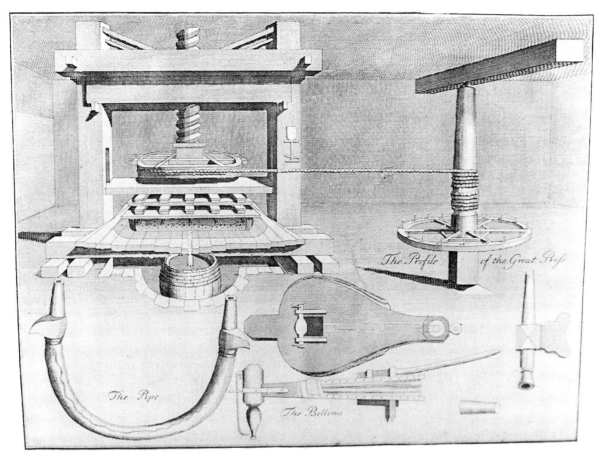

Profile of the Great Wine Press [GD]

produced more cotton than any other and, with a finer staple, Miller reckoned it to be well worth the attention of the inhabitants of British colonies in America. In fact, he did send this seed to America in 1732 and the cotton was eventually cultivated with great success in Georgia, samples of which reached England some forty years later, after Miller's death and too late for his commendation.

The French and Spanish in America cultivated *Cacao* and sold the cocoa to the English at a high price. This irritated Miller and he thought the situation 'might be remedied if the planters in our colonies were the least bit industrious' as little work was involved in the production process. He had difficulty in obtaining fruit from his plants at Chelsea because they were unable to thrive in a cold climate. He had more success with *Vanilla*, easily propagated by cuttings, and felt that the British in Jamaica should set about cultivating the plant, so successfully grown by the Spanish there, but did not suppose that 'persons who were so indolent as to quit the culture of many valuable plants then growing on the spot, would take the trouble of introducing new ones.'

Although the West Indies grew coffee, it was judged inferior to Arabian produce. There might be improvements, Miller suggested, if only planters would try to experiment, as he had, with plants and berries produced in the Physic Garden. Three important points were stressed: soil in which coffee is grown should not be too moist, berries should not be gathered too soon and the greatest care must be taken over drying and in transit. He had known whole cargoes of coffee to be ruined by placing the beans near strong-scented produce like rum and pepper.

Along with the economic advantages to be gained from careful cultivation of cocoa and coffee, Miller mentioned, in the preface of the *Dictionary*, an even more essential commodity, one which 'grows naturally in both Indies, and is there cultivated for its juice which, when boiled, affords that sweet salt which is called Sugar.' He was critical of those growers who left the care of their plantation to overseers and of their methods of drastic overplanting and resultant poor crops. He had discussed cultivation with the owner of a large sugar estate in Jamaica, who had assured him that results beyond expectation had been achieved by using the horsehoe to space the canes further apart and allow for maximum development.

Thoughts on the economic production of timber were also directed abroad. Miller considered that *Swietenia mahagoni*, of the West Indies, whose wood was so widely used in England, warranted cultivation by those settlers whose barren rocky land showed little profit, 'but few of the gentlemen in those islands extend their thoughts so far as to make provision for the rising generation.' Practical Miller, battling with adverse weather at Chelsea, was at a loss to understand why advantage was not taken by those living in more clement conditions to cultivate the produce needed both by themselves and their mother country. However, he would have been gratified to hear of Dr George Young, appointed in 1764 to the military hospital in St Vincents who, with the Governor, General Melville, founded a botanic garden. Young reported on the garden's progress to the Society of Arts and expressed a wish to obtain various plants from royal and botanic gardens in and about London. No doubt Chelsea was in his mind, as he specifically asked for spice plants from the East Indies.

Miller raised many exotic fruits at Chelsea, while he coaxed other new plants for their beautiful flowers and decorative value or for trial in medicine and cookery. It is evident that success with these rarities brought him the greatest pleasure. He considered the pineapple to surpass all known fruits in the world for its rich flavour, listing six varieties and his directions on its propagation take up three pages of the *Dictionary*, although he emphasised that production was well within the scope of the average gardener, as explained to Gilbert White in a letter of 1759. *Carica*, pawpaw, was successfully grown on hotbeds at Chelsea and in three years Miller had plants twenty feet high, producing flowers and fruit in great profusion. He also raised a small white guava, *Psidium pyriferum*, and reckoned it to be preferable to the larger red *P. pomiferum*, rather like the fruit of a pomegranate. The latter, originally nursed with care in greenhouses, became fairly common in English gardens and when planted in strong soil and a warm situation, the beautiful scarlet flowers provided an additional bonus. The mango, *Mangifera*, was usually pickled when unripe and thus brought to England. Miller had heard that it was eaten fresh in India and was considered delicious. He tried propagation from the nuts, but without success, and therefore advocated potting up in their native country and, when a foot high, shipping the plants to England; a method proven by one brought over by a Captain Quick and 'in good health in the Chelsea Garden'.

Miller was enthusiastic over the appearance and culinary use of the fruit of *Capsicum*, Guinea pepper, of which he listed many varieties. He liked them planted in pots, mixed with annuals, and used for the decoration of courtyards. *Capsicum minimum*, known in America as Bird Pepper, was used for 'pepper pots'. These consisted of the ripe pods, dried, pounded, mixed with flour and baked into small cakes, later to be powdered for discriminate use in the kitchen when 'a scruple of this powder put into chicken or veal broth, is greatly commended for comforting cold stomachs'.

One of the most decorative plants at Chelsea was *Caesalpina pulcherrima*, Barbados Pride, a plant used for hedging there and also known as Flower-fence or Spanish Carnation by some of the British inhabitants. The seed, brought annually from the West Indies since Dr Houstoun discovered it, was sown in hot beds, transplanted into successively larger pots, all plunged in beds of tanner's bark. Miller had some plants nearly eighteen feet high in his stoves, producing beautiful flowers in December. Visitors to the Chelsea Garden must have marvelled at the rare fruit and flowers displayed, largely as a result of Miller's correspondence overseas and Pulteney's comment sums up this achievement:

> From the Cape of Good Hope, from Siberia, from North America, and particularly, by means of Dr. William Houstoun from the West Indies, his garden received a plentiful and perpetual supply of rare, and frequently of new species, which his successful culture seldom failed to preserve. It was the remark of foreigners that Chelsea exhibited the treasures of both the Indies.

17 Chelsea's Association with Cambridge

John Martyn was one of Philip Miller's close Chelsea friends. After a good schooling, he had been employed in the counting house of his father, a London merchant, although botany had always ranked high amongst his interests. In this pursuit he was encouraged by Patrick Blair and John Wilmer, often herborising with them. He also joined members of the Society of Apothecaries on their country excursions and himself founded a Society of Botanists, of which Philip Miller became a member, an inclusion possibly marking the fist official recognition of the Chelsea Gardener's ability in the realm of botany. This society was disbanded in 1726, but in the previous year Martyn had begun to lecture in London and, impressed by his ability, Sir Hans Sloane and William Sherard directed him towards Cambridge.

There John Gerard (1545–1612) had advocated a botanic garden in 1588 and Ray had published his *Catalogus Plantarum circa Cantabrigiam nascentium* in 1660 as an aid to the study of botany, but it was not until the end of the seventeenth century that official steps were taken in this direction, when the Vice-Chancellor's accounts contained certain items in connection with a proposed Physicke Garden, of which a plan maybe seen today in the University Library. There is not much evidence of its development, although William Sherard, writing to Richard Richardson in 1722 tells of an eminent physician and botanist Dr Beeston, of Ipswich being in Town [London], at 'Fairchild's, Chelsea, Hampton Court and Eltham ... very curious and knowing in plants and has a fine collection of exotics, which he gives to the new Garden at Cambridge, as he told our gardener.' In the Preface of the *Catalogus Plantarum*, Dr William Beeston (1672–1732) is acknowledged as one of the 'many curious gentlemen which at present are carrying the spirit of gardening to a considerable height'.

Richard Bradley (d. 1732) was the botanist mentioned by Philip Miller in correspondence with Patrick Blair in 1721 and one who was frequently quoted by him in *The Gardener's and Florist's Dictionary* of 1724; including a reference to coffee trees grown under glass in Amsterdam, from a paper presented to the Royal Society in 1715. Bradley was appointed Professor of Botany at Cambridge in 1724 where, contrary to earlier belief, his contribution to the science was considerable, as Dr Max Walters has conclusively shown in *The Shaping of Cambridge Botany* (1981). In the Preface of *A Survey of the Ancient Husbandry and Gardening*, published a year after his

Plate 13

Pawpaw, Papaya, Carica papaya *L.; drawing by G. D. Ehret. Native of tropical America.*

Plate 14

GOSSYPIUM *arboreum foliis palmatis: lobis lanceolatis, caule fruticoso.* Linn.

G. D. Ehret pinxit
1766

Vine-leaved Cotton, Gossypium barbadense L. var. vitifolium (Lam.) Triana & Planchon; drawing by G. D. Ehret. Native of tropical America.

appointment, Bradley expressed a hope that a physic garden might be established where experiments to improve land and subsequent crops at home and abroad might be encouraged. Like Miller, he was anxious to promote economic production in the new colonies. In 1730 Bradley's *Materia Medica* lectures of the previous year were published and mention was made in the Introduction that suitable land had been found for a botanic garden.

Shortly afterwards Mr Brownell of Willingham, a gentleman of considerable means and an interest in botany, came forward with a proposal to sponsor a garden for the University. John Martyn, now established as lecturer, asked his friend Miller for advice on this matter which was not pursued to fruition, probably because Mr Brownell's offer of support was withdrawn. There is no record of payment to Miller in the collection of Vice-Chancellor's vouchers, so it may be assumed that he made no charge for any consultation.

Unicorn-plant, Proboscis flower,
Proboscides louisianica *(Miller)* Thellung; *drawing by J. S. Miller [pl. 286,* FIGS]

John Martyn was still living at Chelsea and, in fact, never resided permanently at Cambridge, commuting back and forth over the years. More than likely he and Miller would ride together over the Gog Magog Hills and take note of wild flowers because the Chelsea Gardener seemed well acquainted with those to be found by the roadside on the way from London to Cambridge (p. 130). While lecturing under Bradley Martyn produced in 1727 a new flora of the area. This was largely based on Ray's earlier work, with two hundred additions to bring it up to date as reliable reference work for students. It was used until the appearance of a third Cambridge flora in 1763, by Israel Lyons, who was later to tutor Joseph Banks at Oxford. This contained a list of over a hundred plants he had found, together with John Martyn and Philip Miller, between 1727 and 1730.

After Bradley's death, Martyn succeeded as Professor in 1733 and although he occupied himself making many translations of classic botanical works, it is evident that very little time was given to the proper instruction of botany at Cambridge. His son, Thomas, a student of mathematics and theology at the University, had considered 'Botany to be rather the amusement of my leisure hours than my serious pursuit'. However, when his father resigned in 1762, he 'had the felicity of taking the lead in introducing the Linnaean system and language to my countrymen by a course of public lectures.' A little is learned of Philip Miller's second son, Charles (1739–1827) from Thomas Martyn's later comments. They had been schoolfriends in Chelsea and would certainly have helped in the Physic Garden, as did Miller's elder son, Philip, who worked there for some years before going to the East Indies, where he died. As their fathers had collaborated in the cause of botany at Cambridge, so the sons strove to establish a botanic garden for the university.

In 1763, Dr Richard Walker, Vice-Master of Trinity, published *A Short Account of the late Donation of a Botanic Garden to the University of Cambridge*, in which John Martyn's work was acknowledged, 'but this Gentleman's private affairs took him from us'. Reference was also made to a 'learned physician', Dr Heberden, and his course of instruction on medicinal plants, but he had left, lamenting 'the want of a public garden furnished with sufficient variety of Plants for making the like experiments'. Dr Walker, 'with the assistance of his friend, Mr. Miller of Chelsea, called in for his great experience and judgement in such an affair', searched for a proper situation and after several abortive negotiations they 'pitched upon and purchased the Mansion House in Free School Lane' for £1600. This had formerly been part of an old monastery and consisted of five acres of walled garden with an ancient water course running through the centre. The land was bequeathed by Dr Walker to the University in perpetuity, 'in trust nevertheless that the premises so given shall be employed for the sole use and purpose of a public Botanic Garden.' As the same time leading university figures were appointed as 'particular Inspectors and Governors of the said Garden, with full power to regulate and govern the same.'

Richard Walker also made provision for the practical officials: he appointed the Reverend Mr Thomas Martyn, now Titular Professor of Botany, to be

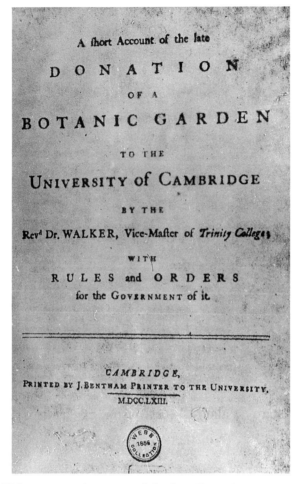

A ſhort Account of the late

DONATION

OF A

BOTANIC GARDEN

TO THE

UNIVERSITY of CAMBRIDGE

BY THE

Rev^d Dr. WALKER, Vice-Maſter of *Trinity College*

WITH

RULES and ORDERS

for the GOVERNMENT of it.

CAMBRIDGE,
PRINTED BY J. BENTHAM PRINTER TO THE UNIVERSITY,
M.DCC.LXIII.

Title page ... Account of the late Donation ..., 1763

the first Reader and Mr Charles Miller, the first Curator or Superintendent of the Works of the Garden, 'believing them to be well qualified for the said Offices'. The purpose of the Botanic Garden was also established: 'as soon as the Stoves and Greenhouses are finished for the reception of tender Plants and the whole Garden perfected for the hardy sorts, Trials and Experiments shall be regularly made and repeated, in order to discover their Virtues, for the benefit of Mankind'. It was proposed that the results of trials should be sent up to the Royal Society and the College of Physicians; thus very much echoing the procedures at Chelsea and maintaining close touch with centres of science in London.

In the *Cambridge University Register* 25.1 there is a MS copy of the *Short Account*, quoted above, and this included a practical note omitted from the printed text: 'We have already introduced about 3000 new plants into the garden, given by Mr Miller of Chelsea and other friends and we have reason to expect many more next spring, which will cost little or nothing more than carriage, but taking care of them will be an additional charge'. Voluntary subscribers were widespread: a list included sums from the Duke of Newcastle, the Bishop of Lincoln, Dr John Fothergill and Dr Hayes of Chester, and a note below read, 'Mr. Peter Collinson gave a large collection of American plants and others from his garden ... but procured a great variety of all species from Mr. Gray, Mr. Williamson and Mr. Gordon, all our principal Nursery Gardeners.'

By 1765 funds for the Garden, hitherto supported and maintained by voluntary subscription, were running low and the Trustees issued a Proposal for an Annual Subscription in Support of the Botanic Garden at Cambridge, 'this foundation so necessary to the study of Natural History and Physic'. The *Proposal* carried assurance that any money collected would be expended with the utmost care and frugality under the Trustees' direction. In spite of this appeal, financial difficulties still prevailed, for when Charles Miller left in 1770, he was not replaced and a note in the Trustees' *Proceedings*, 22 February 1770, records, 'The Revd. Mr. Martyn having been so kind as to offer to be Curator of the Botanic Garden without a salary, this offer was thankfully accepted.'

Thomas Martyn, writing over thirty years later, had this to say of his Curator at Cambridge, 'Having executed this trust during several years to the general satisfaction of the University, he also went to the East Indies whence, more fortunate than his brother [Philip], he returned and is now resident in London.' He added a slight criticism, '... although from his knowledge and experience he is very capable of giving information on many subjects, he has never published anything.' However, in the *Phil. Trans. of the Royal Society* Vol. 58, Sir William Watson gave an account of an experiment conducted by Charles Miller at Cambridge on the increase of wheat from a single grain. In the same volume is an account of Sumatra from Charles Miller, and Thomas Martyn, when writing to a Dr Percy in 1774, also quoted a letter from him describing that island. John Rogers recalled that, after a long spell in India, Philip Miller's second son returned to London and was in 1827 buried in Chelsea churchyard, a stone recording his name, age and parentage, 'together with that of his aged and more distinguished sire'.

After Charles Miller's departure from Cambridge, Thomas Martyn devoted himself wholeheartedly, both as Professor and Curator, to the cause of botany. He completed catalogues of plants in the Botanic Garden, encouraged his pupils and generally performed his duties, all without adequate financial support. However, the Professor wrote to Pulteney in 1776: 'My pupils are but few in number and they are fewer still who give any attention to the science.' He left Cambridge that year and moved first to

Buckinghamshire and then to Bedfordshire, rarely visiting the University, and devoted the latter part of his life to writing and reviving the Martyn/ Miller association.

Nearly ten years had elapsed since the last edition [1768] of the *Gardeners Dictionary*, a decade in which many new plants had been discovered, particularly in the Antipodes. A proposal for a revised edition had been put to William Curtis (1746–1799), editor of *The Botanical Magazine*, by the London booksellers, White and Rivington, and had been turned down. Thomas Martyn undertook the task and hoped to complete it in eleven years. In fact, he took twenty-two years and was paid one thousand guineas for the work, which eventually appeared in four folio volumes from 1803 to 1807. The title was changed to *The Gardener's and Botanist's Dictionary the Whole Collected and Newly Arranged* and although it appeared under Miller's name and the greatest care was taken to give due acknowledgement to the Chelsea Gardener, Martyn tended to give more emphasis to scientific aspects, carefully brought up to date. He wrote to Pulteney in 1786, 'I am determined that the book shall contain in English the *marrow* of Linnaeus's great works' and seven years later, 'If I were to begin the work, it should certainly appear in the order of Linnaeus's system ... but I was to build on Miller's foundation.' Pulteney agreed, 'I more and more lament that it could not have been thrown into a *systemmatic* form'. However, the booksellers remained adamant and, true to their original author, they set the Miller stamp on the revised edition.

The long Preface is valuable in providing comments on Philip Miller's work. Thomas Martyn seemed inclined to reinstate the acclaim which had undoubtedly diminished during the old gardener's last years at Chelsea. He explained that in the new edition, he had paid attention chiefly to rearrangement: the scientific, popular and practical parts being kept separate. With regard to the latter, he added: 'Mr Miller's authority, derived from long and extensive experience, I have generally retained very scrupulously and although nothing is detracted from Mr Miller under this head, yet much is added from authentic books and reputable living authority.' Martyn was generous in praise: 'To his superior skill in his art, the curious owe the culture and preservation of many fine plants, which in less skilled hands would have failed at that time to adorn the conservatories of England.' He went on to emphasise that: 'His objects were not confined to exotics, few were better acquainted with indigenous plants of Britain, of which he successfully cultivated most of the rare species.' A pertinent comment on a more personal aspect of Philip Miller's habits followed: 'He accumulated no wealth from reputable connection with the great or from the numerous editions of his useful works. He was of a disposition too generous and careless of money to become rich and in all his transactions showed more attention to integrity and to honest fame than to any pecuniary advantage.'

MILLER.

De la société Royale de Londres
De l'Académie des Botanistes de florence
Et Directeur du Jardin de Botanique
Des Apothicaires de Chelséa

Philip Miller? The controversial portrait, mentioned by Thomas Martyn,
from the French edition of the Dictionary, 1785.

Thomas Martyn was critical of an illustration in the French edition of the *Dictionary* (1785) and scoffed at 'a fancy portrait of the author in front in a bag wig and ruffles, a costume which must appear truly ridiculous to such as remember the plain old-fashioned English dress in which Mr. Miller always appeared.' Although Martyn, who knew him well, did not question the likeness, it is now believed to be a portrait of the artist, John Miller, who worked closely with Philip, providing many illustrations for his works (p. 108). However, there may have been some facial resemblance between Philip Miller the gardener/author and John Miller, the artist. It has been pointed out that Linnaeus described the calyx of the plant he named *Milleria* as 'Close, short and completely enclosing the seeds' because this echoed the Chelsea Gardener's short, plump figure. The face portrayed is certainly not lean and it would seem that chubbiness was a feature shared by both these gentlemen and this may have contributed to the subsequent confusion.

From his remarks in the Preface to the revised edition of the *Dictionary* (1807) we learn that Thomas Martyn had unsuccessfully approached Charles Miller about this task: 'If he would have undertaken this work, than which no one would have executed it better, the editor would gladly have delegated it to him, having had no other view but of being useful to the public and of doing what honour he could to his worthy father.' However, Thomas Martyn gave Philip Miller all honour due and the updated four-volume *Dictionary* was to prove valuable to botanists and gardeners of the nineteenth century; although it is with Miller's great achievements in the eighteenth that students of today – particularly garden historians – are the more concerned.

18 Miller's Departure

Philip Miller has so far been seen in relation to his friends and correspondents and, occasionally, his own writing, but he was, of course, also an employee of the Worshipful Company of the Apothecaries; a 'servant' to use their designation. Their opinion has been revealed in two Minute Books of the Garden Committees (1731–1771) and these, with Kalm's careful biographical observations, have proved the most valuable source of information on their Gardener.

No detailed Minutes were kept before 1731 and for some time thereafter records of Committee Meetings were scant, somewhat untidy and not of botanical or horticultural importance. They transferred their meeting place from the Garden to the Swan Tavern where, judging from the resultant illegibility of the records, business obviously took a second place. However, records were kept and are of day to day interest. By 1768 official observation and guidance on Garden affairs had declined to such a degree that a further Committee was set up at Blackfriars. The Minute Book of this Committee (from 1769) is precise and orderly and gives a reliable account of the Garden. It also records how Philip Miller was virtually put on trial, dismissed and replaced by one of his former pupils. It is an important assessment of him from his employer's point of view albeit, as we shall see, somewhat unappreciative: no acknowledgement was made of Miller's outstanding industry in producing valuable text books, while at the same time elevating the Chelsea Garden to a place of great eminence in the botanical and horticultural fields.

The first Minute Book sets out the Rules and Orders for the Management of the Physick Garden at Chelsea, approved and confirmed by the Court of Assistants, 21 August 1722. This made provision for a Director, a Gardener, a Catalogue and a subscription from Society members to pay for a new greenhouse, two stoves, a large room over the greenhouse for the 'commodious receiving of books and preserving collections of dry plants'. Repairs were to be made to the gate and wall on the side of the garden next to the Swan Tavern and the ground adjoining the river was to be wharfed with brick. A proper place was to be made for water plants and convenient accommodation provided for the Director and the Gardener. Finally three orders were to be 'fairly written' and hung in the greenhouse: no produce from the Garden was to be sold or exchanged without permission from the

Director, a proper record was to be kept of plants received and no wine or other liquor was to be brought into or consumed in the Garden 'on any account or pretence whatsoever'.

A Committee Report of February 1724 stated that three large stoves had been erected for the preservation of the 'nicer and more curious Exotic Plants', while other conveniences had been supplied for the more hardy plants, and commented on the fact that plants 'both Foreign and Domestick' had been much augmented in the last few years. The Committee also considered that the Garden warranted more attention than they could afford and they recommended the appointment as Director of Mr Isaac Rand 'not only capable of such a status, but a very zealous promoter of Botany'.

By 1725 the Garden Accounts showed a profit of £45, the first credit for many years, and Philip Miller is first mentioned in the Minutes for 5 January 1731, when it was agreed that Mr Rand should order him to prepare a running catalogue of the Garden. In this respect there was a certain amount of competition between Director and Gardener: in 1730 Miller had produced a catalogue of the medicinal plants in the Garden with some 500 entries but Rand, perhaps jealous of his position, capped it with a longer record, together with a map of the Garden.

Bowls at the Swan Tavern, Chelsea 1788

The new greenhouse was completed by 1734, when the Committee met there for the first time, rooms upstairs were occupied by the Director and orderly procedure seemed established. The Garden's library was re-organized: presses, nine feet high, were ordered for the safe keeping of the books and both the Director and Gardener were to have keys. A catalogue was to be compiled, with donors' names inserted in each volume. A minute of June 1735 reads, 'Ordered that thanks be given to Mr Phyllip Miller for his two volumes of the Gardeners Dictionary.' Later that year acknowledgment is made of his presentation of works by Linnaeus and Tournefort – throughout his term of office he donated generously to the library. Alongside these literary references are found notes of the more humdrum tasks of the Gardener: to buy brushes, garden pots and tubs, to seek out the slater of the greenhouse and to produce an estimate for its painting, to cut off branches of the cedars and hedges damaged by the great frost of 1739/40, to procure materials to fill up part of the pond and to have the barge-house doors properly repaired.

Isaac Rand died in 1739 and thereafter meetings of the Committee became spasmodic. They discussed with the City Surveyor, at the Temple Exchange Coffee House in 1741, the question of repairs to the greenhouse, the cost of which was met by Sir Hans Sloane, Philip Miller acting tactfully as a go-between. The Committee forbade the removal of specimens from the Garden, inspected the cabinets of books and dried plants presented by Mrs Rand and, in 1744, reviewed the plants in the Garden and found them to be in good order. However, the attention of the Company's Master was drawn to the fact that for some eight years there had been no serious deliberations and he laid down in 1747 that the Committee should meet in the Garden at least four times a year.

In 1750, almost thirty years after his appointment, Philip Miller received rare praise from the Committee for his industry:

> The Committee, having carefully examined the Garden, found it in very good order and well satisfied with the appearance of a very large number of rare plants wherewith it has been lately furnished, many of which were nondescript, and these were owing to Mr. Miller's great diligence in settling a correspondence and producing seeds and plants from various parts of the world. As such correspondence has been and still is of great expense to Mr. Miller, the Committee resolved unanimously that it would be for the Honour of the Company that Mr. Miller should be reimbursed the expense attending such correspondence and he was accordingly to lay an account thereof before the next committee.

This, amounting to £25.11.6., was paid a month later and in the following year the Committee again decided to ask the Court to pay Miller these expenses.

By 1758 the Committee was meeting only very occasionally and then at the Swan Tavern, thereby ignoring the earlier directive of 1747. It is evident from the Minutes that Philip Miller had assumed responsibility for Garden affairs, there being no appointed Director. In 1760 he was asked to negotiate with the Steward or Agent of the Ladies of the Manor over a contribution towards the cost of moving the south-west wall of the Garden, next to the New Tavern, to the boundary and, provided the sum received

Swan Tavern, Chelsea

did not fall short of twenty pounds, then the work was to proceed. Encouraged perhaps by this apparent trust, Miller decided in 1767 to present a financial statement for the previous year and set out the following:

Salary	£50
Taken at the gate for shewing the garden	31. 4. 0.
	81. 4. 0.
Paid to three men 52 weeks @ 9s per m.	70. 0. 0.
Four man @ 10/–	4. 0. 0
Add to this several parcels of seeds sent by post as also of plants sent by sea	15. 5. 0.
	89. 0. 0.

He added: 'It appears that I am considerably a loser instead of having anything myself and from the inclemancy of this season I have not received four shillings a week on an average since Christmas last.' Miller's point was taken and in September 1768 the Court resolved:

In cons(sideration) of Mr. Miller's Age and Experience, his long and faithful Services, his great Reputation and skill in the Science of Botany; the great number of Indigenous and Exotic Plants with which by his Care, the Company's Garden at Chelsea is stored and adorned, and on account of which it is become famous thro'out Europe and has gained much Honor to the Company, that £50 should be granted and given to him under the mode of a present made him by the Court of Assistants, but which shall not be drawn into a Precedent for any Claim as being part of a settled Salary.

A note at the end of the first Minute Book, dated 17 August 1769, indicates that a new Committee was to be appointed to draw up a *Materia Medica* and make an inventory of all the plants in the Chelsea Garden. A week later, Mr Chandler, who had served on the previous Committee, took the chair and ordered Mr Miller 'to give all due and required assistance to forwarding the taking of such inventory and catalogue, as such in his powers left ...' The concluding proviso set the tone: there was not much confidence in Miller emanating from the new Committee. However, he wrote in agreement and in October, Stanesby Alchorne (1727–1800), reported that the Committee was satisfied with Miller's inventory of plants, tools, etc. although they questioned his claim to all the orange trees in the Garden.

The 1770 *Index Plantarum quo in Horti Medico Chelseano aluntur*, compiled by Miller and the *Praefecus Horti*, William Hudson, is held in the Library of the Garden today. This shows Miller's careful copperplate still to be meticulous and painstaking in that although single species names are listed under the genus, the old polynomials are additionally included.

Early in 1770, Alchorne presented to the Committee a catalogue of 266 volumes and 49 unbound books and pamphlets in the library at Chelsea. These included the 1730 *Index*, the third and sixth editions of the *Dictionary* and the tenth of the *Garden Kalendar*. Following this many books were removed from the Garden's library to the Apothecaries' Hall, despite Miller's objection that 'several donors had appointed that the books should always remain at Chelsea'. He was overruled by the Committee, the argument being that the books had been given to the Company and could be kept wherever they chose; moreover they would remove more if they wished.

In the Garden, his domain for almost fifty years, the old man made his final stand, and there he held out from May to October 1770. The Committee had decided that, in the process of indexing the plants, each was to be marked with a stick. Miller refused to cooperate, maintaining that the new Committee had no jurisdiction over him, and made this very clear by keeping them waiting on two occasions. After a notice from the Master and Wardens in May 1770 he appeared more agreeable and 'struck the table several times to show he would give his assistance', although still insisting that the orange trees and several other plants belonged to him. Over the next few weeks there was more dissension and by the middle of June the Committee's patience was exhausted. The Minute Book stated: ' ... that Mr. Miller has been frequently refractory ... notwithstanding he was acquainted with the said Order ... for his part **he would give the present Committee no assistance therein**.' The argument continued throughout July, August and September, while many more hundreds of marking sticks were ordered. A gratuity of 5s.3d. was given to 'Mr. Miller's man', who had attended the Committtee and given them assistance. Mr. Miller had only made one appearance and continued to treat them with the 'usual rudeness'.

Finally on Friday, 26 October 1770 the case against the Gardener was presented to the Committee by Chandler. It took the form of a judgment on the Minutes of the original Garden Committee (1731–1769) which were minutely dissected and portions presented with a certain amount of relish. The rhetoric resounded, and it is evident from the start that Chandler, with no defence to oppose him, was set to remove Miller. His criticism of the Committee, the Director and the Gardener takes up ten closely written foolscap pages.

The Court of 1722, he said, had required the Director to attend the Garden twice a week to demonstrate on general subjects and on medicinal plants, to attend public and private herborisings and to give the Court an annual account of plants in the Garden. He was to deal with and keep records of the correspondence and finally he was to prepare and deliver the fifty specimens annually to the Royal Society. The Committee of 1724 had changed the attendance to twice a month only in summer in order to demonstrate plants. Chandler than directed his attention to the Catalogue, which was required twice yearly; none appeared until 1731 when Rand had ordered Miller to provide one. Miller had said he did this and Rand made no use of it. In 1749 the Committee resolved that a Catalogue should be taken and reference be made to the Court as to how it should be done.

> Now the mistery is unravelled, how it happened in so many years (27) the catalogue had never appeared. In short the Committee were not equal to the task. They knew not how to take it. In general they were no botanists. Those few persons among them who were, evaded the toil through want of proper assistance in the work. The case stands there. The Court surely never intended or expected to have a business thrown back upon their heads. However, if we may guess by the Court's silence on the reference and the inactivity of the Committee for ten succeeding years, it may seem that both Court and Committee were equally at a loss and incompetent to the service.

Thus, having dismissed in a cursory manner the Director, Committee and even the Court, Chandler turned his attack on the Gardener. He had the original committee Minute Book to hand and noted the day to day instructions given to Miller during the first twenty years of his appointment, concluding with an entry for 28 July 1743, which stated that the Gardener should not order necessities for the Garden without instruction from the Committee, and continued:

> Hitherto the Gardener appears in his proper character – as a servant, giving no order and in due subserviency, although the last mentioned direction seems to imply some past transgression of his duty. But on April 30, 1750, he appears in a different light as the following extraordinary Minute will exemplify.

Chandler then quoted the commendation already given in full (p. 154) and to this added his own interpretation:

> Mr. Miller here appears not as a Gardener to take care of the culture and keep the accounts of the Garden, but as himself the Superintendent Director and sole manager, settling correspondence and procuring seeds and plants without any direction from a superior or from the Committee and without any special appointment in that office ... and it must be observed that the Committee's description is in too general terms to ascertain merit of the Transactions. Had any Catalogue been taken or the particulars of this new furniture of the garden, it would have worn a better countenance.

Having made his point over a presumptuous Gardener, Chandler continued to expound at great length in order to substantiate his claim, and insisted:

> ... that the careful examination mentioned was performed in the short time of one examination ... consisting of taking a walk before Dinner by the side of the Greenhouse and Stoves and then round the Garden, seeing the Walks and Alleys well swept and a general appearance of neatness and order. Also admiring at a fine sight of objects, most of them unknown by name or family. As to the nondescripts, what follows must undoubtedly have been taken on the *ipso dixit* of the Gardener. Indeed, had this representation of the Committee been then or since fairly authenticated, the reimbursement of expenses and a proper reward could never have been postponed as it has been ... It seems that the original appointment of Superintendent or Director was either forgot or was unknown to a young Committee ... indebted to the Gardener for his help in their improvement. No wonder they were disposed to take his word for it and therefore recommend reimbursement.

Chandler continued to argue that particulars of the expenses should have been given by Miller and although the Gardener had again made application in 1754, nothing seems to have been determined until 1767. He was then granted a gratuity of £50 per annum, a sum considered by Chandler to be 'sufficient to induce him to a ready complyance' with future orders and requests.

This concluded the indictment which was to substantiate the case for Miller's removal. Here was a Gardener who had been overstepping the mark for some twenty years and who now, an octogenarian, had shown 'misbehaviour to the Gentlemen who prosecute the Business of fixing the index

Miller's lead cistern in the Chelsea Physic Garden

sticks to the plants of the garden.' This was unpardonable. A further Minute of 30 November 1770 added that he had even threatened to pull up those already fixed and place others in their stead, according to his own method and, an even more glaring example of transgression: a large plane tree in the Garden had been grubbed up and sawn, with no satisfactory reason being given for such waste of the Company's property. This brought matters to a crux and 'Mr. Miller accordingly desired leave to resign the office of gardener to the Company and hoped for their forgiveness and future favour.'

The Court accepted his resignation and he was asked to relinquish all seeds, roots, lists, etc. and every other item that might be thought useful to the Committee or succeeding Gardener although, until that appointment, Miller was to be allowed to live in his house. A week later the Warden and several Gentlemen of the Committee went to Chelsea and found the old man submissive and obliging and ready to comply with their directions: 'to give all necessary orders to the servants and keep in the fires until he received further orders from the Committee.'

John Ellis, whose caustic criticism had been directed at Miller over the years, was even moved to include a modicum of sympathy when writing to Linnaeus:

> Poor Miller, through his obstinacy and impertinance to the Society of Apothecaries, is turned out of the Botanical Garden at Chelsea. I am sorry for it as he is now 79 years of age; they will allow his stipend, but have chosen another gardener. His vanity was so raised by his voluminous publications that he considered no man to know anything but himself, though Gordon, Aiton and Lee have been very long superior to him in the nicer and more delicate part of gardening.

To his transatlantic correspondent, Alexander Garden, Ellis again quoted Miller's impertinence to his masters and continued:

> They have got a much better, one Forsyth, late gardener to the Duke of Northumberland, who has an excellent character and will revive the credit of the garden, which was losing its reputation and everything curious was sent to Mr. Aiton, the Princess of Wales's gardener at Kew.

However, William Anderson, Chelsea's Gardener from 1814 to 1846 considered his predecessor to have been dismissed 'in a most illiberal manner' and in his *Encyclopaedia* (1822) Loudon commented on Miller having no competitor in his long life until the end, when:

> ... several writers took advantage of his unwearied labours of near half a century and fixed themselves upon him as various marine insects do upon decaying shellfish ... all except Hitt and Justice, who are both originals, as is also Hill, after his fashion, but his gardening is not much founded in experience.

The new Gardener took over on 6 February 1771, when Philip Miller surrendered the keys and promised to give him all the assistance he could. The old man retired to live in a house near Chelsea Church, a short walk from his beloved Garden. A Committee Minute dated 10 May 1771 ordered the Gardener 'to supply Mr. Miller occasionally from the Garden with such kitchen herbs as he can conveniently spare for the use of Mr. Miller's own table.' With typical tenacity, the old man stuck to his due and a July Minute laid down that he should be paid for a cistern, if his claim to have bought it for the Committee was proven. By September they were again provoked by Miller's demands for several things already paid for and they could 'only excuse the same upon consideration of the failure of Mr. Miller's memory'. However, the last entry in Garden records concerning him stated that, 'Mr. Dennison reported that upon enquiry according to order, he did not find

Plate 15

IASMINUM *Arabicum, Castaneæ folio, flore albo,*
odoratissimo, cujus fructus Coffy in officinis dicuntur nobis.
Com. Pt 2f.

G. D. Ehret. pinx. 1774.

Arabian Coffee, Coffea arabica L.; *drawing by G. D. Ehret. Native of Aethiopia*
(Abyssinia).

Plate 16

strobus

Weymouth Pine, Pinus strobus *L.; drawing by G. D. Ehret. Native of eastern North America.*

that the leaden cistern behind the dry stove was any part of the Company's property and ordered that Mr. Miller be paid £4.10.' This Cistern, inscribed '1670 W.W.', remains today in the Physic Garden, a secure and substantial reminder of the Miller regime.

He died on 16 December 1771 and was buried on the northern side of Chelsea Churchyard, his grave unmarked and his achievements unrecorded until 1810, when a monument was erected by Fellows of the Linnaean and Horticultural Societies. This memorial, a somewhat gaunt pillar, is topped with a foliage-decorated urn and the inscription reads: 'Philip Miller, Curator of the Botanic Garden, Chelsea and author of the Gardeners Dictionary'. It is thus recorded for posterity that he had, in fact, established himself high above the subservient position to which he was originally appointed and, in both his gardening and his writing, deserved due recognition.

Philip Miller's efficiency and the resultant prosperity of their Chelsea Garden in the mid-eighteenth century meant that the Apothecaries adopted a policy of *laissez-faire* and the Gardener, having been allowed so much free rein, resented a sudden check, with the result that acrimony soured acclaim so long overdue. Had there been earlier altercation over responsibility, Chandler would certainly have capitalized on the point. The old man had behaved very foolishly in the end, but it does seem extraordinary that no tribute was paid to Miller's literary achievements in the course of the inquisition. Admittedly they did not come within Miller's terms of appointment, but the Physic Garden had not been neglected on their account; rather was it enhanced because references to it in his books are legion. Looking back now, two centuries on, a substantial reason for disagreement seems to lie with the Apothecaries through their lack of supervision.

John Rogers, who met Philip Miller through Henry Hewett of Brompton Nurseries, wrote a worthy testimonial as an appendix to his *Vegetable Cultivator* (1839). After a biographical account, he sums up as follows:

In a work devoted to the subject of gardening, the author could not refuse to pass what he conceives to be a just eulogium to the memory of one, whose acquaintance he had the honour to enjoy and to whom his profession is so greatly indebted; for not only did Miller, by his numerous writings, render more easy the previously rugged path of horticulture, but afforded to others the ready means by which further improvement could be effected. With a modesty so often associated with great talent, he laid open to his brother gardeners the knowledge he himself possessed: and the whole tenor of his labours seemed to say, to one and to all, 'Go thou and do likewise'.

19 Followers of Miller

Many passed through the Chelsea school of gardening in Philip Miller's time and subsequently reflected much of his expertise. Some went abroad and remembered their teacher with gratitude, as Miller reported to Linnaeus in 1768, 'I have the *Laurus cinnamonea* [*Cinnamomum camphora*] growing finely in our Garden and am in hopes of getting many other rare plants from India next summer, having a pupil settled there with a large garden and sufficient help to manage it.' Others obtained important positions as gardeners; for instance William Wilson worked for Sir John Cockburn at Petersham and while there he demonstrated his knowledge of one of Chelsea's specialities by writing his *Short Treatise on the Forcing of Early Fruits and the Management of Hot-Walls* (London 1777). This covered peaches, nectarines and vines, with a note on forcing strawberries, of which he judged the scarlet Virginian the best kind.

William Forsyth (1737–1804), a Scotsman who came from Aberdeen to work at Chelsea in 1763, must have proved a competent pupil under Miller, who supported his subsequent appointment as gardener in charge for the Duke of Northumberland at Sion House. On Miller's resignation, there were many applicants for the position and the Garden Committee considered William Forsyth the most promising candidate to recommend to the Court. He was appointed early in 1771 at a salary of £50 a year, with a staff of two under-gardeners and was provided with lodgings in Chelsea, 'until such time as Mr. Miller has quitted his appartments in the greenhouse'. He moved to the Garden in March 1771 after painting, whitewashing and roof repairs had been carried out. The Minute Book confirmed the choice; Forsyth proved 'intelligent and communicative', carrying out his business diligently. That summer Alchorne who had agreed to become Demonstrator of plants 'until a proper person can be found' spent 'perhaps some twenty whole days in the Garden' where he pursued new projects with some enthusiasm. A large load of mould was brought for the intended bog garden and Alchorne reported to the Committee that he had purchased 40 tons of old stone from the Tower of London at his own expense for the purpose of 'raising an artificial rock to cultivate plants which delight in such soil'. The following year Chandler contributed a large quantity of flints and chalk for the project and Joseph Banks presented the Society with pieces of volcanic larva, collected on his recent expedition to Iceland*. This first rock garden in

Page from Alchorne's Index Horti Chelseiani, *1772*

England flourished under Forsyth's care and its remains can be seen in the Physic Garden today.

Alchorne was also busily engaged in compiling a complete inventory of all plants in the Garden, completing it in 1772 as *Index Horti Chelseiani*, arranged alphabetically with binomials only used, and all plants, including those presented by Joseph Banks, are related to a diagram of the Garden indicating exact positions – a very valuable record. This is the only complete list of the garden's plant collection and the first since one of medicinal plants compiled by Miller and Rand forty-two years earlier. Alchorne was succeeded by William Curtis as Demonstrator of Plants in 1773, who held the post for four years.

* A recent investigation by C. Meynell and C. Pulvertafl recorded in *Geographical Magazine* **53**: 433–436 (1981) has revealed that this lava came not from Hekla, but from the coast of Hafnaefjorfhur, south of Reykyavik, apparently taken aboard as ship's ballast.

Systematic Names.	English Names.	Native Country.
Callicarpa.	Nepaul.	Nepaul.
Coffea Arabica.	Coffee Tree	Arabia Felix.
Calycanthus floridus.	Carolina Allspice.	N. America.
Capparis rupestris.	Caper Bush.	S. of Europe.
Citrus Medica.	Lemon Tree.	Asia.
——— Aurantium.	Orange Tree.	East Indies.
Cocos nucifera.	Cocoa-nut Tree.	Both Indies.
Croton Sebiferum.	Tallow Tree.	N. America.
Correa alba.	White flowering.	N. South Wales.
——— speciosa.	Red do.	
——— virens.	Green do.	
Cereus Grandiflora.	Night flow'ring cereus	Africa.
Caryota urens.	Torn-leaved Palm.	East Indies.
Carolinea princeps.	Finger-leaved.	West Indies.
——— insignis.	Great-flowered.	
Coccoloba pubescens.	Downy sea-side grape	
Dioscorea sativa.	Yam.	N. America.
Dracæna Draco.	Dragon Tree.	East Indies.
——— fragrans.	Sweet-scented.	Africa.
——— ferrea.	Purple.	China.
Ficus Bengalensis.	Bengal Fig Tree.	East Indies.
——— elastica.	Indian rubber Tree.	
——— Nymphæifolia.	Water-lily leaved.	
——— Indica.	Indian Fig.	India.
Glycyrrhiza glabra.	Liquorice Plant.	S. Europe.
Gossypium arboreum.	Tree Cotton Plant.	S. America.
Guaiacum officinale.	Lignum-Vitæ Tree.	
Hura strepens.	Sand Box Tree.	
Heretiera littoralis.	Looking-glass Plant.	East Indies.
Ixora grandiflora.	Sessile-leaved.	
——— coccinea.	Scarlet-flowered.	China.
Indigefera tinctoria.	Dyer's Indigo.	East Indies.
Juniperus Virginiana.	Red Cedar Tree.	N. America.
Liriodendron tulipifera.	Tulip Tree.	
Laurus Cinnamonum.	Cinnamon Tree.	Ceylon.
——— Camphora.	Camphor Tree.	Japan.
——— Sassafra.	Sassafras Tree.	N. America.
Latania rubra.	Red Bourbon Palm.	Mauritius.
Myristica moschata.	Nutmeg.	East Indies.
Musa sapientum.	Banana Tree.	West Indies.
Mimosa sensitiva.	Sensitive Plant.	S. America.
Maranta Zebrina.	Zebra Plant.	East Indies.
Musa Paradisiaca.	Plantain Tree.	Both Indies.
Myrica cerifera.	Candleberry Myrtle.	N. America.
Melianthus major.	Great flower.	Cape of G. Hope
——— minor.	Small ditto.	
Nicotiana tabacum.	Virginian Tobacco.	America.
Olea Europæa.	Olive Tree.	S. of Europe.

N 4

Part of Thomas Faulkner's list of plants in the Chelsea Physic Garden, 1829

William Forsyth continued to collect and exchange in the Miller tradition. In 1773 he reported on a visit of the French Royal Gardener to obtain certain plants, with a promise of items in return. Contributions were received from Dr Fothergill, Dr Pitcairn, Aiton, Lee, Gordon and from Miller's old friend at Woodford, Richard Warner. Forsyth would have been instrumental in obtaining plants from Sion House: various *Azalea*, *Kalmia andromeda* and *Magnolia grandiflora* were received from there.

The Gardener at Chelsea still appeared to be overworked and underpaid because in 1775 Forsyth told the Committee that the increased number of plants warranted more labour, that he was dissatisfied with a greenhouse home for his family, 'In a dangerous situation from the great fires in the stoves in winter' and that his income had been unchanged for many years. There are notes in the Minutes of improvements to the greenhouse, but none on Forsyth's salary and, before the year was out, he left to become King's Gardener at Kensington and St James where he was able to concentrate on his chief interest, the cultivation of fruit trees. His *Observations on the Diseases, Defects and Injuries of all Kinds of Fruit and Forest Trees* (1791) was followed by a *Treatise on the Management of Fruit Trees* in 1802 and this ran into three editions before his death two years later. His name is perpetuated by the shrub *Forsythia*, to be seen glowing in countless gardens in early spring. He was followed at Chelsea by John Fairbairn, who remained there many years, making no claims and accepting his lot.

Another Scot, William Aiton (1731–1793), came south from Lanarkshire to study under Philip Miller in 1754. Four years later he was selected by Princess Augusta to establish a botanic garden at Kew House on the lines of the Physic Garden at Chelsea. Since the time of Charles II, when Henry Capel collected rarities to embellish the grounds and glasshouses around his own house at Kew, the garden there had been of some consequence. It brought comment from John Evelyn in 1688 on the excellence of both an orangery and myrtetum and probably such refinements attracted the Prince of Wales, who took a lease on the property in 1730. After his death his widow, the Princess Augusta, continued to live there and it was due to her great enthusiasm for gardening, the wise counsel of her adviser, the third Earl of Bute, a scientific botanist of some repute, and Aiton's sound practical knowledge, that Kew's reputation grew as Chelsea's seemed to diminish.

The Royal Gardens at Richmond were managed in conjunction with Kew, but within a year of Aiton's appointment in 1759, the overall head gardener of both left Kew entirely to Aiton. In 1783 a comprehensive catalogue of all the plants at Kew, entitled *Hortus Kewensis*, was published in three volumes under Aiton's name. Many items were quoted as being introduced into this country by Philip Miller. The actual extent of Aiton's contribution to this work is obscure; it was certainly less than that of Daniel Solander and Jonas Dryander, Sir Joseph Banks's learned botanist librarians and Banks himself. In 1810 William Townsend Aiton, who had succeeded his father at Kew on his death in 1793, brought out a second edition of *Hortus Kewensis*, this time in five volumes and it owed much to Robert Brown, who followed Dryander as Banks's botanist librarian. The younger Aiton said that he was anxious to emulate his father's industry and acknowledge the same kind of learned assistance. Friends had also contributed, 'particularly those who cultivate exotics round London with a degree of success not to be exceeded in any country', with practical information on their cultivation. This could well apply to the Chelsea Garden and, to stress the important part it played, the letters RS were placed against those specimens presented by the Company of Apothecaries to the Royal Society, 'in obedience to Sir Hans Sloane's Will'. Every edition of the *Gardeners Dictionary* is included in the bibliography of this second edition of the *Hortus Kewensis*.

Some beautiful illustrations appeared in the first catalogue of Kew's plants, including *Strelitzia reginae*, introduced from the Cape of Good Hope by Joseph Banks in 1773. Thomas Martyn dedicated the revised edition of the *Gardeners Dictionary* 1807 to this great natural historian – a suitable choice in that as a youth he knew well Chelsea's Physic Garden. In his early years Joseph Banks found constant pleasure in his mother's copy of Gerard's *Herball* and while at Eton he collected plants from the water-meadows beside the Thames, discovering different species on the family estate, Levesby Abbey in Lincolnshire. After his father's death in 1761, his mother, who had always encouraged her son's interest in botany, took a house in Chelsea – 24 Paradise Row, very near to the Garden.

At this time Philip Miller was seventy and endowed with a wealth of experience. The young man, just eighteen, must have been delighted to find such an authority on his favourite subject within a stone's throw of his home and, when down from Oxford, would often be found studying exotics flourishing in the stoves and rare plants growing in the open under Miller's care. Undoubtedly it was there, at the Chelsea Physic Garden, that Banks's interests in travel and collection were stimulated. There, too, he would have met Georg Ehret, whose flower illustrations were among the best in the world and Carl Solander, a botanist sent to England by Linnaeus to work as a librarian in the British Museum, with whom Banks formed a firm friendship. At Oxford he was dismayed to find botany languishing and this country's oldest Botanic Garden much neglected. Ehret had found Humphrey Sibthorp incompetent ten years earlier while, in contrast, Philip Miller, recently called to Cambridge for consultation, knew that botany was reviving there. Banks took the initiative to journey to Cambridge and investigate the possibility of obtaining someone to stimulate the subject at Oxford. It was entirely due to his efforts that Israel Lyons, later author of the third Cambridge flora, was persuaded to lecture at Oxford for a while, where he was at least sure of one enthusiastic undergraduate.

Banks became a Fellow of the Royal Society in 1766 at the age of 23 and in that year joined an expedition to Newfoundland and Labrador. He found botanising in this country equally rewarding and in 1767 he was collecting in the West of England and in Wales, although the following year was to bring him his greatest adventure. With Daniel Solander he joined Captain James Cook on the *Endeavour* to make a journey of exploration and scientific observation to the other side of the world. It was the collections made by

The Botanic Gardens from the river. Drawn from nature on stone by Henry Warren

Banks on this expedition that assured him of a place in botanical history, and the native 'honeysuckle' from New South Wales was called *Banksia* to honour the young scientist. The Minute Book of the Garden Committee shows that in 1771 Banks and Solander presented seeds to the Physic Garden via Mr Lee of Hammersmith and a decade later Forsyth informed the Committee that 500 different kinds of seeds and plants had been presented by Banks to Chelsea. A trip to Iceland was the last of Banks's travels and thereafter he settled down, consolidating his experiences and interests, his house in Soho Square becoming the pivot point of scientific and especially botanical learning. He became President of the Royal Society in 1778 and received a baronetcy in 1781. He encouraged collectors, employed draftsmen, established a magnificent herbarium, embracing Philip Miller's great collection from Chelsea, and generally laid the foundations for Kew's role as the centre for botanical research.

Finally, these three associates of Philip Miller: Banks, Forsyth and Aiton's son, were to come together to establish an even stronger botanical bond, links with which were to stretch far into the future, wide into the world. At the turn of the eighteenth century, John Wedgwood of the great pottery family and a keen gardener, called Forsyth to Bristol to seek his advice on horticultural matters. They probably also discussed the formation of a body to further the interests of gardeners, as soon afterwards Wedgwood wrote to Forsyth asking him to approach Sir Joseph Banks with a proposition. This was approved and a meeting was called at Hatchard's Bookshop in London, and there the idea of a Horticultural Society was conceived in 1804. John Wedgwood, Sir Joseph Banks and Charles Greville represented the authoritative section of those interested, R. A. Salisbury and John Hawkins attended as botanists, while William Forsyth and W. T. Aiton, both in charge of royal gardens, stood for the practical side.

Today, the Royal Horticultural Society's Annual Show is the most important event in the diaries of the gardening fraternity, attracting exhibitors and visitors from all corners of the world. In 1975 conservationists from Kew drew attention to the dwindling cycads with a display of these curious plants. An historic note was struck with a photograph of the ancient *Encephalartos longifolius*, then celebrating its bi-centenary under glass at the Royal Botanic Gardens, having been brought by Masson from South Africa in 1775. This was a reminder of Richard Warner and his damaged *Cycas circinalis* and all those patient plantsmen of the eighteenth century who sought, transported, nurtured and shared rare plants from distant places to embellish our greenhouses and gardens.

At the 1984 Show, Kew Gardens staged another interesting exhibition in the Scientific Section showing foods from foreign lands with, amongst many others, plants of coffee, cocoa, capsicum, orange, pineapple, sugar cane, tea and vanilla. They immediately brought back thoughts of one in particular who persevered with propagation in stove and hotbed of new overseas products for our kitchens and dispensaries. Indeed, it is significant that this great Show is held at Chelsea, where can be savoured the ultimate display of the world's horticulture, fostered by Philip Miller at the Physic Garden, just up the road, two centuries ago.

20 The Botanical Importance of Philip Miller's Publications*

WILLIAM T. STEARN

'Of all gardeners, Micheli alone excepted, the most learned and the most sagacious', so Kurt Sprengel described Philip Miller (1691–1771) in his *Historia Rei Herbariae* (1808), awarding him superlative upon superlative, *doctissimus, sagacissimus, acutissimus, indefessus*, and giving much the same kind of praise to Miller's *Gardeners Dictionary*, 'necessary just as much for botanists as for gardeners ... an immortal compendium', *lexicon ipsius botanicis aeque ac hortulanis necessarium ... opus est immortale etc.* A study of Miller's works together with those of his contemporaries confirms the veracity of these remarks by so learned a botanical historian.

Both for its intrinsic merit as a comprehensive and massive repository of information and for its long-lasting influence, Miller's *Gardeners Dictionary* is the most important horticultural work of the eighteenth century. Its botanically and most important edition is the eighth, the last edition in Miller's life-time and the first to adopt Linnaean binomial nomenclature for species; this was published on 14 April 1768. It is not simply a monument to the industry and knowledge of a great gardener and a good botanist, an expression in horticultural terms of the encyclopaedic spirit of the eighteenth century which also animated such very different men as Chambers, Zedler, Robert James, Pivati, Linnaeus and Diderot; it is also a work still relevant to the nomenclature of many well-known plants. The period from 1722 to 1770, during which Miller had charge of the Chelsea Physic Garden belonging to the Worshipful Company (*or* Society) of Apothecaries, was a period when the overseas expansion of the British, Dutch and French nations provided increasing opportunities for the introduction of new plants from distant countries and, thanks to the happy relations existing between the Chelsea, Leyden, and Paris gardens, most of these plants came into Miller's hands and were grown at Chelsea. The successive editions of his *Gardeners Dictionary* thus record the progress of horticulture in Britain from 1721 to 1768, and by comparing them the approximate dates of introduction of plants into cultivation can be ascertained.

---

* This chapter incorporates material extracted from the writer's publications of 1969, 1972 and 1974; see bibliography.

In 1724 Miller published a two-volume octavo work, *The Gardeners and Florists Dictionary*. In 1731 he superseded this by a folio one-volume work, *The Gardeners Dictionary*, of which a second little altered edition came out in 1733, a third in 1737, with an extra volume in 1739, a fourth edition in 1743, a fifth in 1747, a sixth in 1752 which brought the contents of the former two volumes into one sequence, a seventh in parts between 1756 and 1759, and an eighth in 1768. It was intended to be primarily a practical guide, as its title-page made plain from the start, 'containing the methods of cultivating and improving the kitchen, fruit and flower garden as also the physick garden, wilderness, conservatory and vineyard, according to the practice of the most experienc'd gardens of the present age.' The succession of editions indicates how well it met current needs.

Miller's *Dictionary* contained, however, more than cultural information; it provided much descriptive botanical information, in Miller's own words, 'the history of the plants, the characters of each genus, and the names of all the particular species, in Latin and English, and an explanation of all the terms used in botany and gardening.' Many of the species were then new to science and they had to be given names in order that they could be listed. For many years the *Dictionary* was the unique repository of information about them. In 1768 Miller recorded that the number of kinds of plants cultivated in England had more than doubled since the publication in 1731 of his first edition. The recording of so many plants, with their genera described in an alphabetical sequence, his work being a dictionary intended for easy consultation, forced Miller to study the genera in which they were to be placed and the correct names for these.

The dominant naturalist of the eighteenth century was Miller's Swedish contemporary Carl Linnaeus (1707–1778), whose *Species Plantarum* (1753) and *Genera Plantarum* (1754) have been internationally accepted as the starting point for the scientific naming of plants. Linnaeus's drastic alterations of currently accepted names and his equally disturbing reclassification of genera did not please Miller, who was an older man with more respect for predecessors. He accepted the Linnaean method of naming species with two-word names (binomials) very reluctantly. Introduced by Linnaeus in 1753, it was not adopted by Miller until 1768. He never completely accepted Linnaeus's views on the definition of genera, which were indeed unpopular with many contemporary botanists and gardeners besides Miller. Thus Miller's friend Peter Collinson, a gentle Quaker, wrote to Linnaeus on 20 April 1754: 'my dear friend, we that admire you are much concerned that you should perplex the delightful science of Botany with changing names that have been well received, and adding new names quite unknown to us. Thus Botany, which was a pleasant study and attainable by most men, is now become, by alterations and new names, the study of a man's life, and none now but real professors can pretend to attain it.' Such a lamentation has continued to come from gardeners though not always so mildly expressed. Miller agreed but his conservatism as regards generic concepts now makes him appear in modern nomenclature as a botanical innovator!

Generic Concepts and Nomenclature

The classification and generic nomenclature followed by Miller down to the seventh edition of his *Dictionary* (1756–59) were based on Joseph Pitton de Tournefort's *Institutiones Rei Herbariae* (1700), a work of great originality and scholarship which proved the first comprehensive and logically arranged set of consistently drafted formal definitions of genera of vascular plants (*cf*. Stearn, 1960). In his *Isagoge in rem herbariam* or introduction to botany, Tournefort explained the philosophy and method of his vast under-taking. For establishing the genera of plants he stated that 'we consider both the form of the flower and the fruit in those genera which bear flowers and fruit; calling to our aid other parts when the affinity of flowers and fruits by itself does not appear to satisfy completely our plan. Accordingly we will call genera of the first rank (*genera primi ordinis*) those of which the nature is contained in the flower and fruit alone such as *Aconitum, Ranunculus, Rosa, Viola* etc; the rest to which something other than the structure of the flower and the fruit is to be added will be of the second rank (*secundi ordinis*) ... Roots can be employed for genera of the second rank, *Bulbocast-anum* by the sole form of the root, which is a tuber, differs from most genera of Umbellifere ... Likewise the position and number of leaves ... *Pinus, Abies* and *Larix* agree in their catkins [male cones] and scaly fruits; they differ in the placing of the leaves which are solitary in *Abies*, are dispersed here and there, in *Pinus* arising in pairs, in *Larix* very numerous ... Characters of the stem and the bark sometimes complete the definition of the genus. *Dens Leonis* [i.e. *Taraxacum*] by its fistular and unbranched stem differs from species of *Hieracium*.'

Guided by such considerations Tournefort defined many natural groups, most of which are accepted as genera today, although, owing to the intervention of Linnaeus, often not under the same names. His descriptions were accompanied by excellent copper-engravings of floral structure, etc. by Claude Aubriet and all were based on examination of living plants. The first third of the eighteenth century saw the almost complete acceptance of Tournefort's genera, the middle third their gradual but never complete supersession by Linnaeus's, the last third their restoration in large part (*cf*. Dandy, 1967).

THE

Gardeners Dictionary:

Containing the METHODS of

CULTIVATING *and* IMPROVING

THE

Kitchen, Fruit *and* Flower Garden.

AS ALSO, THE

Phyfick Garden, Wildernefs, Confervatory,

AND

VINEYARD,

According to the PRACTICE of the

Moft *Experienc'd Gardeners* of the *Prefent Age.*

Interfpers'd with

The Hiftory of the PLANTS, the Characters of each GENUS, and the Names of all the particular SPECIES, in *Latin* and *Englifh*; and an Explanation of all the TERMS ufed in BOTANY and GARDENING.

Together with

Accounts of the Nature and Ufe of *Barometers, Thermometers,* and *Hygrometers* proper for GARDENERS; And of the Origin, Caufes, and Nature of METEORS, and the particular Influences of *Air, Earth, Fire* and *Water* upon *Vegetation,* according to the beft NATURAL PHILOSOPHERS.

Adorn'd with COPPER PLATES.

By *PHILIP MILLER,* Gardener to the BOTANICK GARDEN at *Chelfea,* and F. R. S.

———*Digna manet divini gloria ruris.*   VIRG. GEO.

LONDON:

Printed for the AUTHOR;

And Sold by C. RIVINGTON, at the *Bible* and *Crown* in St. *Paul's Church-Yard.*
M. DCC. XXXI.

Title page, Gardeners Dictionary,
1st ed. 1731

THE

Gardeners Dictionary:

Containing the METHODS of

CULTIVATING *and* IMPROVING

THE

Kitchen, Fruit *and* Flower Garden,

AS ALSO THE

Phyfick Garden, Wildernefs, Confervatory,

AND

VINEYARD.

Abridg'd *from the* FOLIO EDITION,

By the AUTHOR, *PHILIP MILLER,*

Gardener to the Worfhipful *Company of Apothecaries,* at their BOTANICK-GARDEN, in *Chelfea,* and F. R. S.

In TWO VOLUMES.

———*Digna manet divini gloria ruris.*
VIRG. GEO.

VOL. I.

LONDON:

Printed for the AUTHOR, and Sold by C. RIVINGTON, at the *Bible* and *Crown,* in St. *Paul's Church-Yard.*
M.DCC.XXXV.

Title page, Gardeners Dictionary ...
Abridgement *1735*

Miller was among those who prefered to follow Tournefort rather than Linnaeus and his *Dictionary* undoubtedly helped to make Tournefort's concepts and names known and accepted in England. As he himself stated in 1768:

... the Names of the Plants were chiefly taken from Tournefort's Institutions as were the Characters of the Genera, these being described by the Author [Tournefort] with great Accuracy, and their Figures were also well graven on Copper Plates. Therefore as the Author [Miller] is far from thinking any system perfect; so he has principally followed that of Tournefort here and only varied from it in those places where his is less perfect; and also to include those Genera which have been discovered since his time.

Linnaeus' *Genera Plantarum* was first published in 1737. It dealt severely with the works of his predecessors although greatly indebted to them. In arrangement, nomenclature, and generic concepts it frequently departed from Tournefort's *Institutiones*, since Linnaeus emphasized the floral characters on which he based his 'sexual system' of classification; he rejected Tournefort's genera of second rank founded primarily on vegetative characters; he changed, moveover, many names used by Tournefort because they did not conform to his own rules as set forth in the *Critica botanica* (1737). Miller, like many of his contemporaries, saw no reason to accept all these innovations. If 'Charles Linnaeus, Doctor of Physic, and Professor of Botany at Upsal in Sweden' chose to ignore the distinctions between *Muscari* and *Hyacinthus*, between *Linaria* and *Antirrhinum*, between *Abies*, *Larix*, and *Pinus*, and between other groups separated by Tournefort, he could do so. Miller, 'Gardener to the Worshipful Company of Apothecaries, at their Botanic Garden in Chelsea', on the basis of his own observations steadfastly kept them separate as Tournefort had done; moreover, he was 'unwilling to introduce any new Names where the old established names were suitable; lest, by this he should rather puzzle, than instruct, the Lovers of Gardens.' This conservatism, strangely enough, has given the fourth abridged edition (1754) of Miller's *Gardeners Dictionary* its great nomenclatural importance.

The Abridgement

In 1735 Miller brought out a two-volume edition 'abridg'd from the folio edition' of 1733, a third volume following in 1740. His object was 'to reduce the Price of the Book so low, as that the Purchase of it might not be too great for the practical Gardeners.' A second edition came out in 1741, a third in 1748, a fourth in 1754, a fifth in 1763, and a sixth in 1771, *i.e.* in the last year of Miller's life. The massive folio edition was clearly intended for the well-to-do owners of big gardens; it cost more money than most head gardeners then earned in a month. The more humble abridgement served as a handbook for men with lesser means. That it had any nomenclatural botanical significance passed completely unnoticed until 1914 when G. C. Druce pointed out that its fourth edition (1754) was the first major work containing descriptions of genera published after Linnaeus' *Species Plantarum* (1753), and that this edition gave valid publication to numerous Tournefortian generic names suppressed by Linnaeus, whose restoration had commonly been attributed to Adanson, Medicus, Moench, and other post-Linnaean authors. Its importance is due to an accident of chronology. Miller, of course, did not set out deliberately to reestablish such genera. He merely continued to do after 1753 the same as he had done before 1753, indeed before Linnaeus had published a word, and paradoxically he thereby

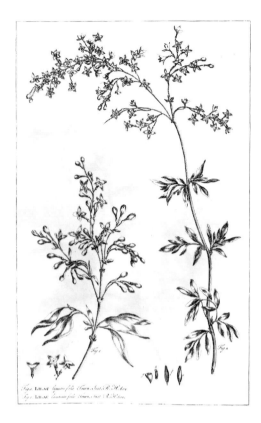

Fig. 1 Persian Lilac, Syringa × persica *L.*
Fig 2 Laciniate Lilac, Syringa × laciniata
Miller; *drawings by R. Lancake [pl. 164,* FIGS]

became an inadvertent innovator, for, as Dandy (1967) has emphasized, by recognizing pre-1753 genera which Linnaeus had reduced, Miller, like his contempories Duhamel du Monceau, Gagnebin, Guettard, Scopoli, and Séguier, in effect founded new genera. At the same time, by retaining Tournefort's names which Linnaeus changed on linguistic grounds, in their opinion wantonly, e.g. by retaining Tournefort's *Alkekengi* instead of Linnaeus' *Physalis*, these early non-binomial authors published in effect new names which have now to be treated as 'superfluous substitutes for the corresponding Linnaean names'.

Because other works of pre-Linnaean character appeared in 1754 and because, as stated by Dandy (1967), Miller's *The Gardeners Dictionary ... abridged from the last folio Edition*, 4th ed. (3 volumes; London, 1754) is 'much the most important source of generic names in the early years following 1753,' it became necessary to ascertain as exactly as possible its date of publication. Fortunately there appeared in the London daily newspaper *The public Advertiser* No. 6007 (28 January 1754) the advertising statement: 'This Day is published, in Three Large Volumes, octavo, The Fourth Edition, corrected and enlarged, of the The Gardeners Dictionary abridged from the last Folio edition.' The price was 18 shillings. This advertisement establishes 28 January 1754 as the date of issue of all three volumes. In consequence of its early publication in 1754, Miller's work can reasonably be accepted as having priority over other works dated 1754.

Dandy (1967) has indexed the large number of generic names for which Miller must be cited as the first post-Linnaean author. Among those established in the abridgement (1754) are:

Abies	Cruciata	Hepatica	Myrrhis
Abutilon	Cydonia	Hermodactylus	Omphalodes
Acacia	Cysticapnos	Inga	Onobrychis
Acetosa	Damasonium	Kleinia	Paliurus
Acinos	Diervilla	Larix	Paronychia
Adhatoda	Dodonaea	Lens	Pereskia
Alnus	Dorycnium	Leucanthemum	Persea
Alyssoides	Dracunculus	Limonium	Persicaria
Ananas	Eruca	Linaria	Polygonatum
Arisarum	Fagopyrum	Luffa	Pulsatilla
Asteriscus	Filipendula	Lycopersicon	Quamoclit
Bernardia	Foeniculum	Majorana	Serjania
Cakile	Frangula	Malus	Silaum
Calamintha	Glaucium	Manihot	Thymelaea
Castanea	Guazuma	Maurocenia	Toxicodendron
Ceiba	Hedypnois	Melilotus	Valerianella
Cereus	Helianthemum	Meum	Vanilla
Cotinus	Helichrysum	Muscari	Ziziphus.

These had not been accepted by Linnaeus but modern botanists accept almost all of them. It will be obvious that many are well-known genera both horticulturally and botanically important.

Also published in the abridgement are many names which must be treated as superfluous substitutes for Linnaean names, e.g. *Acajou* for *Anacardium*, *Acriviola* for *Tropaeolum*, *Alkekengi* for *Physalis*, *Aquifolium* for *Ilex*, *Azedarach* for *Melia*, *Castorea* for *Duranta*, *Lilac* for *Syringa*, *Syringa* for *Philadelphus*, and some names for groups not usually accepted as taxonomically distinct from Linnaean genera, e.g. *Cepa, Moly, and Porrum* now included in *Allium*.

The specific names in this work are phrase-names e.g.: *Rubus major, fructu nigro; Rubus Idaeus spinosus, fructo rubro; Salvia Hispanica, folio lavendulae*; and the occasional accidental binomials (pseudo-binomials) among them, such as *Rubus odoratus, Salvia nigra, Sorbus sativa, Thymbra legitima*, have no validity. The only binomials which can legitimately be attributed to Miller are those in the eighth edition (1768) of his *Dictionary*.

Emphasis on the botanical importance of Miller's 1754 work should not obscure its horticultural interest, as it lists a large number of garden variants under the cultivar names then in use, e.g. 'Hotspur Pea', 'Sickle Pea', 'Green Rouncival Pea', 'Marble Rouncival Pea', 'Rose Pea' or 'Crown Pea' and gives cultural directions exemplifying the best current practice.

THE

GARDENERS DICTIONARY:

CONTAINING

The BEST and NEWEST METHODS

OF

CULTIVATING and IMPROVING

THE

Kitchen, Fruit, Flower Garden, and Nurſery;

As alſo for Performing the

Practical Parts of AGRICULTURE:

INCLUDING

The MANAGEMENT of VINEYARDS,

WITH THE

Methods of MAKING and PRESERVING WINE,

According to the preſent Practice of

The moſt ſkilful Vignerons in the ſeveral Wine Countries in *Europe.*

TOGETHER WITH

DIRECTIONS for PROPAGATING and IMPROVING,

From REAL PRACTICE and EXPERIENCE,

ALL SORTS OF TIMBER TREES.

THE EIGHTH EDITION,

Reviſed and Altered according to the lateſt SYSTEM of BOTANY; and
Embelliſhed with ſeveral COPPER-PLATES, which were not in ſome former Editions.

BY PHILIP MILLER, F.R.S.

Gardener to the Worſhipful Company of APOTHECARIES, at their Botanic Garden
in *Chelſea,* and Member of the Botanic Academy at *Florence.*

. . . . *Digna manet divini gloria ruris.* VIRG. Georg.

LONDON,

Printed for the AUTHOR;

And Sold by JOHN and FRANCIS RIVINGTON, at No. 62, *St. Paul's Church-yard*; A. MILLAR,
J. WHISTON, W. STRAHAN, J. HINTON, R. BALDWIN, B. WHITE, L. HAWES and
W. CLARKE and R. COLLINS, W. JOHNSTON, T. CASLON, S. CROWDER, T. LONGMAN,
B. LAW, C. RIVINGTON, J. DODSLEY, W. GRIFFIN, T. CADELL, T. LOWNDES,
S. BLADON, G. ROBINSON and J. ROBERTS, and T. PAYNE.

M. DCC. LXVIII.

Title page, Gardeners Dictionary, *8th ed. 1768*

The Eighth Edition of the Dictionary

As stated by Pulteney (1790), because Miller had been habituated from his youth onwards to the methods of Ray and Tournefort, 'it was not without reluctance that he was brought to adopt the system of Linnaeus; but he was convinced, at length, by the arguments of the late Sir William Watson and

Mr. Hudson, and embraced it.' His conversion was certainly slow and never wholehearted. In the seventh edition (*1756–59*) of his folio *Dictionary*, he illustrated Linnaeus's 'sexual system' of classification, referred genera to their position in this and adopted the phrase names (polynomials) of the *Species Plantarum* where applicable but not Linnaeus' binomials. In the eighth edition (1768) published when he was 77, he adopted at last the Linnaean system of binomial nomenclature for species but he still declined to accept all Linnaeus's broadly defined genera. The specific epithet or trivial name is here placed in parentheses after the generic name and is followed by a diagnostic phrase, which was sometimes Linnaeus's own procedure. Thus the polynomial or phrase-name '15. VERBENA *diandra spicis carnosis subnudis, foliis lineari-lanceolatis obsolete serratis*' of Miller's 1759 edition became a binomial specific name with diagnosis, '15. VERBENA (*Angusti-folia*) diandra, spicis carnosis subnudis' etc. in his 1768 edition; it is the basionym of *Stachytarpheta angustifolia* (Miller) Vahl. and is represented in the British Museum (Natural History) by three authentic specimens, the best being Chelsea Plants no. 547(1732) grown from Houstoun's Vera Cruz seed.

In the preface to the eighth edition Miller made clear his reasons for accepting Linnaeus's system and nomenclature as a whole while diverging from them in detail. He stated that:

> In the last edition of this work, the author adopted in a great measure the system of Linnaeus, which was the prevailing method of ranging plants then in use among botanists; but as many of the plants which were treated of in the Gardeners Dictionary, were not to be found in any of Linnaeus's works then published, Tournefort's system was also applied to take in such as were not fully known to Dr. Linnaeus; but since that time the learned professor having made great additions to his works, and those additions being generally consulted for the names of plants, the author has now applied Linnaeus's method entirely, except in such particulars, where the Doctor not having had an opportunity of seeing the plants growing, they are ranged by him in wrong classes; as for instance, the Ilex or Agrifolium is ranged in his fourth class, with those plants whose flowers have four stamina or male organs, and four stigmas or female parts of generation; whereas those plants have male flowers upon some, and female upon other plants. The Laurus Linnaeus has placed in his ninth class, with those plants whose flowers have nine stamina or male organs of generation, and one female part; but these plants should also be ranged in his twenty-second class, for all the species of this genus have male and female flowers on different plants. These, with some other alterations from Linnaeus's system, have been made in this edition, where the author has given his reasons for so doing, which he hopes will be approved by the public.

Of the approximately 1300 new binomials published in the eighth edition, many were new combinations made by transferring Linnaean specific epi-thets to Tournefortian generic names when Miller rejected Linnaeus' generic concepts and nomenclature. His procedure was not directly to cite a Linnaean binomial as a synonym of his own but to cite Linnaeus's generic name in a discussion at the head of the article on a given genus and to adopt Linnaeus' specific epithet (trivial name), when it did not duplicate the generic name; Miller's citation of a pre-Linnaean synonym also cited by Linnaeus makes the association clear. Thus under *Castanea* Miller stated that Linnaeus 'has joined this genus to the Fagus ... However as the male flowers of the Chestnut are formed into long katkins, and those of the Beech are globular, they may with propriety be kept separate; and this I choose to do, that it may be more intelligible to common readers.' Linnaeus had included three species in *Fagus*, i.e. *F. sylvatica*, *F. castanea*, and *F. pumila*. Miller restricted *Fagus* to *F. sylvatica*. To avoid the tautonym *Castanea castanea*, he renamed Linnaeus' *Fagus castanea* as *Castanea sativa*, citing as a synonym not *F. castanea* L. but *Castanea sativa* C. Bauhin which was also cited in synonymy by Linnaeus. Again under *C. pumila* Miller did not cite *F. pumila* L. but simply the common synonym *Castanea pumila Virginiana racemosa* Plukenet. His procedure is the same in other genera. Thus under *Foeniculum* Miller remarked, 'Dr Linnaeus has joined this genus to Anethum ... But as the seeds of Fennel are oblong, thick, and channelled, and those of Dill flat and bordered, it is much better to keep them separate than to join them in the same genus.' The difference noted by Miller remains the one by which the two genera are distinguished, for example, in L. H. Bailey's *Manual of cultivated Plants*, 2nd ed. (1949):

> Fruit strongly flattened, the lateral ribs distinctly winged ... ANETHUM (Dill)
> Fruit not strongly flattened, the ribs not winged ... FOENICULUM (Fennel)

The pre-Linnaean synonym *Foeniculum vulgare germanicum* C. Bauhin common to Linnaeus' protologue of *Anethum foeniculum* and Miller's of *Foeniculum vulgare* establishes their connexion. Likewise the pre-Linnaean synonym *Damasonium stellatum* Dalechamps connects *Alisma damasonium* L. and *Damasonium alisma* Miller. The importance of common synonyms in linking nomenclaturally the works of Linnaeus and his contempories has long been recognized but tends to be overlooked by the uninitiated having little acquaintance with eighteenth-century botanical procedures. Such new names and new combinations are validly published by indirect reference in accordance with the *International Code of Botanical Nomenclature* (1988, article 32.4) to Linnaeus's *Species Plantarum* 'printed at Stockholm in 1753 and the Second Edition in 1765' which Miller listed as works referred to. The text of the *Dictionary* makes evident Miller's intimate knowledge of these and earlier Linnaean works.

Linnaeus had used a number of Tournefort's generic names as specific epithets in his binomials, thereby preserving a little nomenclatural continuity in the midst of upheaval. Miller's restoration of the Tournefortian genera concerned if accompanied by retention of the Linnaean specific epithets would have resulted in such tautonyms as *Linaria linaria* (based on *Antirrhinum linaria* L.) which Miller, unlike his contemporary John Hill, presumably regarded as ridiculous. Hence Miller had to provide new specific epithets. Some examples are *Acetosa pratensis* (*Rumex acetosa* L.), *Asarina procumbens* (*Antirrhinum asarina* L.), *Damasonium alisma* (*Alisma damasonium* L., *Damasonium damasonium* (L.) Ascherson & Graebner), *Diervilla lonicera* (*Lonicera diervilla* L., *Diervilla diervilla* (L.) MacMillan), *Foeniculum vulgare* (*Anethum foeniculum* L., *Foeniculum foeniculum* (L.) Karsten), *Frangula alnus* (*Rhamnus frangula* L.), *Helianthemum chamaecistus* (*Cistus helianthemum* L.), *Larix decidua* (*Pinus larix* L., *Larix larix* (L.) Karsten), *Limonium vulgare* (*Statice limonium* L., *Linaria vulgaris* (*Antirrhinum linaria* L., *Linaria linaria* (L.) Karsten), *Lycopersicon esculentum* (*Solanum lycopersicum* L., *Lycopersicum lycopersicum* (L.) Karsten), *Muscari racemosum* (*Hyacinthus muscari* L., *Muscari muscarimi* Medicus), *Paliurus spina-christi* (*Rhamnus paliurus* L., *Paliurus paliurus* (L.) Karsten), *Pereskia aculeata* (*Cactus pereskia* L., *Pereskia pereskia* (L.) Karsten). *Persea americana* (*Laurus persea* L., *Persea gratissima* Gaertner f.), *Persica vulgaris* (*Prunus persica* L.), *Pulsatilla vulgaris* (*Anemone pulsatilla* L., *Pulsatilla pulsatilla* (L.) Karsten), and *Ziziphus jujuba* (*Rhamnus zizyphus* L).

No edition has page numbers, but the articles are arranged alphabetically, with the genera entered under their scientific names and the species individually numbered. Thus, while a citation such as *Verbena angustifolia* Miller, Gard. Dict. ed. 8, art. Verbena, no. 15 (1768) indicates precisely the place of publication, in fact the brief citation *Verbena angustifolia* Mill, could suffice, as this eighth edition of 1768 is the only work by Miller in which he published binomials.

Miller grew many species from South Africa, North America, and the West Indies, as well as from Europe, which Linnaeus had never seen or had failed to separate from other species and consequently had not named. To such new species Miller was obliged to give names of his own, *e.g.*, *Aconitum orientale*, *Acer opalus*, *Aloe africana*, *Aloe arborescens*, *Aloe barbadensis*, *Aloe carinata* (now *Gasteria carinata*), *Aloe glauca*, *Aloe herbacea* (now *Haworthia herbacea*), *Aloe mitriformis*, *Aloe obscura*, *Aloe verrucosa* (now *Gasteria verrucosa*), *Anagallis foemina*, *Anthericum altissimum* (now *Bulbine altissima*), *Arum italicum*, *Convallaria odorata* (now *Polygonatum odoratum*), *Convolvulus elegantissimus* (now C. *althaeoides* var. *pedatus*), *Cornus foemina*, *Corylus maxima*, *Crocus biflorus*, *Crotalaria pilosa*, *Cyclamen coum*, C. *orbiculatum*, C. *persicum*, *Cytisus alpinus* (now *Laburnum alpinum*), *Datura innoxia*, *Galeopsis speciosa*, *Gladiolus italicus*, *Helianthus tracheliifolius*, *Hemerocallis minor*, *Hypericum inodorum*, *Lamium moschatum*, *Limonium humile*, *Linum anglicum*, L. *bienne*, *Lycium chinense*, *Nerium indicum*, *Ophrys sphegodes*, *Paeonia peregrina*, *Pinus echinata*, P.

halepensis, P. palustris, P. rigida, P. virginiana, Populus tacamahaca, Pulmonaria saccharata, Rhus africana, Ribes americanum, Scilla hispanica (now *Hyacinthoides hispanicus*), *Silene orientalis, Solidago fistulosa, Stachys italica, Tilia cordata, Toxicodendron altissimum* (now *Ailanthus altissima*), *Tragacantha massiliensis* (now *Astragalus massiliensis*), *Tragopogon minor* (now *T. pratensis* subsp. *minor*), *Veronica orientalis, Watsonia humilis, Watsonia meriana, Xanthoxylum americanum, Xeranthemum inapertum, Xeranthemum oriental* (now *Chardina orientalis*) and *Zizyphus oeniplia*. When in his experience a taxon remained unaltered when raised from seed Miller often gave it a binomial; thus he distinguished six species of *Cyclamen* (of which three *C. coum, C. persicum* and *C. purpurascens*, are accepted) and ten species of *Capsicum* (apparently variants of *C. frutescens*), following the need of cultivators.

Miller's friendship with the Scottish surgeon William Houstoun (1695–1733), who was in Jamaica and Mexico between 1729 and 1733, led to the introduction of many plants from there into the glasshouses of Chelsea and so to their recording by Miller, to whom Houstoun bequeathed his manuscripts, drawings, and herbarium and from whom they passed to Sir Joseph Banks and so ultimately to the British Museum (Natural History), London. One of these Houstoun specimens, the type of *Maurocenia americana* Miller and hence of *Bumelia americana* is illustrated in the *Journal of the Arnold Arboretum 49*: 280–289 (1968). Thus many tropical American plants first received binomials in the eighth edition of Miller's *Gardeners Dictionary*. Among these may be mentioned: *Acacia macracantha* Humb. & Bonpl. (*Mimosa lutea* Miller, *A. lutea* (Miller) Britton, non Leavenw.); *Acrocomia spinosa* (Miller) H. E. Moore, Jr. (*Palma spinosa* Miller, *A. fusiformis* (Swartz) Sweet); *Aeschynomene biflora* (Miller) Fawc. & Rendle (*Cassia biflora* MIller *Ae. brasiliana* DC.); *Ageratum houstonianum; Anonna cherimola; Baccharis rhexiodes* Kunth (*Conyza spicata* Miller, non *Baccharis spicata* Hieron), *Conyza trinervia* Miller, non *Baccharis trinervis* Pers.); *Bumelia americana* (Miller) Stearn (*Maurocenia americana* Miller, *Bumelia retusa* Swartz); *Calliandra houstoniana* (Miller) Standley (*Mimosa houstoniana* Miller, *C. houstonii* Benth.); *Canna coccinea; Cassia bahamensis, C. fruticosa* (*C. bacillaris* L.f.), *C. pentagonia, C. uniflora* (*C. sericea* Swartz). *C. villosa; Cestrum diurnum* L. var. *venenatum* (Miller) O. E. Schulz (*C. venenatum* Miller); *Conyza viscosa* (*C. lyrata* Kunth); *Copernicia prunifera* (Miller) H. E. Moore, Jr. (*Palma prunifera* Miller, *C. cerifera* (Arruda) Mart.); *Crotalaria sagittalis* L. var. *fruticosa* (Miller) Fawc. & Rendle (*C. fruticosa* Miller); *Crusea hispida* (Miller) Britten (*Crucianella hispida* Miller, *Crusea rubra* Bartl.); *Daphnopsis americana* (Miller) J. R. Johnston (*Laurus americana* Miller, *D. bonplandiana* (Kunth) Meisner); *Desmodium intortum* (Miller) Urban (*Hedysarum intortum* Miller, *D. uncinatum* DC.), *Desmodium procumbens* (Miller) Hitchcock (*Hedysarum procumbens* Miller, *H.*

spirale Swartz), *Eleutherine bulbosa* (Miller) Urban (*Sisyrinchium bulbosum* Miller, *Moraea plicata* Swartz); *Erythrina americana; Eupatorium betonicifolium; E. morifolium; Gnaphalium americanum; Harrisia gracilis* (Miller) Britton (*Cereus gracilis* Miller); *Lantana angustifolia* (*L. stricta* Swartz); *Lendneria verticillata* (Miller) Britton (*Erinus verticillatus* Miller, *Lendneria humilis* (Aiton) Minod); *Lippia alba* (Miller) N. E. Brown (*Lantana alba* Miller, *Lippia geminata* Kunth); *Mecardonia procumbens* (Miller) Small (*Erinus procumbens* Miller, *Herpestis chameadryoides* Kunth); *Opuntia spinosissima; Physalis cordata; Physalis maxima; Roystonea altissima* (Miller) H. E. Moore (*Palma altissima* Miller, *R. jamaicana* L. H. Bailey); *Solanum jamaicense; Stachytarpheta angustifolia* (Miller) Vahl (*Verbena angustifolia* Miller); *Teucrium vesicarium* (*T. inflatum* Swartz); *Tithonia rotundifolia* (Miller) Blake (*Tagetes rotundifolia* Miller, *Tithonia speciosa* (Hook.) Griseb.); *Vernonia remotiflora* Rich. (*Conyza uniflora* Miller non *V. uniflora* Schulz-Bip.).

This list is not exhaustive and takes no account of the many names published by Miller which are commonly placed in the synonymy of species named earlier by Linnaeus and Jacquin. Some of these may prove to be nomenclaturally important. Thus since the name *Prunus communis* (L.) Arcangeli (1882) based on *Amygdalus communis* L. (1753) must be rejected as a later homonym of *Prunus communis* Hudson (1778), Miller's *Amygdalus dulcis* supplies the earliest available epithet for the almond, now *Prunus dulcis* (Miller) D. A. Webb.

Date of Publication of Eighth Edition of the Dictionary

Because some of Miller's names may conflict with those of other authors published in 1768, e.g. N. L. Burman's *Flora Indica* (probably late March, certainly before 6 April 1768; *cf.* Stearn, 1961), it is desirable to ascertain the exact date of publication of the eighth edition of Miller's Dictionary. Fortunately five contemporary London newspapers carried advertisements. Thus the *St James Chronicle* No. 1, 109 (7–9 April 1768) announced that '*This Month will be published*, Neatly printed in one large Volume, Folio, the Eighth Edition ... of the Gardeners Dictionary ... by Philip Miller F.R.S.' *The Gazetteer and New Daily Advertiser* No. 12,205 (14 April 1768) stated 'This day is published, price 31.3s bound, Neatly printed in one large volume, folio, the Eight edition ... of the Gardeners Dictionary.' The *St James Chronicle*, No. 1,112 (14–16 April 1768) also stated that it 'This day was published'. *Lloyd's Evening Post* No. 1,683 (18–20 April 1768), the *London Evening Post* No. 15,312 (19–21 April 1768) and *The Public Advertiser* No. 10,444 (20 April 1768) also recorded its publication. Thus 14 April 1768 can be accepted as the date of publication. According to *The Public Advertiser* No. 10,441 (16 April 1768) the twelfth volume of Hill's *The Vegetable System* was published on that day.

Herbarium Specimens

Miller's descriptive notes accompanying his new names are sometimes inadequate to establish unquestionably the application of his names today. In view of the many new species named by Miller, it is fortunate that herbarium specimens and illustrations made from plants grown at Chelsea during Miller's curatorship still exist. Miller himself formed a large private herbarium (*cf.* Britton, 1913) to which he referred in a letter of 1758 to John Bartram. Sir Joseph Banks purchased this in 1774, i.e. three years after Miller's death, and it was incorporated into the Banks herbarium by his botanist librarian Daniel Solander. The specimens had presumably been kept loose until then between folded sheets of paper, on which Miller may have written their names; if so, these were discarded when the specimens were mounted for Banks and a note indicative of origin such as 'Herb. Miller', 'Hort Chels.', or 'Hort.' was written on the back of the herbarium sheet, following Linnaean precedent. These specimens passed to the British Museum in accordance with Banks's bequest and are now in the Department of Botany, British Museum (Natural History), London. They include many specimens collected in the Caribbean region by William Houstoun. An example is one from the Palisadoes at Kingston, Jamaica, called *Frangula folio subrotundo rigido subtus ferrugineo* by Houstoun, which is the type of *Maurocenia americana* Miller (1768) and thus of *Bumelia americana* (Miller) Stearn (1968) as mentioned above. Another less important source is a collection of specimens given by Miller to Sir Hans Sloane between 1727 and 1739 and contained in vols. 228–30, 244, 293–6, 316, 317, 323, 324, of the Sloane Herbarium (*cf.* Dandy 1958). By no means are all of Miller's new species represented in these collections.

A more important relevant collection in the British Museum (Natural History) consists of specimens grown in the Chelsea Physic Garden when Miller was preparing the successive editions of his *Dictionary*. They were presented to the Royal Society of London in accordance with Sir Hans Sloane's 1722 deed of conveyance of the Chelsea Physic Garden to the Society of Apothecaries. The cost of maintaining the garden continuously worried the Apothecaries, who held the garden under lease, it being part of the Manor of Chelsea bought by Sloane in 1712. When they made their financial difficulties known to Sloane they found him a sympathetic but shrewd landlord. He transferred the land to them in perpetuity but subject to a yearly rental of 'five pounds of Lawfull Brittish money' and various conditions (*cf.* Stearn 1972).

A very important condition was that the Apothecaries should render yearly and every year to the Royal Society of London 'fifty specimens or samples of distinct plants well dried and preserved and which grew in the said garden the same year together with their respective names or reputed

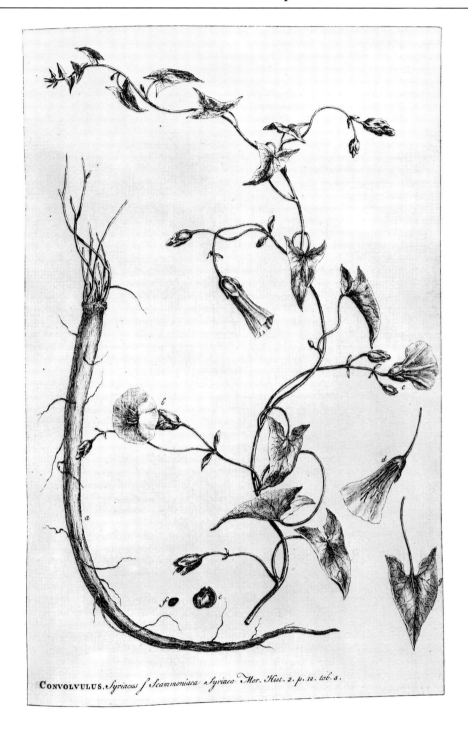

CONVOLVULUS, *Syriacus f Scammoniaca Syriaca Mor. Hist. 2. p. 12. tab. 8.*

Levant Scammony, Convolvulus scammonia *L.; drawing by R. Lancake* [*pl. 102*, FIGS]

QUAMOCLIT, *foliis tenuiter incisis & pennatis Tourn. Inst. R. H. 116.*

Cardinal Climber, Ipomoea quamoclit *L.; drawing by J. S. Miller [pl. 214,* FIGS]

names and so as the specimens or samples of such plants to be different or specifically distinct and no one offered twice until the compleat number of two thousand plants shall have been delivered'. The legal intent of this condition was to provide annual evidence that the Apothecaries' Company was maintaining the garden as a physic garden 'for the Improvement of their Members in the Knowledge of Botany'. Its psychological effect was to ensure a dynamic attitude towards the garden by making necessary the continual introduction of new plants. For posterity, it created a first-hand record of plants cultivated at Chelsea during the most important period of its history, when Philip Miller had charge. Most of these specimens must have been cut from the very plants at Chelsea recorded by Miller; they can serve as types or representative specimens in the absence of a specimen preserved by Miller himself. This indeed is their prime importance. In 1781 the neglected state of the Royal Society's 'Repository' at Crane Court, London, led the Society to transfer these specimens to the British Museum for better storage and they are now incorporated in the General Herbarium of the Department of Botany, British Museum (Natural History), within the covers holding cultivated plants. Although some listed specimens are no longer extant, this collection helps substantially to typify many of the binomial specific names published by Miller in 1768.

From 1722 onwards the keeper or *praefectus* of the Chelsea Garden presented annually to the Royal Society, as directed, fifty herbarium specimens of plants grown in the garden and his list of these, under names current at the time, was published later in the Royal Society's *Philosophical Transactions*. Isaac Rand (d. 1743) supplied the list of specimens 1–900 (for 1722–39) printed in *Phil. Trans.* 33–41 (1724–40); Joseph Miller (d. 1748) specimens 901–1250 (for 1740–6) in *Phil. Trans.* 42–6 (for 1744–9); John Wilmer (d. 1769) specimens 1251–2150 (for 1747–64) in *Phil. Trans.* 46–55 (1750–66); William Hudson (1730–93) specimens 2151–2200 (for 1765–9) in *Phil. Trans.* 56–60 (1767–71); Stanesby Alchorne (1727–1800) specimens 2401–2500 (for 1770–1) in *Phil. Trans.* 61–3 (1771–3); William Curtis (1746–99) specimens 2501–2550 (for 1772) in *Phil. Trans.* 64 (1774). These received polynomial phrase-names down to no. 2150 (1764), as did the plants, mostly grown at Chelsea, recorded in Miller's *Dictionary* down to its seventh edition (1759). Since Miller cited under the binomials of his eighth edition the polynomials of previous editions, the association of earlier specimens with his 1768 names can be easily established. Although not types in the strict modern sense, none being annotated by Miller's own hand, they represent the plants he grew, studied and named. These specimens thus provide valuable evidence as to the application of Miller's names. A specimen (Chelsea Physic Garden plants No. 1,843), gathered in 1758, representing *Datura innoxia* Miller, is illustrated by A. S. Barclay in *Harvard*

University Botanical Leaflet 18: 253, t.52(1959); this bears the polynomial *Stramonium Americanum maximum flore albo*, etc.

In 1950 George H. M. Lawrence (1910–1978) worked for several months searching the British Museum (Natural History) herbaria for Miller specimens and photographing them on behalf of the Bailey Hortorium of Cornell University, Ithaca, N.Y., U.S.A.

Illustrations

Illustrations made from plants cultivated at Chelsea also provide valuable information. The most important are the coloured engravings published in Miller's *Figures of the most beautiful, useful and uncommon Plants described in the Gardeners Dictionary, exhibited on three hundred Copper Plates* (1755–1760). These were drawn by J. Bartram, G. D. Ehret, W. Houstoun, R. Lancake and J. S. Miller (Müeller). The names on them are the polynomials such as Miller used before 1768. The accompanying descriptions often provide more information than is given in the *Dictionary*. An important example is Miller's plate and description of a new species from Madagascar received by way of Paris, which he grew at Chelsea and named *Vincafoliis oblongo-ovatis integerrimis tubis floris longissimo, caule ramoso fruticoso* in *Figures* 2:124, t. 186 (1757). In 1759 Linnaeus named this species *Vinca rosea*, basing the name on Miller's account and plate, which is accordingly the type. Among the Chelsea plants sent to the Royal Society in 1758 is no. 1849 taken from the same cultivated stock and hence the typo-type of the name *Vinca rosea* L. Alkaloids from this species, now named *Catharanthus roseus* (L) G. Don, are valuable in cancer treatment (*cf.* Stearn, 1975).

Georg Dionys Ehret (1708–70), the German botanical artist who settled in England and married Miller's sister-in-law in 1738, also drew many Chelsea plants for his patron C. J. Trew (1695–1769) of Nürnberg, who published some of them in *Plantae selectae* (1750–92), *Hortus nitidissimis* (1750–86), *Cedrorum Libani Historia* (1751) and *Plantae rariores* (1763–84). There remain, however, unpublished drawings by Ehret which may also help to elucidate some of Miller's names. Thus no authentic specimen exists of *Verbascum ferrugineum* Miller, *Gard. Dict.* ed. 8, art. Verbascum, no. 10 (1768). Miller received this plant from Paris under the name *Blattaria flore ferrugineo* and the British Museum (Natural History) possesses an unpublished coloured drawing by Ehret under the name *Blattaria flore ferrugineo* which agrees with Miller's account of his *V. ferrugineum*, and which can be taken to represent this. According to Dr I. K. Ferguson it fits no species now known, but combines features of several, e.g. flowers of the *V. virgatum* group and foliage of the *V. lychnitis* group and thus may be a hybrid no longer extant.

It seems unjust that Magnol and Garden are commemorated by such conspicuous plants as *Magnolia* and *Gardenia* whereas Miller, whose contributions to botany and gardening much exceeded theirs and who grew so many remarkable plants, nevertheless had his name unworthily attached to a small-flowered weedy species, *Milleria quinqueflora*, introduced by his friend William Houstoun from Central America and illustrated from a Chelsea plant by another friend John Martyn in his *Historiae Plantarum XXX Decas*, 7.39 (1732–36). This is the only species of the genus *Milleria* (Compositae), as *Milleria biflora* is now *Elvira biflora*.

Rusty Mullein, Verbascum V. ferrugineum *Miller, with South American grasshopper* Tropidacris collaris (Stoll); *drawing by G. D. Ehret, 1747*

Continuing Importance of Miller's Work

Miller's works remain scientifically important for their contents, for the names of plants first established in them to which reference must continually be made in the course of nomenclatural research. They are historically important on account of the models they provided for later works and for their influence upon these. Botanically, of Miller's many contributions to horticultural knowledge and progress, his *Gardeners Dictionary ... abridged*, 4th ed. (1754) and his *Gardeners Dictionary*, 8th ed. (1768) stand as his most important achievements, the one for generic, the other for specific nomenclature. The first valid publication of generic names attributed to Miller is in his 1754 abridgement, of specific names in his 1768 folio edition of the *Gardeners Dictionary*, rightly described by E. A. Bowles as 'that marvellous example of one man's work'. Its influence did not, however, end with the eighteenth century but has continued into the twentieth, by providing directly and indirectly the foundation for later encyclopaedic horticultural works. Thus Thomas Martyn (1756–1825) in 1807 expanded it into a four-volume work, *The Gardener's and Botanist's Dictionary*. Later the copyright holders of this work gave George Don the younger (1798–1856) the task of preparing a new edition. Don abandoned Miller's alphabetical arrangement and followed instead a natural system of classification; he acknowledged his debt to Miller by entitling his work *A general System of Gardening and Botany ... founded upon Miller's Gardener's Dictionary* (4 vols., 1831–38) and this was long known as 'Don's Miller'. Miller's work also provided inspiration and information for lesser dictionaries and encyclopaedias. The deficiencies of these led William Roberts (1862–1940) to propose in 1882 to the London publisher L. Upcott Gill the publication of a new dictionary of gardening. In 1882, to quote his own words, he was 'a youth of 20 with little or no practical experience, a smattering of English botany and such knowledge of exotic plants as could be picked up in visits to the gardens in and around Penzance', but he had enthusiasm and industry, and the enterprising Gill, chief proprietor of *The Bazaar and Exchange and Mart*, to which James Britten, D. T. Fish and W. J. May contributed articles, evidently liked the scheme, for he set Roberts to work on the compilation of this horticultural dictionary. Roberts's best quarry of information was 'Don's Miller'. He kept at this task until December 1884, then left Gill's employ to become a journalist and an author of works about book-collecting and of catalogues of pictures; in the course of time he acquired an extraordinarily detailed knowledge of British horticultural history. The text thus compiled by Roberts did not wholly satisfy either Roberts or Gill. Fortunately Gill then obtained the services of George Nicholson (1847–1908), curator of the Royal Botanic Gardens, Kew, who revised and extended Roberts's text on the basis of his own wide experience and knowledge with the help of other experts at Kew and elsewhere. It was published in parts between 1884 and 1888 as *The Illustrated Dictionary of Gardening*; a *Century Supplement* appeared in 1901. Nicholson's Dictionary gave gardeners the same good service as Miller's Dictionary had provided in the eighteenth century, but by 1936 the large number of new plants introduced from Western China and elsewhere since 1901 had made it an inadequate guide. The Royal Horticultural Society of London accordingly set up a committee in 1936 to consider ways and means of producing a new edition. Work on this began in October 1938 under the editorship of Frederick James Chittenden (1873–1950), a worthy successor of Miller in knowledge, experience, and sturdy conservatism, but he was soon much handicapped in his great undertaking by the outbreak of World War II in 1939 and the subsequent difficult conditions, and later by ill-health. The articles of Nicholson's *Dictionary* were pasted on to sheets and either revised by the editor or submitted to collaborators. When Chittenden died in 1950, the arduous task of completing the work passed to Patrick M. Synge (d. 1982) and me with instructions to finish it in the shortest possible time. Up to the letters SO (i.e. vol. 4, p. 1969) the text was in page proof, beyond that in galley proof or unwritten. The revision and completion of articles from SO onwards to ZY included for me the description of roughly some 500 species within six months and in association with concurrent routine library tasks brought me to the brink of a nervous breakdown. The Royal Horticultural Society's *Dictionary of Gardening; a practical and scientific Encyclopaedia of Horticulture* was published at Oxford in four volumes in 1951, with a preface indicating its descent through the works of Martyn, Don and Nicholson from Miller's *Gardeners Dictionary*. Thus two centuries after the publication of the eighth edition, the world of horticulture still remains indebted to Philip Miller *hortulanorum princeps* for that monumental work and to the Society of Apothecaries and Sir Hans Sloane for the Chelsea Physic Garden wherein he grew with skill and recorded, with an industry then comparable only to that of his contemporary botanical encyclopaedist Carl Linnaeus *princeps botanicorum*, so many diverse plants from so many diverse regions.

Pomegranate, Punica granatum *L.; drawing by G. D. Ehret*

Appendix

Editions of Miller's Works

The utility of Philip Miller's publications and their consequent popularity are evident from the numerous editions published during his lifetime. Thus there were 8 editions of *The Gardeners Dictionary* between 1731 and 1768; 6 editions of its Abridgement between 1735 and 1771; 15 editions of *The Gardeners Kalendar* between 1731 and 1769; there were also pirated versions published in Dublin. Blanche Henrey in her monumental *British Botanical and Horticultural Literature 3*: 89–93, entries 1096–1147 (1975), gives particulars of them all. F. A. Stafleu & R. S. Cowan in their likewise monumental *Taxonomic Literature 3*: 491–499, entries 6035–6061 (1981), provide more detail regarding *The Gardeners Dictionary*. Further bibliographical information is to be found in A. Stevenson's *Catalogue of Botanical Books in the Collection of Rachel McMasters Miller Hunt 2*. ii: entries 563, 566 and 601 (1961). The following is accordingly an abbreviated list with the entry numbers of the above works inserted.

The Gardeners Dictionary

1724	*The gardeners and florists dictionary, or a complete system of horticulture*, etc. 2 vols. London. Henrey, 1110; Stafleu & Cowan, 6035.
1731	*The Gardeners Dictionary; containing the methods of cultivating and improving the kitchen, fruit and flower garden*, etc. London. Henrey, 1101; Stafleu & Cowan, 6038. A pirated version of this was published in Dublin in 1732 (Henrey, 1102).
1733	——Second edition, corrected, London. Henrey, 1103; Stafleu & Cowan, 6039.
1735	*An appendix to the gardeners dictionary, containing several articles which were omitted*. London. Henrey, 1104; Stafleu & Cowan, 60392.
1737	*The Gardeners Dictionary ... Third edition corrected London*. Henrey 1105; Stafleu & Cowan, 60396

1739   *The second volume of the gardeners dictionary; which completes the work.* London.
Henrey 1106; Stafleu & Cowan, 6040.

1740   —— *Second edition. London.*
Henrey 1107; Stafleu & Cowan, 6040.

1741   *The Gardeners Dictionary ... Fifth edition.* Dublin.
Henrey, 1108; Stafleu & Cowan, 6042.
Evidently a pirated issue.

1743   —— *Fourth edition.* 2 vols London.
Henrey 1109; Stafleu & Cowan 6041.

1752   —— *Sixth edition; carefully revised and adapted to the present practice. Illustrated.* London.
Henrey 1110; Stafleu & Cowan, 6043.

1756–59   —— *Seventh edition, revised and altered according to the latest system of botany.* Illustrated London.
Stevenson, 563; Henrey, 1111; Stafleu & Cowan, 6044.
According to Henrey, this was issued in 112 parts between October 1756 and March 1759. A pirated Dublin version was published in 2 vols. in 1764.

1768   —— *Eighth* edition. London.
Stevenson, 601; Henrey, 1113; Stafleu & Cowan, 6043.

1795–1807   *The gardeners and botanists dictionary ... By the late Philip Miller ... to which are now first added a complete enumeration and description of all plants hitherto known ... By Thomas Martyn.* 2 vols. London.
Henrey, 1114; Stafleu & Cowan, 6048.

Translations of 'The Gardeners Dictionary'

1745   *Groot en algemeen kruidkundig, hoveniers, en bloemisten woorden boek*, etc. 2 vols. Leiden.
Stafleu & Cowan 6047.
Dutch translation with preface by Adriaan van Royen.

1750–58   *Das english Gartenbuch*, etc. 3 vols. Nürnberg.
Stafleu & Cowan, 6048.
German translation of the fifth edition.

1776?   *Le grand dictionnaire des jardiniers et des cultivateurs*, etc. 8 vols. octavo. Paris.
Stafleu & Cowan, 6050.
French translation, updated, of 8th edition.

1785   *Dictionnaire des jardiniers*, etc. 8 vols, quarto. Paris.
Stafleu & Cowan, 6051.
French translation of 8th edition.

1786–89   *Dictionnaire des jardiniers, et des cultivateurs.* Bruxelles.
Stafleu & Cowan, 6052.

The Gardeners Kalendar

1731	The Gardeners Kalendar, directing what works are necessary to be done every month. London.
	Henrey, 1124.
	According to Henrey, although dated 1732, this was published in 1731. There were three 1732 Dublin issues (Henrey 1125, 1126, 1127)
1733	—— Second Edition. London.
	Henrey, 1128.
1734	—— Third edition. London.
	Henrey, 1129.
1737	—— Fourth edition. London.
	Henrey, 1131.
1739	—— Fifth edition. London.
	Henrey 1132.
1743	—— Sixth edition. London.
	Henrey 1133.
1745	—— Seventh edition. London.
	Henrey, 1134.
1748	—— Eighth edition. London.
	Henrey, 1135.
1751	—— Ninth edition. London.
	Henrey, 1136.
1754	—— Tenth edition. London.
	Henrey, 1137.
1757	—— Eleventh edition. London.
	Henrey, 1138.
1760	—— Twelfth edition. London.
	Henrey, 1139.
1764	—— Thirteenth edition. London.
	Henrey, 1140.
1765	—— Fourteenth edition. London.
	Henrey, 1141.
	There was also a 1766 Dublin issue (Henrey 1142)
1769	—— Fifteenth edition. London.
	Henrey, 1143.
1775	—— Sixteenth edition. London.
	Henrey, 1144.
1792	—— Seventeenth edition. Dublin.
	Henrey, 1145.

Abridgement of The Gardeners Dictionary

1735	The Gardeners Dictionary ... Abridg'd from the folio edition. 2 vols. octavo. London.

Henrey 1117; Stafleu & Cowan, 6053.

1740–41 —— *Second edition.* 3 vols. octavo. London.
Henrey, 1119; Stafleu & Cowan, 6054.

1748 —— *Third edition.* 3 vols. octavo. London.
Henrey, 1120; Stafleu & Cowan, 6055.

1754 —— *Fourth edition.* 3 vols. octavo. London.
Henrey, 1121; Stafleu & Cowan, 6056. [facsimile, Lehre, 1969]

1763 *The Abridgement of the Gardeners Dictionary*, etc. Fifth edition. Quarto. London.
Henrey, 1121; Stafleu & Cowan, 6057.

1771 —— *Sixth edition. Quarto. London.*
Henrey, 1123; Stafleu & Cowan, 6058.

Figures of Plants

1755–60. Figures of the most beautiful, useful and uncommon plants described in the Gardeners Dictionary. 2 vols. 300 plates. London.
Stevenson, 566; Henrey, 1097; Stafleu & Cowan, 6059.

1768–82. Abbildungen der nütlichsten, schönsten und seltensten Pflanzen welche in seinem Gartner-Lexicon vorkommen. 2 vols. 3 plates, Nürnberg.
Stafleu & Cowan, 6060.

Trumpets, Sarracenia flava *L.; drawing by G. D. Ehret*

Bibliography

The following have been referred to throughout:

AMHERST, A., 1876. *A History of Gardening in England*. London.
HADFIELD, M., 1969. *A History of British Gardening*. London.
JOHNSON, G. W., 1829. *A History of English Gardening*. London.
KALM, P., 1748. *Visit to England on the Way to America*. [Trans. Joseph Lucas, 1892. London.]
MILLER, P, 1768. *The Gardeners Dictionary*. Eighth Edition. London.
PULTENEY R., 1790. *Historical and Biographical Sketches of Progress of Botany in England from its Origin to the Introduction of the Linnaean System*. 2 vols. London.

Additional Works consulted for relevant chapters:

2 The Apothecaries and their Garden

BARRETT, C. R. B., 1905. *History of Society of Apothecaries of London*. London.
DREWITT, F. G. D., 1922. *The Romance of the Apothecaries' Garden at Chelsea*. London.
FIELD, H. & SEMPLE, R.H., 1878. *Memoirs, Historical and Illustrative, of the Botanick Garden at Chelsea belonging to the Society of Apothecaries of London*. London.
GILMOUR, J. S. L., 1944. *British Botanists*. London.
HAWKS, E., 1900. *Pioneers of Plant Study*. London.
KEW, H. W. & POWELL, H. E., 1932. *Thomas Johnson, Botanist and Royalist*. London.
STEARN, W. T., 1971. Sources of information about botanic gardens and herbaria. *Biological Journal of the Linnaean Society* 3: 225–233.
STEARN, W. T., 1972. Philip Miller and the Plants from the Chelsea Physic Garden presented to the Royal Society of London, 1723–1796. *Transactions of the Botanical Society of Edinburgh* 41: 293–307.
WALL, R. C. B., CAMERON, H. C. & UNDERWOOD, E. A., 1963. *History of the Worshipful Society of Apothecaries, 1617–1815*. London.

3 The Garden's Benefactor

BROOKS, E. ST. J., 1954. *Sir Hans Sloane*. London.
SLOANE, *Sir* HANS., 1707–1725. *A Voyage to the Islands of Madeira ... and Jamaica ... 2 vols*. London.
WELD, C. R., 1948. *History of the Royal Society*. London.

4 Philip Miller in Chelsea

BEAVER, A., 1892. *Memorials of Old Chelsea*. London.
BRYAN, G., 1869. *Chelsea in the Olden and Present Time*. London.
Chelsea Parish Records. Archives of Greater London Council.
FAULKNER, T., 1829. *Historical and Topographical Description of Chelsea*. London.
ROGERS, J., 1839. *The Vegetable Cultivator*. London.

5 Correspondence in England and Scotland

SHERBURN, G. W. (Ed.), 1956. *Correspondence of Alexander Pope*. 5 Vol. Oxford.
TURNER, D. (Ed.), 1835. *Extracts from the Literary and Scientific Correspondence of R. Richardson ...* Yarmouth.
WHITE, GILBERT, 1751–1771. *Garden Kalendar*. Ed. by John Clegg. London, 1975.
WHITE, GILBERT, 1877. *Natural History of Selborne*. Ed. by Thos. Bell. London.

6 European Exchange

LINDEBOOM, G. A., 1968. *Herman Boerhaave, the Man and his Work*. London.
LINDEBOOM, G. A., 1970. *Boerhaave and his Time*. Leiden.

7 Some Noble Estates

CLUTTON, *Sir* G. & MACKAY, C., 1970. Old Thorndon Hall, Essex: a History and Reconstruction of its Park and Gardens. *Garden History Society Occasional Paper*. No. 2: 27–38.
HENREY, B., 1986. *No Ordinary Gardener. Thomas Knowlton, 1691–1781*. Ed. by A. O. Chater. London.
RAMSBOTTOM, J., 1938. Old Essex Gardeners and Their Gardens. *Essex Naturalist* **26**: 65–103.

8 Collinson, Bartam and Fothergill (also 9 & 10)

BRETT-JAMES, N. G. [1926] *Life of Peter Collinson*. London.
CHESTON, EMILY READ., 1938. *John Bartram, 1699–1777, his Garden and his House William Bartram, 1739–1823*. Johnson Press, Ambler, PA.
DARLINGTON, WILLIAM., 1967. *Memorials of John Bartram and Humphry Marshall*. (Facsimile of 1849 ed.) New York.
HINGSTON FOX, R., 1918. *Dr. John Fothergill and his Friends*. London.
SAVAGE, H., 1970. *Lost Heritage*. New York.
SWEM, E. G., 1949. Brothers of the Spade: Correspondence of Peter Collinson of London and John Custis of Williamsburg, Virginia, 1734–1746. *American Antiquarian Society Proceedings* **April 1948**: 17–201.

11 The Gardeners Dictionary and its Abridgement

MILLER, P., 1754. *Gardeners Dictionary Agridged*. 4th ed., London.
STEARN, W. T., 1969. *The Abridgement of Miller's Gardener's Dictionary*. Lehre.

STEARN, W. T., 1974. Millers Gardener's dictionary and its abridgement. *Journal of the Society for the Bibliography of Natural History* 7: 125–141.

12 Miller's Other Works

MILLER, P., 1724. Gardener's and Florist's Dictionary. 2 vol. London.

MILLER, P., 1730. *Catalogus Plantarum Officinialum quae in Horto Botanico Chelseyano aluntur.* London.

MILLER, P., 1732–69. *Gardener's Kalendar.* London.

MILLER, P., 1755–60. *Figures of Plants.* 2 vol. London.

SOCIETY OF GARDENERS, 1730. *Catalogus Plantarum.* London.

13 Illustrators at Chelsea

BLUNT, W., 1950. *The Art of Botanical Illustration.* London.

CALMANN, G., 1977. *Ehret, Flower Painter extraordinary; an illustrated Biography.* London.

MACKENNA, F. S., 1951. Botanical Painting on Chelsea Porcelain. *Apollo,* **July 1951**: 7–10.

SYNGE-HUTCHINSON, P. G. D., 1959. Ehret's Botanical Designs on Chelsea Porcelain. *The Consise Encyclopaedia of Antiques* 4: 73–78.

TJADEN, W. L., 1970. Georg Dionysius Ehret (1708–70) Flower Painter Supreme. *Journal Royal Horticultural Society* **95**: 385–389, 1970.

14 The Most Valuable Flowering Shrub

As Chapter 11 & 12.

MILLER, P., 1770. Index Plantarum quo in Horto Medico Chelseano aluntur, (MS).

15 Collection in the Countryside

CLAPHAM, A. R., TUTIN T. G. & WARBURG E. F., 1962. *Flora of the British Isles* 2nd ed. Cambridge.

16 Agriculture, Forestry and Specialised Husbandry

DOSSIE, R., 1767–82, *Memoirs of Agriculture and other Economical Arts.* 3 vol.

FUSSEL, G. D., 1947. *Old English Farming Books.* London.

FUSSEL, G. D., 1950. *More Old English Farming Books.* London.

ROYAL SOCIETY OF ARTS. *Guard Books* 4 and 5.

17 Chelsea's Association with Cambridge

Cambridge University Register 25.1.

PRESTON, F. G., 1940 The University Botanic Garden, Cambridge. *Journal Royal Horticultural Society* 65: 171–181.

WALKER, RICHARD, 1763. *A short Account of the late Donation of a Botanic Garden to the University of Cambridge.* Cambridge.

WALTERS, S. M., 1981. *The Shaping of Cambridge Botany.* Cambridge.

18 Followers of Miller

Chelsea Physic Garden Committee Books, 1731–1862 Guildhall Library MS 9223, 1–4.

FELTON, S., 1830. *Portraits of English Authors on Gardening*, 2nd ed. London.

19 Followers of Miller

AITON, W.T., 1789. *Hortus Kewensis*. London.

AITON, W. T., 1810–13. *Hortus Kewensis*, sec. ed. London.

ALCHORNE, S., 1772. *Index Horti Chelseiani* (MS).

CARTER, H., 1988. *Sir Joseph Banks, 1743–1820*. London.

DONALD, D., 1987. William Curtis at the Chelsea Physic Garden. *Kew Magazine* **4**.

FLETCHER, H. R., 1968. *Story of the Royal Horticultural Society 1804–1968*. London.

LYSAGHT, A. M., 1971. *Joseph Banks in Newfoundland and Labrador, 1766*. London.

SIMMONDS, A., 1948. *Horticultural Who was Who*. London

SMITH-LANE, E., 1911. *Life of Sir Joseph Banks*. London.

20 The Botanical Importance of Phillip Miller's Publications

BARCLAY, A. S., 1959. New considerations in an old genus, *Datura*. *Botanical Museum* Leaflet, Harvard Univ. **18**; 245–272

BRITTEN, J., 1898. The Conyzas of Miller's Dictionary (ed. 8). *Journal of Botany*. (London) 36: 53–55

BRITTEN, J., 1912. The Linums of Miller's Dictionary (ed. 8) (1768). *Journal of Botany* (London) **50**; 245–247

BRITTEN, J., 1913. Philip Miller's plants. *Journal of Botany* (London) 51: 132–135.

BRITTEN, J. & BAKER, E. G., 1897. Houstoun's Central American Leguminosae. *Journal of Botany* (London) **35**: 225–234.

CALMANN, C., 1977. *Ehret, Flower Painter extraordinary; an illustrated Biography*. London.

DANDY, J. E., 1967. *Index of generic Names of vascular Plants 1753–1774 (Regnum Vegetabile* 51). Utrecht (International Bureau of Plant Taxonomy).

DANDY, J. E., 1958. *The Sloane Herbarium*. London.

DRUCE, G. C., 1914 The abridgement of Miller's Gardeners dictionary. *Botanical Exchange Club and Society of the British Isles* 3: 426–436.

HENREY, B., 1975. *British botanical and horticultural Literature before 1800*. Vols 2 & 3. London & Oxford.

MARTYN, T., 1807. *The Gardener's and Botanist's Dictionary*: Vol. 1, preface. London.

MOORE, H. E., 1963. The typification and species of *Palma* Miller (1754). *Gentes Herbarum*. **9**: 235–244.

PULTENEY, R., 1790. *Historical and biographical Sketches of the Progress of Botany in England*. 2 vols. London.

STAFLEU, R. A. & COWAN, R. S., 1981. *Taxonomic Literature* Vol. 3. Utrecht (Bohn, Scheltema & Holkema), The Hague (W. Junk)

STEARN, W. T., 1957. An introduction to the 'Species Plantarum' and cognate botanical works of Carl Linnaeus. Prefixed to Ray Society facsimile of Linnaeus *Species Plantarum* ed. 1, 1753. Vol. 1. London (Ray Society)

STEARN, W. T., 1960. Notes on Linnaeus's 'Genera Plantarum'. Prefixed to facsimile of Linnaeus, *Genera Plantarum*, fifth edition 1754. Weinheim (H. R. Engelmann (J. Cramer)) & Codicote (Wheldon & Wesley)

STEARN, W. T., 1961. Botanical gardens and botanical literature in the eighteenth century. *In* Stevenson, A. H. (comp.) *Catalogue of botanical Books in the Collection of Rachel McMasters Miller Hunt*, vol 2, pp. xli–cxl. Pittsburgh, Pa. (Hunt Botanical Library)

STEARN, W. T., 1969. The abridgement of Miller's 'Gardeners Dictionary'. Prefixed to facsimile of Miller, *Gardeners Dictionary abridged*. Vol. 1. pp. i–xvi. Lehre (J. Cramer).

STEARN, W. T., 1972. Philip Miller and the plants from the Chelsea Physic Garden presented to the Royal Society of London, 1723–1796. *Transactions of the Botanical Society of Edinburgh* **41**: 293–307

STEARN, W. T., 1974. Miller's Gardeners Dictionary. *Journal of the Society for the Bibliography of Natural History* **7**: 125–141

STEARN, W. T., 1975. A synopsis of the genus *Catharanthus* (Apocynaceae). *In* Taylor, W. I. & Farnsworth, N. R. (Eds), *The Catharanthuus Alkaloids*, pp. 9–44. New York.

Narcissus tazetta; *drawing by G. D. Ehret*

Acknowledgements

The following provided information, criticised various sections, helped with transcription of difficult MSS, checked typescript and I am grateful for their generous assistance: Dr M. V. Angel, Dr T. H. Angel, Mrs Mavis Batey, Professor G. R. Batho, Mr Wilfrid Blunt, Dr C. H. Brock, Mr. H. B. Carter, Mrs J. Collins, Mrs M. Draper, Miss Joan Edwards, Mr R. M. Gard, Mr J. S. L. Gilmour, Mr D. Graham, Mr E. W. Groves, Dr John Harvey, Mr R. Holden, Mr A. Jewell, Mr D. Legg Willis, Mr R. P. S. Le Rougetel, Mr W. G. M. McKenzie, Miss P. Minay, Mr A. Paterson, Dr M. C. Payne, Mr E. M. Rose, Miss B. Rouse, Mrs Ruth Stearn, Dr Max Walters, Mrs L. A. West, Mr R. R. Wilson.

From overseas I have received great courtesy and would like first to express appreciation of the valuable advice given by the John Bartram Association of Philadelphia. Also from the United States help has come from Mr Whitfield J. Bell (American Philosophical Society), Miss Elizabeth Hall (Horticultural Soceity of New York), Miss J. Morris (Pennsylvania Horticultural Society), Miss Mary-Grace Stewart, Mr N. B. Wainwright (Historical Society of Pennsylvania) and Miss Elizabeth Vining. In Europe I have corresponded with and am grateful to Professor Pier Virgilio Arrigoni, Firenze; Professor G. S. Lindeboom, Amsterdam; Professor R. E. G. Pichi Sermolli, Genova; Professor Dr F. A. Stafleu, Utrecht; and Dr Ir. A. C. Zevan, Wageningen.

I have worked at or corresponded with the following libraries of local authorities and institutions and to their staff I owe sincere thanks: Bedford County Record Office, Bedford Estates, Bodleian, British Museum, Botany Department British Museum (Natural History), Cambridge University, Cambridge University Botanic Garden, Chelsea Physic Garden, Edinburgh University, Goodwood Estate Company Limited, Greater London Council, Guildhall, Haslemere Educational Museum, Ipswich Central, Royal Borough of Kensington and Chelsea (Chelsea Library), Royal Botanic Gardens Kew, Royal Horticultural Society, Linnaean Society, Public Record Office, Royal Society, Royal Society of Arts, Science Museum, Sheffield City, St. Martins, U.S. Embassy Information Service, Gilbert White Museum, Wellcome Trust and Westminster City.

Sources of Illustrations

Illustrations from the *Gardeners Dictionary* 8th ed. 1768 are annotated [GD].

Illustrations from *Figures of ... plants described in the Gardeners Dictionary* (1755–60) are annotated [FIGS].

The drawings by G. D. Ehret are in the British Museum (Natural History).

J. Martyn, *Historiae Plantarum Variorum ... Decas*, pl. 39 (1732–36) **p. 8**; Thomas

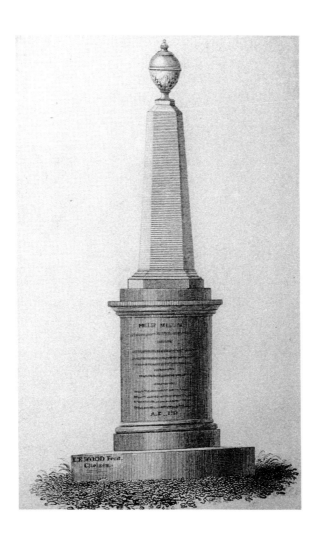

Index

Index

Index

Index

Index

Index

Index